SHADOW

OF THE

CROSS

365 DEVOTIONALS FROM THE GOSPEL OF MARK

PHIL WARE

LEAFWOOD
PUBLISHERS

The Shadow of the Cross
365 Devotionals from the Gospel of Mark
Published by Leafwood Publishers

Copyright 2010 by Phil Ware

ISBN 978-0-89112-642-3
LCCN 2009941500

Printed in the United States of America

Cover design by Marc Whitaker

Scripture quotations are from the Holy Bible: Easy-to-Read Version (Revised Edition)
copyright 2005 by the World Bible Translation Center, Inc. and used by permission.
www.wbtc.org

For information:
Leafwood Publishers, Abilene, Texas
1-877-816-4455 toll free
Visit our website: www.leafwoodpublishers.com

10 11 12 13 14 15 / 7 6 5 4 3 2 1

FOR LYNN ANDERSON, PAUL FAULKNER,
& NEIL LIGHTFOOT

three friends & mentors who helped me learn to listen to & love the voice of Jesus

Acknowledgements

My love for the Gospels goes back more than three decades ago to a time when Dr. Neil Lightfoot asked me to survey the library holdings on the four Gospels and make recommendations for additional volumes. This wasn't a job or an assignment; it was a labor of love and an undeserved opportunity.

Dr. Lightfoot's constant encouragement for me to be in the text and my walk with books on Jesus for a whole summer forever changed me. During that same time, Dr. Lynn Anderson invited me into a graduate mentoring group as he preached through the Gospel of John focusing on Jesus' personal ministry to people. About the same time, Dr. Paul Faulkner grabbed my heart with his earthy descriptions of Jesus' ministry and teaching. Reading through the Gospel of Mark in the original language catalyzed these experiences into a passion to know Jesus and hear his voice through the four Gospels. Thank you, dear brothers for your influence on me, as well as your investment in me.

The Heartlight.org community has shaped these devotionals by reading and responding to them with questions, insights, and confessional stories. Special thanks to these folks, scattered all over the world, who have encouraged me to get these devotionals into book form. I am still amazed that others love them so.

I want to especially thank Ray Butts and E.R. Holley, volunteer proofreaders, encouragers, and helpers. Their corrections, questions, and hours of investment in these devotionals and many other pieces of the Heartlight.org ministry have enriched everything we do.

Thanks again to Leonard Allen and Leafwood Publishers for encouraging me to get each of the four daily devotional books on the Gospels in print.

Each of the four evangelists told the story of Jesus for a specific reason and with a very unique style. The more I read them, the more clearly I hear both Jesus' voice and the passion each writer has for us to know the Lord more fully. I encourage you to regularly read through Mark's Gospel in one sitting as you use this devotional book for your daily reflection. Get a sense of feel for the flow of the story for yourself, spontaneously taking a moment to reflect on the story and thank the Father for Jesus and for Mark, who introduced us to the literary form we call Gospel. We would be short-changed without Mark's vibrant telling of Jesus, the Son of God and our powerful Messiah who lived His whole earthly life in the shadow of the cross.

Thanks to all of these, who along with my physical family and my church family have enriched my life in ways far beyond what I deserve!

Phil

A Walk with Mark in
the Shadow of the Cross

Jesus and his follower Mark, the one who first wrote down the good news story about Jesus, lived in a time intoxicated with power. Jesus' own people, the Jews, longed for the power they once had under the mighty King David. The Romans had power and used it, sometimes with brute force, to keep their version of peace in a fragile and fractured world. While the Romans ruled, the Jews longed for a powerful redeemer who would deliver them with power!

Mark sought to communicate the power of Jesus and explain the cross of Jesus to folks caught up in the collision of Roman power and Jewish expectation. Jesus' followers would live in the middle of these colliding worlds. Ominous clouds were forming on the horizon for the followers of Jesus. How could they understand the amazing miracle-working power of Jesus and their own struggles, persecutions, and trials?

Mark's words are clear, precise, and action-oriented. He moves the story along with the often-repeated word "immediately." His story of Jesus is the shortest of the four gospels . Mark's Gospel shares the story of Jesus in three parts and I believe he shares his story of Jesus for a reason.

The clue to understanding Mark's story of Jesus involves the healing of two blind men. The first blind man is caught up in one of the most bizarre miracles we find in Scripture (Mark 8:22-26). The blind man is not healed at once like everyone else Jesus heals. Instead, Jesus has to perform a second step to his miracle before the blind man begins to see clearly.

We get so infatuated with the power of Jesus that, if we are not careful, we miss the real Jesus. We seem him incompletely. Yes, Jesus is powerful. Yes, Jesus is the living demonstration of God's compassion and might sent to save us. However, Jesus is much more than this. His work involves much more than demonstrating God's power; it also involves the demonstration of God's sacrificial love.

After this blind man fully receives his sight, Jesus begins working with his closest followers to help them receive their spiritual sight. Over the next few chapters, Jesus will tell his apostles three times that he we will go to the cross, suffer, die, and be raised from the dead. They struggle to understand this. They cannot comprehend why someone with such great power would ever face such humiliation and suffering.

Jesus completes his instruction on the way of the cross by saying, "Follow my example: Even the Son of Man did not come for people to serve him. He came to serve others and *to give his life to save* many people" (Mark 10:45 ERV, emphasis added). The highlighted phrase has often been translated, "give his life as a ransom." Jesus came as God's powerful Son, the Christ, who has power over demons, death, disease, and the terrors of the deep. Yet some things can only be remedied by sacrifice. The Jesus way involves power used for compassionate and redemptive purposes, but it also requires the power of a willing sacrifice.

Immediately after Jesus' statement, we meet Bartimaeus, the other blind man (Mark 10:46-52). He is seeking Jesus and will not be denied an audience with the Son of David, this powerful one God had sent. This time, when Bartimaeus is healed of his blindness the healing is immediate. He is ready to follow Jesus on the way, the way that ultimately leads to the cross—the way we are called to follow.

When we recognize this movement of the story of Jesus in Mark, then suddenly we understand how the story is told:

Mark 1:1-8:21	The Way of Power & Compassion
Mark 8:22-10:52	The Way of Jesus & His Followers
Mark 11:1-16:20	The Way of the Cross & Sacrifice

For Mark, all of the life of Jesus is lived in the shadow of the cross. Jesus is the great reminder that power can be seen in wonderful and amazing miracles. Yet an even greater power is seen in Jesus' statement in the garden, "*Abba*, Father! You can do all things. Don't make me drink from this cup. But do what you want, not what I want" (Mark 14:36). Jesus reminds us that wrongs can't be righted, broken lives won't be mended, and rebellious hearts won't be ransomed by power alone. These fractures can't be fully healed until we follow Jesus in the shadow of the cross.

So as we journey each day through this remarkable and powerful story of Jesus' life, never forget Mark's underlying message. Marvel at Jesus' miracles. Wonder at his power and might. But let God have your heart at the cross. Here you see Jesus , the Son of God, withhold his power to accomplish a greater good: paying your ransom and liberating you from the notion that power alone can accomplish God's will. The shadow of the cross falls across the whole ministry of Jesus and rests upon any who would follow Jesus today.

Come, like Bartimaeus, and follow Jesus with eyes wide open as we live in the shadow of the cross.

By God's grace,

Phil Ware

Day 1

GOOD NEWS!

MARK 1:1
The Good News about Jesus Christ, the Son of God, begins . . .

KEY THOUGHT

We are beginning a journey through the Gospel of Mark. Gospel means "good news." Mark wants us to know four things about our journey with him through the life of Jesus. First, it is a journey about God's good news. Second, it is about a very human person named Jesus; his humanity is revealed throughout Mark's Gospel. Third, this Jesus is also the Messiah (or Christ) promised in the Old Testament. Fourth, Jesus is the Son of God. Never lose sight of the fact that Mark is telling us the good news of God in the story of Jesus that he shares with us. Sometimes the words and stories will be challenging and hard to understand. Yet at the heart of each story, event, or teaching is an implicit conviction that God has brought us something very good in Jesus!

TODAY'S PRAYER

Father, as I make the journey through the next year, please help me know Jesus better. Help me see Jesus as the embodiment of your good news. Open my eyes and help me see Jesus, in whose name I pray. Amen.

CONTEXT: MARK 1:1-11

RELATED PASSAGES: PSALM 96:2; ISAIAH 52:7-10; MARK 8:35

Day 2

PREPARE THE WAY

MARK 1:1-3

The Good News about Jesus Christ, the Son of God, begins with what the prophet Isaiah said would happen. Isaiah wrote: "Listen! I will send my messenger ahead of you. He will prepare the way for you. There is someone shouting in the desert: 'Prepare the way for the Lord. Make the road straight for him.'"

KEY THOUGHT

Where does the Gospel actually begin? Where does God's good news originate? Matthew and Luke begin their accounts of Jesus' life with the stories surrounding his birth. John begins with the creation of the world where the Son of God was not only present, but also did the creating. Mark, with his focus on good news, chooses to begin at a different place. If folks are going to be open to God's good news, then someone is going to have to be a servant and prepare the way for Jesus to come and for his word to be heard. In many ways, the good news always begins in this place. The real question is whether we are willing to be used as servants like John the Baptizer—who is introduced in the next verse—and prepare the way for the good news about Jesus to be heard by our friends.

TODAY'S PRAYER

Father in heaven, please use my life to prepare the way for Jesus to come with his good news into the lives of my friends, acquaintances, and family. I pray this in the name of Jesus Christ, the Son of God. Amen.

CONTEXT: MARK 1:1-11

RELATED PASSAGES: MARK 1:14-15; JOHN 3:26-30; MARK 8:35

Day 3

Turn from Your Sins!

Mark 1:4

So John the Baptizer came and was baptizing people in the desert area. He told them to be baptized to show they wanted to change their lives and then their sins would be forgiven.

Key Thought

God's messenger was John. He was called The Baptizer because he baptized people who came to him wanting to change their lives to align with the will of God. John's mission was to prepare people for the coming of the promised Christ. The purpose of this baptism was to demonstrate a person's turning away from sin to God and to receive God's forgiveness. What can we learn from John's mission for our lives today? First, God uses human messengers to reach the hearts of those who are seeking him. Someone is out there seeking for God and God can use you or me to be that messenger! Second, seeking God involves two things: we turn to God and we turn away from our sins. Third, everyone needs God's forgiveness; none of us is righteous and holy on our efforts. In other words, we need God's gracious forgiveness. Have I come to God to receive his forgiveness and grace? Have I truly turned to God and away from sin? And to whom will I be God's messenger?

Today's Prayer

Father in heaven, you are holy and righteous. As I think about praying to you, I am humbled that you would hear me. Thank you for the gracious forgiveness you have given me through the gift of your Son. I turn my back on sin in an effort to flee its grip on me. As a recipient of your grace, please help me see the people for whom I can be your messenger. In Jesus' name. Amen.

Context: Mark 1:1-8

Related Passages: Acts 19:14; Acts 3:17-21; Acts 2:36-39

Day 4

FROM ALL OVER

MARK 1:5

All the people from Judea, including everyone from Jerusalem, came out to John. They confessed the bad things they had done, and he baptized them in the Jordan River.

KEY THOUGHT

John didn't choose the most accessible location for his ministry. Instead, he was located in the wilderness. Yet people came long distances to hear him. Why? Because they were hungry for spiritual food. They longed to hear the voice of God through one of his servants, a true prophet. Distance was no barrier. Confession of their sins and baptism were not barriers. They were hungry for God. Are we hungry for God today? What barriers do we let keep us away from seeking God with all of our hearts?

TODAY'S PRAYER

Father, I hunger to know you better and to serve you more faithfully. Please help me destroy any barriers that I have put between your grace and my need for it. Please, dear Father, never let my pride keep me from hearing your call in my life. In Jesus' gracious and powerful name I pray. Amen.

CONTEXT: MARK 1:1-11

RELATED PASSAGES: MARK 3:7-8; MARK 11:27-32; LUKE 7:24-28

Day 5

A LIFE IN SERVICE

MARK 1:6-7

John wore clothes made from camel's hair and a leather belt around his waist. He ate locusts and wild honey.

This is what John told the people: "There is someone coming later who is able to do more than I can. I am not good enough to be the slave who stoops down to untie his sandals."

KEY THOUGHT

John's whole life was defined by his service to God and to God's Son. His clothing, his food, and his tasks were all defined by his mission—to prepare the way for the Lord. How could he live his whole life for someone else? He defined himself as unworthy to even be the servant or slave of this coming one who was so much greater than he. Jesus comes to us and asks us in our day to let him define our lives as well. That's what it means to call Jesus Lord—we see ourselves as unworthy to be his servants and slaves; yet, because of his grace, we are called his brothers and sisters. For such blessings, we offer our lives in service to him and his kingdom.

TODAY'S PRAYER

Gracious Father, thank you for being so gracious to me. Please accept my life in service to you as my thanks and praise. I pray this in the name of Jesus, your Son and my Lord. Amen.

CONTEXT: MARK 1:1-8

RELATED PASSAGES: ROMANS 12:1-2; MATTHEW 7:21; MARK 3:31-35

Day 6

THE HOLY SPIRIT

MARK 1:8

*"I baptize you with water, but the one who is coming
will baptize you with the Holy Spirit."*

KEY THOUGHT

Jesus has the power and authority to send the Spirit and make us new. John could talk about the Holy Spirit and operate by the power and inspiration of the Holy Spirit, as well as promise the coming of the Holy Spirit. However, he could not baptize in the Holy Spirit. It wasn't part of his baptism. Only Jesus can make us new by the power of the Holy Spirit. Each of us need to consider seriously whether we have let him make us truly new.

TODAY'S PRAYER

Father in heaven, thank you for the gift and power of the Holy Spirit that is at work in your children. Thank you for sending this Spirit into our lives. Holy Spirit, I pray that you will mold me and make me into the person I need to be to properly share God's grace with others. In the name of Jesus and through the intercession of the Holy Spirit, I pray. Amen.

CONTEXT: MARK 1:1-11

RELATED PASSAGES: JOHN 3:3-7; TITUS 3:3-7; ACTS 2:32-33

Day 7

BAPTIZED

MARK 1:9

About that time Jesus came from the town of Nazareth in Galilee to the place where John was. John baptized Jesus in the Jordan River.

KEY THOUGHT

Jesus was a real person who came from a real place called Nazareth in the province of Galilee. He was baptized in a real river, the Jordan. In other words, Jesus story is more than a story; it is history. Yet more than history, it is Jesus' saving history. A special part of that history is Jesus' baptism. His baptism is important for a number of reasons. It is a signal of the beginning of Jesus' ministry. It is an opportunity for God to affirm his Son, as we will see in subsequent verses. It is a way for Jesus to identify with people seeking to be ready for the coming of the Messiah and the Kingdom of God. It is a way for Jesus to fulfill righteousness. For us, however, there is another great truth about Jesus' baptism: it is something we can join him in doing if we truly turn our lives toward God as did those who came to John. God's saving history demonstrated in Jesus can intersect our lives. What a blessing of grace!

TODAY'S PRAYER

Father in heaven, thank you for giving me the opportunity to share in the life of Jesus. Help me know your will more fully as I study Jesus' life in the Gospel of Mark. Thank you for letting my life intersect the life of your Son through baptism. Dear Father, please conform me to the character of your Son through the Holy Spirit. In the holy name of Jesus I pray. Amen.

CONTEXT: MARK 1:9-20

RELATED PASSAGES: LUKE 1:1-4; JOHN 1:14-18; HEBREWS 1:1-3

Day 8

SPLIT OPEN

MARK 1:10
*As Jesus was coming up out of the water, he saw the sky torn
open. The Spirit came down on him like a dove.*

KEY THOUGHT

Something dramatic, earthshaking, and eternally significant happened in Jesus' baptism. All who witnessed this event, and all of us who read about it, can't escape the power and significance of this moment. Heaven is opened. The distance between God in heaven and mortals is collapsed. The Holy Spirit descends in the form of a dove on Jesus to show God's approval, blessing, and anointing as God's Son, the King. Jesus' baptism is a turning point—not just for Jesus, but for us as well. Our baptism, though clearly not as dramatic as the Lord's, is a turning point, too. We need to think about the significance of both the Lord's baptism and our own.

TODAY'S PRAYER

Father, I thank you for a clear marker in my past that designates the turning point of my life. Jesus is my Lord. You are my Father. The power of the Holy Spirit lives in me. I praise you and thank you for a fresh start and the power to have a new beginning. Please help me share this freshness of your grace with others. In the mighty name of Jesus I pray. Amen.

CONTEXT: MARK 1:9-20

RELATED PASSAGES: 2 CORINTHIANS 5:16-21; ACTS 22:6-16; GALATIANS 2:20

Day 9

FULLY PLEASED

MARK 1:11
*A voice came from heaven and said: "You are my Son,
the one I love. I am very pleased with you."*

KEY THOUGHT

Isn't this what we all need to hear from the ones we love the most? Look at what is being said. I claim you as my child! I love you! I am completely pleased with you! God shared these incredible affirmations with his Son. In the subsequent verses, Jesus will face the temptations of Satan in the wilderness armed with the understanding that his Heavenly Father lovingly and proudly claims him as his child. When we were baptized, I can't help but believe that God said the same things about you and me!

TODAY'S PRAYER

Loving and adoring Father, I know I do not merit your love and grace. Yet, dear Father, I am overwhelmed with them and thankful for them. As your child, please know that I love and adore you—even in those times when I make wrong choices and when I succumb to temptation's power. Father, do not ever let the evil one strip my love for you from me or let him cloud my eyes to your love. I pray this in the name of Jesus, your beloved Son. Amen.

CONTEXT: MARK 1:9-20

RELATED PASSAGES: ROMANS 8:15-16; GALATIANS 3:26-29; JOHN 3:1-8

Day 10

LED BY THE SPIRIT

MARK 1:12
Then the Spirit sent Jesus into the desert alone.

KEY THOUGHT

Jesus was led and guided by the Holy Spirit—in both good times and bad times. Just as Jesus goes to face temptation in the wilderness immediately after his baptism, we too find ourselves facing powerful temptation after a major spiritual experience, a deepened spiritual commitment, or a special time of devotion. This does not mean the Holy Spirit has abandoned us. Rather, it means that the Spirit goes with us to lead us through the time of testing and temptation. The Spirit takes what Satan intended for our harm and turns it into something that can strengthen our faith and mature us in our discipleship.

TODAY'S PRAYER

Father, give me the courage to believe that your Holy Spirit leads and guides me. Help me believe that I am not alone—not in the good times when I feel strong and not in the tough times when I feel abandoned. Use all the events in my life to mature me more and more into the character, compassion, and commitment of Jesus, in whose name I pray. Amen.

CONTEXT: MARK 1:9-20

RELATED PASSAGES: JOHN 4:30-36; ROMANS 8:14-17; 5:22-26

Day 11

CARE UNDER FIRE

MARK 1:13

*He was there for 40 days, being tempted by Satan. During this time he was
out among the wild animals. Then angels came and helped him.*

KEY THOUGHT

When you feel alone, abandoned, and under attack, where do you turn
for help? Jesus trusted in his relationship with his Father. He was being led by
the Spirit. However, this passage reminds us of a truth we often forget: God
does send his angels to help his faithful servants in times of trial. Jesus faced
Satan in the wilderness and among the wild animals, but he was not alone.
Angels attended to him. The question now is whether each one of us believes
that God will bless us with the same kind of support when we experience
wilderness times?

TODAY'S PRAYER

*Father, I thank you that, as your child, I will never have to face the times of
temptation and trial alone. I thank you for your Holy Spirit that lives in me.
Although I may not see them, I thank you for the angels I trust are sent to assist
me. Most of all, dear God, I rely upon your promise never to abandon me. Please
give me the faith to believe that I am never alone or abandoned as your child.
In the name of Jesus, who victoriously faced temptation, I pray. Amen.*

CONTEXT: MARK 1:9-20

RELATED PASSAGES: HEBREWS 1:14; ROMANS 8:14-17, 38-39; HEBREWS 13:5-6

Day 12

The Near Kingdom

Mark 1:14-15

After John was put in prison, Jesus went into Galilee and told people the Good News from God. He said, "The right time is now here. God's kingdom is near. Change your hearts and lives, and believe the Good News!"

Key Thought

Mark wants us to see that Jesus' baptism by John, Jesus' temptations in the wilderness, and John's arrest lead to the beginning of Jesus' ministry. Jesus goes to Galilee, the place of ministry in Mark's Gospel. He begins to preach "God's Good News" about the nearness of God's Kingdom. This nearness of the Kingdom and this presentation of Good News mean people must respond by turning away from their sins. God's will must reign in our hearts if we are to receive this Kingdom. So the question comes to you and to me: have I welcomed the Good News and turned away from my sins?

Today's Prayer

Holy and righteous Father, God of mercy and grace, I believe that your Son has brought me your Good News. I believe you want the power of your Kingdom to reign in my heart and be seen in the fruit of righteousness produced in my life. I gladly offer my heart, soul, strength, and mind to show my love for you and my desire to honor you. In the name of the one who is good news, Jesus of Nazareth, I pray. Amen.

Context: Mark 1:9-20

Related Passages: Acts 8:4-8, 12; Galatians 5:16-21; 1 Thessalonians 2:12

Day 13

A New Kind of Fishing

Mark 1:16-18

Jesus was walking by Lake Galilee. He saw Simon and his brother, Andrew. These two men were fishermen, and they were throwing a net into the lake to catch fish. Jesus said to them, "Come, follow me, and I will make you a different kind of fishermen. You will bring in people, not fish." So they immediately left their nets and followed Jesus.

Key Thought

I don't know about you, but I love to fish. However, fishing is a hobby, not my livelihood. Jesus is saying to these fishermen that he is going to take their livelihood and transform it into a way to change people's lives for God. Now these fishermen completely left their fishing boats behind, at least for awhile. Most of us, however, he asks to stay in our vocations and let him show us how to bless others and bring God into their lives. If we are going to follow Jesus, then we should see his transforming power show up in our workplace and in our influence among those around us. "Follow me!" Jesus is asking you and me. Will we follow him . . . especially at work and school?

Today's Prayer

Dear Heavenly Father, give me the vision to see the opportunities you place before me to bless others and share your grace. In the name of the Lord Jesus I pray. Amen.

Context: Mark 1:9-20

Related Passages: Matthew 28:18-20; 1 Peter 3:13-16; Acts 8:4-5

Day 14

LEFT BEHIND

MARK 1:19-20

Jesus continued walking by Lake Galilee. He saw two more brothers, James and John, the sons of Zebedee. They were in their boat, preparing their nets to catch fish. Their father Zebedee and the men who worked for him were in the boat with the brothers. When Jesus saw the brothers, he told them to come. They left their father and followed Jesus.

KEY THOUGHT

There is a cost to following Jesus. Some people won't understand. Some of those who won't understand may even be in our own families. However, we are called to follow, knowing that others we love might not be willing to face the cost of that discipleship. Don't be fooled, dear friend, by preachers promising everything while implying there will not be heartbreak or hardship. Some we love will not follow with us. However, our hope and prayer is that their reluctance will be only temporary and that through us they will come to know the Jesus we follow. The first step, however, is to follow . . . no matter the cost!

TODAY'S PRAYER

Give me courage, dear Father, to follow Jesus as my Lord no matter the cost. Please use me to influence those I love to come to know Jesus as their Lord. In the name of Jesus, whom I follow. Amen.

CONTEXT: MARK 1:9-20

RELATED PASSAGES: LUKE 9:23-26, 62; 1 PETER 3:1-2; 1 PETER 4:3-4

Day 15

SABBATH TEACHING

MARK 1:21-22

Jesus and his followers went to Capernaum. On the Sabbath day, Jesus went into the synagogue and taught the people. They were amazed at his teaching. He did not teach like their teachers of the law. He taught like someone with authority.

KEY THOUGHT

Jesus went to church! Well, not exactly church as we know it, but he did go to the assembly of God's people at the synagogue. Weren't there hypocrites, sinners, and worse in those meetings? Yes! But Jesus went to the synagogue because these people were searching for God, despite their failures and problems. He used his visits as opportunities to teach the people. They recognized his authority. Do we? Are we responding to Jesus' words of comfort, challenge, and conviction?

TODAY'S PRAYER

Holy God and righteous Father, thank you for Jesus' example of going to meet with your people and blessing them with your truth. As I go to the assembly of people who honor your name and praise Jesus for his sacrifice, I pray that Jesus' teaching and will are obeyed. In the authoritative name of Jesus I pray. Amen.

CONTEXT: MARK 1:21-28

RELATED PASSAGES: 1 CORINTHIANS 4:20; LUKE 4:16-21; LUKE 3:7-9

Day 16

EVEN THE DEMONS CONFESS

MARK 1:23-24

While Jesus was in the synagogue, a man was there who had an evil spirit inside him. The man shouted, "Jesus of Nazareth! What do you want with us? Did you come to destroy us? I know who you are—God's Holy One!"

KEY THOUGHT

One of the things that we will see again and again in the Gospel of Mark is that the demons know who Jesus is: the Son of God. They know he is more powerful than they are: he casts them out and they obey his commands. Jesus is stronger than Satan and he can defeat Satan and his demonic cohorts. Even though the demons know who Jesus is, Jesus doesn't permit them to spread the news because he doesn't want the testimony of demons. Jesus will define his own identity by his life of service offered to others and given to honor God.

TODAY'S PRAYER

Holy God, guard my heart from desiring titles, accolades, and earthly notoriety. I know, dear Father, that Satan can use my pride to bring me to ruin. I also know, dear God, that the evil one can twist my reputation and use it to keep others from the Gospel. Holy Father, please protect my reputation and guard my heart so that my life can be used to bless others and help them know the truth about your Son. In Jesus' name, your Holy One, I pray. Amen.

CONTEXT: MARK 1:21-28

RELATED PASSAGES: MARK 3:22-27; MARK 1:35-39; JAMES 2:19

Day 17

POWER OVER EVIL

MARK 1:25-26

Jesus, his voice full of warning, said, "Be quiet, and come out of him!" The evil spirit made the man shake. Then the spirit made a loud noise and came out of him.

KEY THOUGHT

Jesus had power over the evil one and the vile power he seeks to wield. He defeated him during the temptation in the wilderness. He defeated him in every encounter during his life. Most importantly, he defeated him in the place of Satan's greatest power—death. Jesus' victory over Satan and death will be most gloriously realized when he comes again in glory with victory for all of his disciples.

TODAY'S PRAYER

O LORD, God Almighty, the Sovereign God of Israel, thank you for giving me victory through Jesus over Satan, sin, and death. I praise you for your grace that has saved me. I praise you for your Spirit that indwells me and gives me power. I praise you for the coming glorious return in which I will share. To you belongs all glory and honor, now and forevermore, in the name of your Son, Jesus. Amen.

CONTEXT: MARK 1:21-28

RELATED PASSAGES: HEBREWS 2:14-15; MARK 6:5-8; 1 CORINTHIANS 15:25-26, 56-58

THE AUTHORITATIVE VOICE

MARK 1:27-28

The people were amazed. They asked each other, "What is happening here? This man is teaching something new, and he teaches with authority! He even commands evil spirits, and they obey him." So the news about Jesus spread quickly everywhere in the area of Galilee.

KEY THOUGHT

Jesus has authority. Not just rank so he can give orders. Not just power so he can obliterate his enemies. No, Jesus has true authority—rank, power, and integrity so that he can authentically rule over and destroy evil. This authority should not just be admired. This authority should not leave us spell-bound. No, this authority should lead us to watch Jesus and learn from his actions, because they are gracious and compassionate as well as mighty. This authority should make us listen to what he says, because Jesus' words are not only true, they are also life-giving and liberating. We should be excited. We should tell others about Jesus. Most importantly, we should obey him and follow his example of sacrificial service.

TODAY'S PRAYER

My dear and precious Father, the One True and Living God, please give me the courage to believe and obey the words of Jesus and to follow his example of sacrificial service. In Jesus' mighty name I pray. Amen.

CONTEXT: MARK 1:21-28

RELATED PASSAGES: MATTHEW 28:18-20; MARK 10:42-45; MARK 3:31-35

Day 19

GONE IN AN INSTANT

MARK 1:29-31

Jesus and the followers left the synagogue. They all went with James and John to the home of Simon and Andrew. Simon's mother-in-law was very sick. She was in bed and had a fever. The people there told Jesus about her. So he went to her bed. Jesus held her hand and helped her stand up. The fever left her, and she was healed. Then she began serving them.

KEY THOUGHT

Jesus leaves no doubt about his power over illness; he sees the illness and cures it. It is gone in an instant. With the touch of Jesus' hand and the power of his grace, Peter's mother-in-law goes from bedridden to healthy hostess preparing a meal. As impressive as this kind of miracle is, think about the change that same grace brings in our spiritual lives. Salvation is a great miracle in each life touched by God's grace and Jesus' love. Our sin is gone in an instant. Our future is changed for the better in an instant. Our hopes are raised in an instant. While our own life as a disciple will be a gradual transformation to become more like Christ, God's view of us is changed in an instant. Such is the power, love, and grace of our Lord!

TODAY'S PRAYER

Father in heaven, thank you for the life-changing power of your grace demonstrated to me in the sacrifice of Jesus and the work of your Holy Spirit. In Jesus' name I pray. Amen.

CONTEXT: MARK 1:29-39

RELATED PASSAGES: 2 CORINTHIANS 5:17; 2 CORINTHIANS 3:17-18; 1 CORINTHIANS 6:9-11

Day 20

THE MAGNET OF GRACE

MARK 1:32-33

*That night, after the sun went down, the people brought to Jesus many
who were sick. They also brought those who had demons inside them.
Everyone in the town gathered at the door of that house.*

KEY THOUGHT

When people see the power of Jesus to change a person's life, they are
drawn to him. As believers whose lives have been touched by Jesus, the power
of Jesus in our lives is just as powerful. People can be drawn to the grace of
our Lord when they see his power at work transforming us. He asks us to be
ready to share the hope that he has given us through his power in our lives
and to live in a way consistent with his character and grace. Let's display and
proclaim what his power has done for us so that others will be drawn to him.

TODAY'S PRAYER

*O LORD God, my Abba Father, let the power, grace, and beauty of Jesus be seen in my
life so that others can come to know him. In the name of Jesus, Lord of all, I pray. Amen.*

CONTEXT: MARK 1:29-39

RELATED PASSAGES: 1 CORINTHIANS 4:20; REVELATION 12:10;
1 PETER 3:15-16

Day 21

POWER UNLIMITED

MARK 1:34

Jesus healed many of those who had different kinds of sicknesses.
He also forced many demons out of people. But he would not allow
the demons to speak, because they knew who he was.

KEY THOUGHT

Jesus' power was not limited. As the Son of God, he had power over
all different kinds of diseases and he had power over all different kinds of
demons. The demons knew who Jesus was so Jesus wouldn't let them speak.
Jesus would reveal his own identity and not let his enemies do it. Jesus would
define what it meant to be the Christ, the Son of God, and not let Satan and
his demonic hordes define him. So Jesus healed diseases and he ordered
demons around and refused to let them have any kind of power. His power
could not, and cannot, be limited by his opposition. He has all the power.

TODAY'S PRAYER

Loving and righteous Father, it is comforting for me to know that Jesus has power over
all demonic power. I ask now that he use that power in several people about whom I am
concerned. I fear that they have succumbed to temptation and have made themselves
vulnerable to the influence of the evil one because of their association with evil people,
harmfully addictive chemicals, out-of-control greed, or uncontrollable lust. Father, I
want to pray for several of these people by name . . . . Bless them and empower them.
I ask this in the mighty name of Jesus Christ, your Son and my Savior. Amen.

CONTEXT: MARK 1:29-39

RELATED PASSAGES: COLOSSIANS 1:11-13; JAMES 4:7; 1 JOHN 4:4

Day 22

QUIET TIME WITH GOD

MARK 1:35

The next morning, Jesus woke up very early. Jesus left the house while it was still dark. He went to a place to be alone and pray.

KEY THOUGHT

Jesus had a regular, disciplined time to be alone with his Father each day. His quiet time with his Father was intentional; it was a priority he built into his day and it required his effort—effort to wake up early before everyone else, and effort to go out away from everyone else so he could talk with God by himself. How intentional is your daily time with the Father?

TODAY'S PRAYER

O loving and tender Father, God Almighty who has the power to save, forgive me for those periods in my life when I have let my time with you suffer. I confess that I let other things and the hectic pace of my life steal away my time with you. Empower my resolve to put you first in my heart and in my daily schedule. In Jesus' name I pray. Amen.

CONTEXT: MARK 1:29-39

RELATED PASSAGES: LUKE 5:15; LUKE 22:39-42; PSALM 59:16

Day 23

PRESSURES OF THE CARING

MARK 1:35-37

The next morning Jesus woke up very early. He left the house while it was still dark and went to a place where he could be alone and pray. Later, Simon and his friends went to look for Jesus. They found him and said, "Everyone is looking for you!"

KEY THOUGHT

The more ministry involves working with people, the more we need quiet time with God. In the previous verses in Mark 1, Jesus has been highly involved in people-intensive ministry as he teaches, preaches, heals, and casts out demons. This is exhausting work. Yet there is always more work with people than any one of us can complete. There will always be another need, broken heart, hurting soul, and desperate problem. For us to continue to minister, we desperately need to get alone with God to renew our relationship, to restore our souls, and to rekindle our passion in the presence of God.

TODAY'S PRAYER

Father, I don't have the pressure or crush of people that your Son faced in his ministry. However, I know I need to follow his example and get away to center myself in your will and be rekindled by time in your presence. Help me become more disciplined as I commit my life to serving others as my Lord did. In Jesus' name and for his cause I pray. Amen.

CONTEXT: MARK 1:29-39

RELATED PASSAGES: MARK 6:30-31; PSALM 23:1-3; LAMENTATIONS 3:22-26

Day 24

DOING THE MISSION

MARK 1:37-38

They found him and said, "Everyone is looking for you!"

Jesus answered, "We should go to another place. We can go to other towns around here, and I can tell God's message to those people too. That is why I came."

KEY THOUGHT

Jesus came with a mission to accomplish. Knowing our mission in life helps us clarify our daily commitments and center our efforts on the things God has called us to do. It helps keep us on track and focused. It enables us to say "No!" to things that are merely good so that we can do the essential ones. We don't normally think about Jesus' turning down an opportunity to teach, preach, serve, and heal folks. Yet in this situation, he does just that— not because he didn't love them, but because God sent him to proclaim the good news of the Kingdom in many cities and towns. Therefore, he couldn't get bogged down being just a miracle-man in one location. Let's focus on our purpose and ask God to clarify for us what our mission is so that we can accomplish it. Like Jesus, it will help us not get bogged down in things that are just good, when there are really essential things to accomplish. Of course, as we will see later in this context, having a mission never means we neglect the needs of those God places in our paths.

TODAY'S PRAYER

Father God, the Almighty who knows me better than I know myself, please help me come to a better understanding of my mission in life. Help me as I make the choices and commitments of each day. I want to do what you have called me to do and not just what I feel compelled by urgency to do. May my life bring you glory and may I fulfill your purpose for me. In Jesus' name I pray. Amen.

CONTEXT: MARK 1:29-39

RELATED PASSAGES: PSALM 139:13-16; EPHESIANS 1:11-12; JOHN 4:34; 19:28-30

Day 25

The Place and the Plan of Ministry

MARK 1:39

So Jesus traveled everywhere in Galilee. He spoke in the synagogues, and he forced demons out of people.

Key Thought

In the previous verses, Jesus recommits to his mission to preach in the villages and cities. He goes all over Galilee sharing the message of the Kingdom. He goes to the people in the synagogues and continues his powerful mastery over demons. He has a plan to fulfill his God-ordained purpose. He executes this plan, not just because he is committed to a plan, but because he also has a heart for people and a commitment to honor God's will. What is your plan for honoring God's will in your life? What is he calling you to do to serve him and his children?

Today's Prayer

Holy and loving Father, I want to honor your will for my life. However, dear Father, I need the guidance of your Spirit to help me recognize your will for me and to help me develop a plan for doing your work and fulfilling your purposes for me. In the name of Jesus, who has power over all things, I pray. Amen.

Context: Mark 1:29-39

Related Passages: Acts 9:17-20; Acts 17:2; Acts 1:8

Day 26

FAITH FINDS ITS HOPE

MARK 1:40

*A man who had leprosy came to Jesus. The man bowed on his knees
and begged him, "You have the power to heal me if you want."*

KEY THOUGHT

Sometimes we come to the Lord for help simply out of habit. Sometimes
we come with a sense of entitlement, arrogantly approaching him as if he
owes us something. Humility is not really part of our modern vocabulary.
Begging is not in our nature or in our experience. We very much need to
learn from this leper: we come to God out of great need, begging for healing,
and fully confident that he can heal if he chooses to do so. When was the last
time we threw ourselves on the mercy of the Lord? When was the last time
we physically knelt in prayer in the presence of the Lord? Let's throw off the
shackles of our false pride and pseudo-sophistication and recognize our place
in the presence of the Almighty God and his Son and our Savior.

TODAY'S PRAYER

*Almighty God, the One True Holy God, I bow before you in prayer. I thank
you for your grace given to me in the gift of your Son. I recognize that I am not
worthy on my own to approach you. Yet, dear Father, I know that as your child
who is filled with your Spirit I have the opportunity to approach you boldly.
Have mercy on me, dear Father, for I need your presence and power in my life
if I am ever going to be all that you want me to be. In Jesus' name. Amen.*

CONTEXT: MARK 1:40-45

RELATED PASSAGES: MARK 10:46-52; PSALM 57:1; PSALM 86:16

Day 27

COMPASSIONATE POWER

MARK 1:40-42

*A man who had leprosy came to Jesus. The man bowed on his knees
and begged him, "You have the power to heal me if you want."*

*Jesus felt sorry for the man. So he touched him and said, "I want to heal you. Be
healed!" Immediately the leprosy disappeared, and the man was healed.*

KEY THOUGHT

This translation uses the expression "felt sorry," but the better translation
is probably "felt compassion." In his heart, in his "gut," Jesus feels the anguish
of this man afflicted with leprosy. So before he speaks healing into the man's
life, he does the unthinkable: he touches the leprous man. By Jewish law,
Jesus makes himself unclean by touching the man. Yet Jesus wants to show
the compassion he feels in a way this man would understand. Jesus spoke the
words of healing only after he has connected to the man's deepest emotional
need and bridged the barrier that enforced this man's isolation. Mark has two
messages for us in this story. First, he wants us to know that Jesus has come
and bridged the distance between us and God and he will let nothing separate
us from his love. Second, he wants us to do the same with others.

TODAY'S PRAYER

*Dear Father in heaven, thank you for your mercy and grace. Thank you for
bridging the distance between your holiness and my weakness by sending Jesus.
Use me to help others find their way to Jesus, in whose name I pray. Amen.*

CONTEXT: MARK 1:40-45

RELATED PASSAGES: JOHN 20:21; LUKE 17:11-19; 1 JOHN 3:16-18

DO WHAT YOU ARE COMMANDED

MARK 1:43-44

Jesus told the man to go, but he gave him a strong warning: "Don't tell anyone about what I did for you. But go and let the priest look at you. And offer a gift to God because you have been healed. Offer the gift that Moses commanded. This will show everyone that you are healed."

KEY THOUGHT

"Offer the gift that Moses commanded." Two principles are at work here. First, the man cleansed of his leprosy needs to do what is required to regain the right to enter into daily public life. Second, his going to the priests would validate Jesus' authority over disease. Jesus is no charlatan. He is the comforting, validating, and affirming Lord and Savior we all need.

TODAY'S PRAYER

Holy God and precious Lord Jesus, help me see what I need to do to show those around me that you are not only my Lord, but that you want me to do what is right, good, honest, fair, and just. To you, O God, and to you, the triumphant Son, I offer my praise and thanks forever and ever. Amen.

CONTEXT: MARK 1:40-45

RELATED PASSAGES: ROMANS 13:1-7; 1 PETER 2:13-15; PHILIPPIANS 1:27; 3:20

Day 29

Disobedience Hinders God's Plan

MARK 1:45

*The man left there and told everyone he saw that Jesus had healed him.
So the news about Jesus spread. And that is why he could not enter a
town if people saw him. He stayed in places where people did not live.
But people came from all the towns to the places where he was.*

KEY THOUGHT

Many times we think we know what is best. Unfortunately, some of those times we actually disobey the clear teaching of the Lord because we think we know a better way. Invariably, our attempts at doing good by disobeying the Lord end up hindering his will. Certainly God can overcome our misguided attempts at helping his cause for he is sovereign and all-powerful. That's not the point. We need to obey him even when we can't understand the reasons behind the command and when we think we may know a better way to help and honor the Lord. The man who had leprosy disobeyed Jesus and told those around him about what Jesus had done. Instead of being able to fulfill God's purpose for him by going to the cities and villages and proclaiming the word there (see vs. 38-39), Jesus now has to stay in secluded spaces. People came to him, but he was cut off from going to them. The man's disobedience, though well intentioned, interfered with Jesus' desire to fulfill his mission. In the same way, our disobedience of the Lord today often interferes with the Lord's desire to accomplish his mission in us.

TODAY'S PRAYER

*Father, forgive me when I do not obey you. I know my disobedience hinders
my own growth and can also interfere with your work in building the
Kingdom and reaching the lost. In Jesus' name I pray. Amen.*

CONTEXT: MARK 1:40-45

RELATED PASSAGES: 1 SAMUEL 15:10-15, 19-23; MATTHEW 7:21; JOHN 15:14

Day 30

A LARGE CROWD FINDS GOOD NEWS

MARK 2:1-3

A few days later, Jesus came to Capernaum. The news spread that he was back home. A large crowd gathered to hear him speak. The house was so full that there was no place to stand, not even outside the door. While Jesus was teaching, some people brought a paralyzed man to see him.

KEY THOUGHT

Once again, the crowds swarmed to see Jesus, presumably because of what they had heard about his miraculous power to cure lepers, to heal the sick, and to cast out demons. However, Jesus chose to teach rather than to heal with such a great crowd assembled. He was called to preach (Mark 1:38). His focus was giving people the good news of God's Kingdom and calling them to repentance (Mark 1:15). Rather than gaining fame, Jesus wanted to win hearts to God. While we all may be tempted to try to impress large crowds and to win fame for ourselves, Jesus' example is a powerful reminder that the most important thing we can do is to help people understand the message of God by our words and our actions.

TODAY'S PRAYER

Holy and tender Father, give me the courage and the sensitivity to share your message with others and to call them to change their lives to honor you. Give me wisdom, dear God, to know how best to do this with gentleness and respect. Help me discern the best time and the best method to share this good news with the people around me. Thank you for your help and guidance in this important task. In the gracious name of Jesus I pray. Amen.

CONTEXT: MARK 2:1-12

RELATED PASSAGES: MARK 1:14-18; ACTS 4:12; 1 PETER 3:14-16

Day 31

FAITHFUL FRIENDS

MARK 2:2-5

While Jesus was teaching, some people brought a paralyzed man to see him. He was being carried by four of them. But they could not get the man inside to Jesus because the house was so full of people. So they went to the roof above Jesus and made a hole in it. Then they lowered the mat with the paralyzed man on it. When Jesus saw how much faith they had, he said to the paralyzed man, "Young man, your sins are forgiven."

KEY THOUGHT

Notice the basis of this miracle. "Seeing THEIR faith . . . ." The four men were the ones who helped make this miracle possible. It wasn't just their willingness to help the man, but it was their faith that if they got their friend to Jesus then the Lord would do great things for him. They were right. The question, however, is whether or not we will be so bold in our faith with our friends.

TODAY'S PRAYER

Father, please strengthen my faith and use me to bring those who are broken, lost, and hurting to experience the gracious and powerful gift of your Son's love. In Jesus' name. Amen.

CONTEXT: MARK 2:1-12

RELATED PASSAGES: MARK 9:20-24; MATTHEW 8:5-10; MARK 5:35-42

Day 32

ONLY GOD CAN!

MARK 2:6-7

Some of the teachers of the law were sitting there. They saw what Jesus did, and they said to themselves, "Why does this man say things like that? What an insult to God! No one but God can forgive sins."

KEY THOUGHT

Yes, the statement is correct: "Only God can forgive sins!" This startling statement was made by the religious opponents of Jesus, but it is intended for us as well. While we need to forgive each other, only God can completely forgive sins. That's the point. Jesus is the Christ, God's Son, who came among us. He is God in human skin. If we want to know how God values people, all we have to do is look at Jesus and we know. Even more important, if we want to know how our sins can be forgiven, we can look to him.

TODAY'S PRAYER

LORD God Almighty, I believe that you walked the roads of Galilee and Judea, getting your feet dirty with the dust of our mortality and your robe soiled with the sins of folks like me. Thank you for showing me your incomparable love and grace in Jesus, in whose name I praise and thank you. Amen.

CONTEXT: MARK 2:1-12

RELATED PASSAGES: JOHN 1:14-18; LUKE 7:11-16; JOHN 14:8-11

Day 33

Blasphemy? I Think Not!

Mark 2:8-11

Jesus knew immediately what these teachers of the law were thinking. So he said to them, "Why do you have these questions in your minds? The Son of Man has power on earth to forgive sins. But how can I prove this to you? Maybe you are thinking it was easy for me to say to the crippled man, 'Your sins are forgiven.' There's no proof it really happened. But what if I say to the man, 'Stand up. Take your mat and walk'? Then you will be able to see if I really have this power or not." So Jesus said to the paralyzed man, "I tell you, stand up. Take your mat and go home."

Key Thought

Jesus heals people for many different reasons and under many different circumstances. The bottom line is this: Jesus heals people because he loves them and wants to bring them to God. In this instance, however, Jesus is moved by two additional things. First, he sees the faith of this man's friends and he is touched by their concern. Second, he is frustrated with the cynicism and opposition from those who are present only to criticize him. They doubt his authority, so he demonstrates it: he heals the man! Then he emphasizes that the miracle he has done shows he has the authority to forgive sins. The real challenge for you and me is to recognize that Jesus' authority doesn't extend just to his power to teach and command, but also to heal, mend, help, forgive, and bless.

Today's Prayer

Holy and Almighty LORD of the ages, thank you that your authority has been powerfully demonstrated in Jesus. Help me open my heart to him fully and not only to respond with obedience to Jesus' commands, but to also let him in to nurture and bless. In the name of Jesus, the one who has power to forgive and cleanse, I pray. Amen.

Context: Mark 2:1-12

Related Passages: Mark 1:22; Mark 11:27-33; Mark 1:27

Day 34

PRAISE AT SEEING GRACE

MARK 2:12

Immediately the paralyzed man stood up. He picked up his mat and walked out of the room. Everyone could see him. They were amazed and praised God. They said, "This is the most amazing thing we have ever seen!"

KEY THOUGHT

The lives in which Jesus works bring praise to God. So . . . are we allowing Jesus to work in our lives and are we helping bring others to Jesus so he can work in their lives as well?

TODAY'S PRAYER

Father, use me to open people's hearts to Jesus. In fact, dear Father, please open my heart to allow Jesus to act with complete authority in my life. In the amazing name of Jesus I pray. Amen.

CONTEXT: MARK 2:1-12

RELATED PASSAGES: MATTHEW 28:18-20; JOHN 1:35-41; JOHN 4:28-30, 39-42

Day 35

LEAVING IT BEHIND

MARK 2:13-14

Jesus went to the lake again, and many people followed him there. So Jesus taught them. He was walking beside the lake, and he saw a man named Levi, son of Alphaeus. Levi was sitting at his place for collecting taxes. Jesus said to him, "Follow me." Then Levi stood up and followed Jesus.

KEY THOUGHT

Two exciting things happen in these two short verses. First, Jesus shows that the call to follow him should be offered to all kinds of people: many we may think wouldn't follow him are actually open to his call. Second, the call to follow Jesus means we are willing to leave all of our bases of security behind and follow him. Levi was willing, are we?

TODAY'S PRAYER

Father, please increase my courage and open the hidden places in my heart that I have not fully offered to the Lordship of your Son and my Savior. In Jesus' name I pray. Amen.

CONTEXT: MARK 2:13-17

RELATED PASSAGES: MARK 9:34-38; MARK 10:17-22; LUKE 14:27

Day 36

AMONG SINNERS

MARK 2:15-17

Later that day, Jesus and his followers ate at Levi's house. There were also many tax collectors and others with bad reputations eating with them. (There were many of these people who followed Jesus.) When some teachers of the law who were Pharisees saw Jesus eating with such bad people, they asked his followers, "Why does he eat with tax collectors and sinners?"

When Jesus heard this, he said to them, "It is the sick people who need a doctor, not those who are healthy. I did not come to invite good people. I came to invite sinners."

KEY THOUGHT

Jesus came to save sinners. Yes, all of us are sinners. Unfortunately, many try to pretend they are not sinners or defend the sins they have committed as "normal failures" or "mistakes." This is true even of people who consider themselves religious. Jesus reminds us that he came to rescue sinners. He came for us. He came to call us to join him in the work. Will we respond?

TODAY'S PRAYER

Righteous Father, thank you for sending Jesus to save me from my sins. Without your grace, I know that I would be lost. Please use me to help others find their way to your grace. In the name of Jesus, who came to call sinners like me to repentance, I pray. Amen.

CONTEXT: MARK 2:13-17

RELATED PASSAGES: 1 TIMOTHY 1:12-17; 1 JOHN 1:8-10; LUKE 19:9-10

Day 37

UNDER SCRUTINY

MARK 2:18

*The followers of John and the Pharisees were fasting. Some people
came to Jesus and said, "John's followers fast, and the followers of
the Pharisees fast. But your followers don't fast. Why?"*

KEY THOUGHT

As today's passage and the verses on either side of it indicate, Jesus is in a
time of close scrutiny as people try to understand him and his message. Even
at this early stage of his ministry, many of the questions move from sincere
truth-seeking and quickly become an opportunity to try to trap him. Other
questions carry some implicit accusation that Jesus' teaching and expectations
are lax on holiness and dedication. While the critical questions of others
should make us go back and re-examine our positions and practices, we do
not need to compromise our commitments and values. Truth and genuine
commitment have always been criticized.

TODAY'S PRAYER

*LORD God Almighty, give me the courage not to turn back from my convictions
when I am criticized, doubted, and questioned. Help me to know your truth
and put it into practice each day of my life. In Jesus' name I pray. Amen.*

CONTEXT: MARK 2:18-28

RELATED PASSAGES: JOHN 8:31-32; GALATIANS 1:10; JOHN 7:14-18

Day 38

SOMEDAY HE WILL BE TAKEN AWAY

MARK 2:19-20

Jesus answered, "At a wedding the friends of the bridegroom are not sad while he is with them. They cannot fast while the bridegroom is still there. But the time will come when the bridegroom will be taken from them. Then they will fast."

KEY THOUGHT

The reason Jesus' disciples didn't fast (see the previous verses) was related to the timing of his ministry, not their piety. They would fast when he was taken from them—the first hint that Jesus will face a painful ending to his life. While he was present with them physically, however, they would not fast. Instead, they would enjoy his presence and celebrate his love.

TODAY'S PRAYER

Father, help me know the proper time for each of my spiritual activities— feasting and fasting, rejoicing and weeping, comforting and being comforted, celebrating and repenting contritely. This I ask in the name of Jesus. Amen.

CONTEXT: MARK 2:18-28

RELATED PASSAGES: ECCLESIASTES 3:1-11; EPHESIANS 5:15-17; MATTHEW 6:16-18

Day 39

New Wineskins Needed

Mark 2:21-22

"When someone sews a patch over a hole in an old coat, they never use a piece of cloth that is not yet shrunk. If they do, the patch will shrink and pull away from the coat. Then the hole will be worse. Also, no one ever pours new wine into old wineskins. The wine would break them, and the wine would be ruined along with the wineskins. You always put new wine into new wineskins."

Key Thought

Jesus wants us to know that being his follower is not just another take on the same old religious agenda. Jesus wants us to know that his words and his way of life are not just another new thing to tack onto the same religious teaching. Jesus brings something new, fresh, and comprehensive. Trying to mix it into the other religious interests in our lives is to miss the point. What Jesus brings is bigger, bolder, and new! Let's realize that to call Jesus our Lord means we surrender every part of our lives to him . . . and that ultimately means we surrender the "religious" parts, too.

Today's Prayer

LORD God Almighty, I offer you myself—all of myself, body, soul, spirit, and mind— to serve you. I want you to have complete rule in my life. Please tear down any idols that I have so that only you reign in my heart. Open my eyes to see your truth in fresh and new ways. In the name of Jesus, who can make me new, I pray. Amen.

Context: Mark 2:18-28

Related Passages: Romans 12:1-2; 2 Corinthians 5:16-17; Romans 6:3-4

Day 40

CRITICAL EYES

MARK 2:23-24

On the Sabbath day, Jesus and his followers were walking through some grain fields. The followers picked some grain to eat. Some Pharisees said to Jesus, "Why are your followers doing this? It is against the law to pick grain on the Sabbath."

KEY THOUGHT

There are some who watch others who are committed to Christ only trying to find fault in them. Critical sniping at Jesus' followers—"nit-picky-ness" as I call it—is not a virtue. Jesus condemns judging others' hearts on the basis of traditions and from a harsh spirit, looking to catch them in minor points of law. The way we judge others becomes the standard of judgment used on us by God. As Christians, we have been liberated from law-keeping; let's also liberate ourselves from a harsh, judgmental, and nit-picky spirit. May the spirit that made some of the Pharisees so harsh not be found among us!

TODAY'S PRAYER

Holy God, forgive me and help me leave behind a critical, harsh spirit of judgment. Teach me to be gracious and never let my faith get lost in Pharisaism. In the name of the Lord Jesus, I pray. Amen.

CONTEXT: MARK 2:18-28

RELATED PASSAGES: MATTHEW 7:1-5; JAMES 2:12-13; GALATIANS 5:1

Day 41

FOR THE BENEFIT OF PEOPLE

MARK 2:25-27

*Jesus answered, "You have read what David did when he and the people
with him were hungry and needed food. It was during the time of Abiathar
the high priest. David went into God's house and ate the bread that was
offered to God. And the Law of Moses says that only priests can eat that
bread. David also gave some of the bread to the people with him."*

*Then Jesus said to the Pharisees, "The Sabbath day was made to help
people. People were not made to be ruled by the Sabbath."*

KEY THOUGHT

Did God need a day to be honored or did his human creations need a day
to rest? Well, God doesn't "need" anything. It seems clear that the Sabbath
was a day to remember and recognize the blessings God had given the
Israelites. At the same time, we human creatures need to rest. Without rest
we make ourselves vulnerable to temptation due to fatigue and exhaustion.
Without rest we can damage our own physical health. Most of all, without rest
we are tempted to forget the one from whom we've received all of our many
blessings. Then we feel that everything depends upon us and this feeling puts
more pressure on us to perform. God didn't make the Sabbath for himself,
but gave Sabbath as a gift to his human creations. While many don't keep the
literal Sabbath (the seventh day or Saturday) as a religious observance, we
would do well to remember this Sabbath principal as the rhythm of God's
universe and take time to rest, remember, and refresh.

TODAY'S PRAYER

*Forgive me, dear Father, for trying to cram too much into my short days.
I confess that I am sometimes overly anxious to do too many things. I am
honestly seeking your help so that I can live a more balanced and holy life.
Help me as I seek to find times of rest that you have created for me and my
spiritual, physical, and emotional needs. In Jesus' name. Amen.*

CONTEXT: MARK 2:18-28

RELATED PASSAGES: COLOSSIANS 2:16-17; JOHN 5:16-23; EXODUS 31:15-17

Day 42

MASTER OF EVERY MOMENT!

MARK 2:28

"So the Son of Man is Lord of every day, even the Sabbath."

KEY THOUGHT

Jesus is Lord! He has authority over everything! He is the Master and Commander of all things. His word, his teaching, his will about the Sabbath set the standard for us. So what Jesus does on the Sabbath, says about the Sabbath, and teaches regarding the Sabbath are our examples, instructions, and truths regarding the Sabbath. We seek Jesus, not the Sabbath! He is the one who provides genuine rest and renewal.

TODAY'S PRAYER

Holy God, my heavenly Father, thank you for giving us the principle of the Sabbath. I know I need to rest more and I need to remember that every good thing comes from you. However, dear Father, I realize now more than ever that I need Jesus. I need his comfort, power, rest, and grace. Come Lord Jesus! Amen.

CONTEXT: MARK 2:18-28

RELATED PASSAGES: MATTHEW 11:25-30; MARK 6:31; HEBREWS 4:7-10

Day 43

COMPASSIONATE EYES

MARK 3:1

Another time Jesus went into the synagogue. In the synagogue there was a man with a crippled hand.

KEY THOUGHT

Jesus touched many people with his compassion, healing, comfort, and teaching. How did he reach so many people? Some came to him for healing because they had heard of his power over demons and disease. Others, however, were simply present and Jesus saw them with his "compassionate eyes." He looked into their eyes, their lives, and their hearts and then he acted to make a difference in their lives. Will we see and act to bless those around us who need Jesus' compassionate care?

TODAY'S PRAYER

Father in heaven, please help me to see those who need Jesus' touch of grace and then to share your love in a personal way with them. In Jesus' name. Amen.

CONTEXT: MARK 3:1-6

RELATED PASSAGES: MARK 2:1-5; MARK 10:17-25; LUKE 19:5

Day 44

CONDEMNING EYES

MARK 3:2

*Some Jews there were watching Jesus closely. They were waiting to
see if he would heal the man on a Sabbath day. They wanted to see
Jesus do something wrong so that they could accuse him.*

KEY THOUGHT

The opposite of Jesus' compassionate eyes (see Mark 3:1) were the
condemning and critical eyes of Jesus' opponents. The opponents were
looking to use the occasion of this man's healing on the Sabbath as the
basis of their arrest and condemnation of Jesus. In other words, the man's
humanity was forgotten; he was no more than a prop for the opponents
of Jesus to use in their drama of anti-Jesus hatred. If we are honest with
ourselves, we'll recognize that we can get so caught up in justifying, defending,
and protecting our religious faith that we become blind to the needs of
those around us for God's grace. Truth is then abandoned in the name of
preservation. God forbid that it should ever be so in us!

TODAY'S PRAYER

*Father, please don't let me ever become so focused on my religious self-
preservation that I forget my search for your truth and abandon
the character of your Son. In Jesus' name I pray. Amen.*

CONTEXT: MARK 3:1-6

RELATED PASSAGES: JOHN 9:1-3; JOHN 5:39-44; JOHN 8:1-11

Day 45

ANGRY EYES

MARK 3:3-5

Jesus said to the man with the crippled hand, "Stand up here so that everyone can see you."

Then Jesus asked the people, "Which is the right thing to do on the Sabbath day: to do good or to do evil? Is it right to save a life or to destroy one?" The people said nothing to answer him.

Jesus looked at the people. He was angry, but he felt very sad because they were so stubborn. He said to the man, "Hold out your hand." The man held out his hand, and it was healed.

KEY THOUGHT

Jesus becomes angry with his critics because they had lost the whole sense of the Sabbath. Instead of making the Sabbath a day to bless and refresh God's human creations, they had made it a day full of rules to the point of harming people. Jesus is angry and disturbed because of their hard hearts and their inability to see how they had perverted something God had intended for good. When religion goes astray, when what is called faith becomes a tool for hurting those whom God intends to bless, then it must be confronted. That is precisely what Jesus does!

TODAY'S PRAYER

Father in Heaven, please never let my heart become hardened because of my religious zeal. I want to be passionate in my faith, but I never want to become so blind that I distort your will and end up hurting those you want to bless. Keep my heart soft—open to you and to those whom you want me to touch with your grace. In the name of the Healer, my Savior Jesus, I pray. Amen.

CONTEXT: MARK 3:1-6

RELATED PASSAGES: ROMANS 10:2-4; MARK 6:1-6; JOHN 7:22-24

Day 46

MURDEROUS INTENTIONS

MARK 3:6

Then the Pharisees left and made plans with the Herodians about a way to kill Jesus.

KEY THOUGHT

When we get into a defensive posture toward those who disagree with us religiously, we can very quickly find ourselves looking to destroy their argument, destroy their faith, and yes, even destroy them. The Pharisees and the supporters of Herod were bitter enemies. Yet their common hatred of Jesus brought them together to plan evil against him. Hatred and a hard heart go together. Both lead to death—not necessarily the death of the target of our hate, but our own spiritual death. When we find ourselves siding with others who dislike us and when we find ourselves scheming what we know is evil, we must immediately be open to God and ask him to change our ways. We must seek his wisdom and his insight into the situation.

TODAY'S PRAYER

Holy and righteous God, please guide me into your truth. I want to honor and serve you with my heart, soul, mind, and strength. I don't want my religious passions to be used to lead me astray. Even more, dear Father, I don't want my religious zeal to cause harm to anyone, especially those who are seeking you. In Jesus' name. Amen.

CONTEXT: MARK 3:1-6

RELATED PASSAGES: MARK 10:16-20; LUKE 22:2; JOHN 12:9-11

Day 47

Checking Out Jesus

Mark 3:7-8

Jesus went away with his followers to the lake. A large crowd of people from Galilee followed them. Many also came from Judea, from Jerusalem, from Idumea, from the area across the Jordan River, and from the area around Tyre and Sidon. These people came because they heard about all that Jesus was doing.

Key Thought

So often the people who think they don't believe in Jesus have never been exposed to the real Jesus. Jesus meets us in many ways, but there are at least two ways that are crucial for most unbelievers. One crucial way to meet Jesus is by experiencing him through the Gospels—Matthew, Mark, Luke, and John. A second way for outsiders to experience Jesus is through the presence of Jesus in the world today—through the compassion, care, and character of Jesus' Body, the people of his church. In both of these cases, the invitation is nearly always the same: "Come. See for yourself!" We need to encourage people to meet Jesus and not just trust what they've heard about him. So let's invite people to do this by giving away free copies of the Gospels to others (the Bible societies offer these very economically), taking them to appropriate movies, or giving them historically accurate video copies of Jesus' life. Let's invite folks to come "meet" Jesus and "see" him for themselves.

Today's Prayer

Father, use me to invite people to come meet Jesus. Open my eyes to see those searching for him and fashion my life so that it is an appropriate example to them in their search. I pray this in Jesus' name. Amen.

Context: Mark 3:7-12

Related Passages: John 1:35-39; John 1:43-46; John 7:16-17

Day 48

MORE THAN A TITLE

MARK 3:9-12

Jesus saw how many people there were, so he told his followers to get a small boat and make it ready for him. He wanted the boat so that the crowds of people could not push against him. He had healed many of them, so all the sick people were pushing toward him to touch him. Some people had evil spirits inside them. When the evil spirits saw Jesus, they bowed before him and shouted, "You are the Son of God!" But Jesus gave the spirits a strong warning not to tell anyone who he was.

KEY THOUGHT

Jesus was more than a miracle maker and was never a title seeker. Instead, Jesus ministers to show God's love and compassion, yet does not want his ministry of preaching the Gospel of the Kingdom thwarted by those who think they know who he is. In times of distress, we want him to be our miracle maker. Jesus, however, is Lord and Master. We come to him and receive his grace, salvation, comfort, life, and Spirit. Yet Jesus is still Lord. He is not our servant boy and he is much more than any title. He will define who he is by what he does. In Mark's Gospel, this means that he will go to the cross and define what it means to be Son of God and the Christ (Messiah). In the process, he also sets us an example for how we should live—a life of sacrificial service to bring others to God. So if Jesus is to be more than a title for us, then his life must be seen in us!

TODAY'S PRAYER

Holy and loving God, my Abba Father, let the beauty, passion, conviction, love, commitment, and obedience of your Son be seen in my life. Teach me what it means for Jesus not only to be my Savior, but also to be my Lord. In Jesus' mighty name I pray. Amen.

CONTEXT: MARK 3:7-12

RELATED PASSAGES: LUKE 6:40-46; JOHN 13:12-17; JOHN 8:32

Day 49

No Accidental Band

MARK 3:13

*Then Jesus went up on a hill and invited those he wanted
to go with him. So they joined him there.*

KEY THOUGHT

We call this "invited" group the twelve apostles. As we meet them, we need to know that they are not an accidental band of misfits. Jesus chose them prayerfully. They answered his call and followed him. He chose them carefully because he was about to invest his remaining time in training them. They would go with him and learn by being at his side—not just hearing his message, but seeing his life. What are we to learn from this? Several lessons are important. First, Jesus chooses how he will use those of us who follow him—he is Lord and that is his right and responsibility. Second, we have to answer his call to follow; he will not force us. Third, the diversity and seeming insignificance of those he chose is purposeful: Jesus sees things in us and in others that we cannot see and longs to use us in his cause in special ways.

TODAY'S PRAYER

Loving God, the giver of every good and lasting gift, please help me see those things you have created me to do. Even more, dear Father, move me to do those things whether I think they are menial or glorious, for I know that you will use everything I offer you to your glory and for the blessing of others. In the life-changing name of Jesus I pray. Amen.

CONTEXT: MARK 3:13-19

RELATED PASSAGES: PSALM 139:13-16; EPHESIANS 4:7-13; ROMANS 8:28-30

Day 50

THE PURPOSE OF THE TWELVE

MARK 3:14-15

And he chose twelve men and called them apostles. He wanted these twelve men to be with him, and he wanted to send them to other places to tell people God's message. He also wanted them to have the power to force demons out of people.

KEY THOUGHT

Jesus selected the Twelve for several clear purposes. First, they were to be his companions; they would learn by being with him. Second, he sent them out to do what he had been doing—preaching the Gospel of the Kingdom. Third, he gave them authority and power to serve. His plan for the development of these disciples, most of whom became leaders after his death, is a good one for us to follow. If we want leaders who can make a huge difference in the world, we need to train them, task them, and trust them. *Training* means that we don't just give them a manual or a book, but that we help them learn by serving as apprentices to proven leaders. *Tasking* means that we give them a clear mission or task to perform and hold them accountable to fulfill that task. *Trusting* means that we actually give them authority and power to do what needs to be done. Unfortunately the whole Body of Jesus is not turned loose to work as it could because we are afraid that some leaders won't live up to the holy task they are given. So let's be honest with Jesus' example. Did these Twelve all live up to their holy task? How long did it take for them to get it right? How many of them failed at some point? How many of them failed completely? Get the point? Let's follow Jesus' example.

TODAY'S PRAYER

Father, forgive us. We have limited your people because we have not called more to lead; and the few whom we have called to lead we often limit because of our lack of faith in them and our lack of direction and accountability to them. Dear Father, please raise up more leaders and open our eyes to their presence. In the name of the Lord Jesus I pray. Amen.

CONTEXT: MARK 3:13-19

RELATED PASSAGES: ACTS 6:1-7; ACTS 13:1-3; 1 PETER 4:10-11

Day 51

EVERYBODY KNOWS YOUR NAME

MARK 3:16-19

These are the names of the twelve men Jesus chose: Simon (the one Jesus named Peter), James and his brother John, the sons of Zebedee (the ones Jesus named Boanerges, which means "Sons of Thunder"), Andrew, Philip, Bartholomew, Matthew, Thomas, James, the son of Alphaeus, Thaddaeus, Simon, the Zealot, Judas Iscariot (the one who handed Jesus over to his enemies).

KEY THOUGHT

People in God's family have names, histories, and futures. They are different in their interests and their vocations. Yet they all have one thing in common: Jesus! Let's not limit our expectations or dreams for people in the Kingdom of God because of their pasts, their names, their occupations, or their reputations. Let's trust that Jesus can and will use anyone who fully yields his or her life to his purposes.

TODAY'S PRAYER

Father, forgive me for the sin of prejudice. Open my heart to see that you want all kinds of different people in your family so that others can be touched by what they see and so that your church can be fully energized with all the various kinds of people you have created. In Jesus' name I pray. Amen.

CONTEXT: MARK 3:13-19

RELATED PASSAGES: 1 CORINTHIANS 12:4-7; 1 CORINTHIANS 3:5-9; REVELATIONS 7:9-10

Day 52

OUR CRAZY BROTHER

MARK 3:20-21

Then Jesus went home, but again a large crowd gathered there. There were so many people that he and his followers could not eat. His family heard about all these things. They went to get him because people said he was crazy.

KEY THOUGHT

Sometimes those people who are most difficult for us to reach with the grace of Jesus can be found in our own families. Fortunately we are not alone in that challenge. The early Christians found themselves in difficult family situations and so there are some very clear things taught about how to handle these situations. Most comforting of all, however, is the realization that Jesus spent much of his ministry being misunderstood by his own family, many of whom would not believe in him until after his death and resurrection. Let's not be discouraged; instead, let's go to the Lord and ask him to lead us and show us how to minister to, serve, and respect those around us so that we can reach them with God's grace.

TODAY'S PRAYER

Mighty Shepherd of your sheep, please give me the wisdom, patience, and character I need to lead the unbelievers in my family to you. In Jesus' name I pray. Amen.

CONTEXT: MARK 3:20-30

RELATED PASSAGES: JOHN 7:1-5; 1 CORINTHIANS 7:12-16; 1 PETER 3:1-2

Day 53

I'M THE STRONGER MAN

MARK 3:22-27

And the teachers of the law from Jerusalem said, "Satan is living inside him!
He uses power from the ruler of demons to force demons out of people."

So Jesus called them together and talked to them using some stories. He said, "Satan
will not force his own demons out of people. A kingdom that fights against itself will not
survive. And a family that is divided will not survive. If Satan is against himself and
is fighting against his own people, he will not survive. That would be the end of Satan.

"Whoever wants to enter a strong man's house and steal his things must
first tie him up. Then they can steal the things from his house."

KEY THOUGHT

Jesus makes it clear that his ability to cast out demons comes from one
source: himself! He is more powerful than the demons could ever imagine him
to be because he is the Son of God. They can't stand up to his presence and
power. Jesus is stronger than the demons and he demonstrates his power over
them again and again throughout his life.

TODAY'S PRAYER

Father, I trust in Jesus' power to save from all forms of evil, sin, and bondage. I
open my heart to let him reign over my emotions and desires. I open my mind so
that he can purify, redeem, and control my thoughts. I open my soul so that he
can rule in every area of my being. Thank you for sending your Son as my Savior,
my Lord, and my Almighty King. In Jesus' powerful name I pray. Amen.

CONTEXT: MARK 3:20-30

RELATED PASSAGES: MATTHEW 28:18-20; COLOSSIANS 1:11-14;
HEBREWS 2:17-18

Day 54

Unforgivable

Mark 3:28-30

"I want you to know that people can be forgiven for all the sinful things they do. They can even be forgiven for the bad things they say against God. But anyone who speaks against the Holy Spirit will never be forgiven. They will always be guilty of that sin."

Jesus said this because the teachers of the law had accused him of having an evil spirit inside him.

Key Thought

Many people have shared a concern that they may be guilty of this unforgivable sin. Take heart, dear friend, and let Jesus' word come to you clearly. The sin is to keep saying that what Jesus did was done by an evil spirit or a demon rather than by the Spirit of God. Even if you may have assigned Jesus' works to something evil at one time in your life, you are not doing so now. You are not guilty. Look on the positive side of this command. If you want to see what the Spirit of God does in a human being when the Holy Spirit takes control, look at Jesus! What Jesus does in his daily life is a demonstration of God's will empowered by the Holy Spirit. If the example of Jesus seems out of our reach, let's consider Paul the Apostle who killed Christians before becoming one and Peter who repeatedly denied knowing Jesus. The Holy Spirit transformed and empowered them to make a huge difference in the world!

Today's Prayer

Father in heaven, I recognize that the greatest gift given to me was my salvation as demonstrated through the forgiveness of my sins and through the gift of the Holy Spirit that dwells in me. Please help the Spirit's fruit to be seen in my life as your Spirit conforms me to be more and more like your Son. In Jesus' holy name I pray. Amen.

Context: Mark 3:20-30

Related Passages: Luke 11:13; 2 Corinthians 3:17-18; Matthew 12:28

Day 55

JESUS' FAMILY

MARK 3:31-35

Then Jesus' mother and brothers came. They stood outside and sent someone in to tell him to come out. Many people were sitting around Jesus. They said to him, "Your mother and brothers are waiting for you outside."

Jesus asked, "Who is my mother? Who are my brothers?" Then he looked at the people sitting around him and said, "These people are my mother and my brothers! My true brother and sister and mother are those who do what God wants."

KEY THOUGHT

Jesus' family can be found where the words of Jesus and the will of God are cherished and obeyed. This is not said to slight those with whom we have biological family ties. However, it is a reminder that our family relationship in the Spirit of God is stronger than physical family. Jesus' family is the forever-family of people who love him, obey him, and allow his Holy Spirit to lead, guide, and empower them.

TODAY'S PRAYER

Precious God and Righteous Father, forgive me for my disobedience in the past. Empower and encourage me to be more passionate for your will in the future. Dear Father, I want to show my love to you, and to your Son, by doing what you ask and obeying what you command of me. In Jesus' name I pray. Amen.

CONTEXT: MARK 3:31-35

RELATED PASSAGES: JOHN 8:31-32; JOHN 14:21-23; MARK 4:35-41

Day 56

TELLING STORIES

MARK 4:1-2

Another time Jesus began teaching by the lake, and a large crowd gathered around him. He got into a boat so that he could sit and teach from the lake. All the people stayed on the shore near the water. Jesus used stories to teach them many things. One of his lessons included this story . . . .

KEY THOUGHT

I find it interesting when a good preacher or Bible teacher is criticized for telling too many stories. Yes, there are some speakers who go only for the "emotional tug" on people's hearts by telling one story after another. But we need to pay attention not only to *what* Jesus taught, but also *how* he taught it. Jesus engaged people's imaginations and made everyday events, images, and experiences into hooks on which he could hang God's truth about the Kingdom. One of the reasons that he attracted large crowds was his miracles. But Jesus is very careful not to allow himself to become "The Miracle Man." Interestingly, Jesus is not called the Healer, but the Teacher! His words were powerful because they were true. His teaching was influential because it carried with it the ring of heaven's truth. But let's not forget that his teaching was popular because he knew how to engage people's hearts, minds, and imaginations when he taught. One of the ways he did that was telling stories. These stories still speak powerfully to us today!

TODAY'S PRAYER

Loving Father and Almighty God, please help me grow in my ability to teach the truth of Jesus. I want to teach it through the example of my life. I want to communicate it to those in my sphere of influence. Father, I offer myself to be used by you to teach others about Jesus in any fashion you choose. And when my opportunities to teach your truth come, please help me to teach in ways that engage the hearts and minds of those I'm trying to reach. In the name of the Teacher, the Lord Jesus, I pray. Amen.

CONTEXT: MARK 4:1-20

RELATED PASSAGES: MATTHEW 28:18-20; MARK 1:21-22; MARK 6:34

Day 57

TELLING STORIES

MARK 4:3-9

"Listen! A farmer went out to sow seed. While he was scattering the seed, some of it fell by the road. The birds came and ate all that seed. Other seed fell on rocky ground, where there was not enough dirt. It grew quickly there because the soil was not deep. But then the sun rose and the plants were burned. They died because they did not have deep roots. Some other seed fell among thorny weeds. The weeds grew and stopped the good plants from growing. So they did not make grain. But some of the seed fell on good ground. There it began to grow, and it made grain. Some plants made 30 times more grain, some 60 times more, and some 100 times more."

Then Jesus said, "You people who hear me, listen!"

KEY THOUGHT

One of the most important questions we need to ask ourselves is this: "Am I willing to truly listen to Jesus, hear what he says, and do what he asks of me?" The parables are powerful learning stories that plant the Word of Jesus deep in our hearts. But we must be committed to hearing what is said so that it takes root, grows, and produces fruit. We determine the type of soil we offer to the good news of Jesus. So let's ask the Father to help us to hear Jesus' words and put them into practice.

TODAY'S PRAYER

Almighty God, my Abba Father, open my heart to the teaching of Jesus. Remove the barriers that I have placed between your will and my proper hearing of your truth. I so much want your Son's words to come to life in me and bear fruit. Mold me, correct me, and mature me as I open my heart, my life, and my will to the words of your Son. In Jesus' name I pray. Amen.

CONTEXT: MARK 4:1-20

RELATED PASSAGES: MARK 6:11; MARK 7:14; MARK 9:2-7

Day 58

FOR YOUR UNDERSTANDING

MARK 4:10-11

*Later, Jesus was away from the people. The twelve apostles
and his other followers asked him about the stories.*

*Jesus said, "Only you can know the secret truth about God's kingdom.
But to those other people I tell everything by using stories."*

KEY THOUGHT

Why would Jesus conceal his message from outsiders? First, they can't
understand it properly. If his disciples had a hard time understanding Jesus,
then how would those who don't share their passion for the work of God
understand it? Second, Jesus is redefining his followers' understanding of
the Kingdom of God. His terms and ideas would be distorted and misused
by others. Third, he is entrusting his message to them, his chosen followers,
to share the message with others later in their ministry when he is gone. Not
every message is appropriate to share with everyone. Certain times are more
appropriate for sharing some information than other times. So we ask God to
give us the sense of time and message to be useful servants for his kingdom.

TODAY'S PRAYER

*Father, please give me wisdom in knowing when to speak and when to be silent. I want
to share your message in the proper way, at the proper time, to the proper people. Give
me patience so that I can keep my mouth shut when silence is needed. Give me courage to
speak when the time is right to speak. May the words of my mouth and the meditations
of my heart be pleasing to you and a blessing to others. In Jesus' name I pray. Amen.*

CONTEXT: MARK 4:1-20

RELATED PASSAGES: PROVERBS 15:23; TITUS 1:3; JAMES 1:19

Day 59

OUTSIDERS AND INSIDERS

MARK 4:12-13

"I do this so that, 'They will look and look but never really see; they will listen and listen but never understand. If they saw and understood, they might change and be forgiven.'" Then Jesus said to the followers, "Do you understand this story? If you don't, how will you understand any story?"

KEY THOUGHT

Certain messages are appropriate for those who are inside the faith, but make no sense to those outside the faith. These messages are not going to be understandable to those who do not share our faith and the worldview that arises from it. For instance: Christians see the story of the cross as a story of great power and sacrifice; non-believers see it as a sign of weakness and defeat. Jesus is preparing his specially selected followers for their ministries. He is focusing on giving them messages they can understand but which those outside their group will not understand. This is a great reminder that those who do not know Jesus will not understand many things we believe, teach, and say. We shouldn't get discouraged; this has always been true. Rather than becoming frustrated, we need to give thanks that God has made these things known to us and then find effective ways to introduce the people in our world to the grace of Jesus.

TODAY'S PRAYER

Father, I know that many people in the world do not understand many of the things I dearly believe. Please give me patience and courage to face their questions, attacks, and rejections. Use me to break down the barriers between them and me so that they can come to know Jesus as their Lord and Savior. In Jesus' name I ask this. Amen.

CONTEXT: MARK 4:1-20

RELATED PASSAGES: LUKE 10:21; 1 CORINTHIANS 2:9-15; COLOSSIANS 1:25-26

Day 60

GOSPEL FARMERS

MARK 4:14
"The farmer is like someone who plants God's teaching in people."

KEY THOUGHT

Jesus explains his parable of the soils. One key component is the farmer in the story. The farmer is the person who shares the good news of God with others. Jesus' parable assumes his followers are going to be sowing the good news of God into the lives of their family, friends, and acquaintances. In fact, the Lord is trusting that they will share the message with all those with whom they have an opportunity. The question we need to ask ourselves is this: are we seeking to be farmers in God's Kingdom and share the good news of Jesus with others?

TODAY'S PRAYER
Father, help me be more effective as a farmer in your Kingdom. Help me see opportunities to sow your good news about Jesus into the hearts of the people around me. In Jesus' name I pray. Amen.

CONTEXT: MARK 4:1-20

RELATED PASSAGES: 1 PETER 3:15-16; ROMANS 10:14-16; ROMANS 1:16

Day 61

FACING THE ADVERSARY

MARK 4:15

*"Sometimes the teaching falls on the path. That is like some people
who hear the teaching of God. As soon as they hear it, Satan comes
and takes away the teaching that was planted in them."*

KEY THOUGHT

Our efforts to share the good news of God's Kingdom don't happen in a
vacuum. Satan is an active adversary. He opposes or seeks to dilute, distort,
and derail every effort made to advance the Kingdom of God in the hearts of
lost people. Let's not forget that we have an adversary. This shouldn't make
us afraid or discouraged, but it should motivate us to feel urgency for the
lost men and women around us. It should awaken us that those who come to
Christ will face difficult challenges as they try to begin their new walk with
the Lord. It should move us with compassion as we see the battle going on in
people's hearts between the influences of Satan and the invitation extended
by Jesus. Satan will try to steal that message from them. We must do all we can
to help them hear and respond to Jesus' message!

TODAY'S PRAYER

*O Father, how you must grieve for those who struggle to receive your grace.
How it must anger you to see the evil one come in and steal away the good news
from the hearts of those who so much need it. Use me as one of your messengers
to help those who are battling Satan. In Jesus' name I pray. Amen.*

CONTEXT: MARK 4:1-20

RELATED PASSAGES: EPHESIANS 2:1-2; 1 THESSALONIANS 3:1-13; EPHESIANS 6:12

Day 62

FOLDING UNDER FIRE

MARK 4:16-17

"Other people are like the seed planted on rocky ground. They hear the teaching, and they quickly and gladly accept it. But they don't allow it to go deep into their lives. They keep it only a short time. As soon as trouble or persecution comes because of the teaching they accepted, they give up."

KEY THOUGHT

We get easily excited about new things, especially new spiritual undertakings. But when the going gets tough we tend to bog down and give up. Self-discipline has never been a commodity found in abundance. People will find difficulty awaiting them when they first respond to Jesus. There is no way to avoid this. At the very least, new believers will find themselves in a culture clash as the values of the Kingdom conflict with the values of the world around them. Often the world around new Christians pushes back. Sometimes it persecutes with incessant ridicule or condescension or worse. If Jesus faced a time of trial for forty days after his baptism, we must know that new followers of Jesus will also face trials. Persecution will come for most believers! (See John 16:33)

TODAY'S PRAYER

Give me strength, O heavenly Father, to withstand the ridicule, persecution, and opposition of others. Help me to encourage new believers so they do not give up when pressures and persecution come. I pray this in the name of the Lord Jesus. Amen.

CONTEXT: MARK 4:1-20

RELATED PASSAGES: MATTHEW 5:10; ROMANS 8:35-37; 2 THESSALONIANS 1:7

Day 63

THE CARES OF THE CROWDED HEART

MARK 4:18-19

*"Others are like the seed planted among the thorny weeds. They hear
the teaching, but their lives become full of other things: the worries of
this life, the love of money, and everything else they want. This keeps the
teaching from growing, and it does not produce a crop in their lives.*

KEY THOUGHT

I hate thorns. Spending part of my time growing up in West Texas, we had
to deal with all sorts of spiny, cactus-like plants. Then in East Texas, where I
spent the other part of my childhood, there were briars. I hate thorns. They
seem to grow better in droughts than most other plants . . . but then they grow
better than most other plants in wet times too! This is just a reminder that our
hearts can easily be distracted from what is important by what is pervasive.
For many of us, the stuff we own may soon begin to own us and choke out our
heart's openness to God.

TODAY'S PRAYER

*Father, please help me keep my priorities correct as I battle with the
cares of this life, the lure of money, and the desire to have nice things.
Bless me as I seek you and your Kingdom first and as I trust that you
will supply what is most needed in my life. In Jesus' name. Amen.*

CONTEXT: MARK 4:1-20

RELATED PASSAGES: MATTHEW 6:31-34; 1 TIMOTHY 6:6-10; PSALM 37:4

Day 64

GREAT HARVEST!

MARK 4:20

*"And others are like the seed planted on the good ground. They hear the
teaching and accept it. Then they grow and produce a good crop—sometimes
30 times more, sometimes 60 times more, and sometimes 100 times more."*

KEY THOUGHT

Jesus wants us to be productive in our service to his Kingdom. In fact, he
is working in the lives of those who are fully yielded to him to bring about
a great harvest. Like a small seed, the power of the Kingdom is multiplied
through the lives of those fully yielded to Jesus.

TODAY'S PRAYER

*O LORD God, help me yield myself completely to your will. May the
things I do in my life bring you glory. In Jesus' name. Amen.*

CONTEXT: MARK 4:1-20

RELATED PASSAGES: 2 PETER 1:5-8; HEBREWS 10:12; 2 CORINTHIANS 9:10-13

Day 65

You'll See It Clearly One Day!

MARK 4:21-23

Then Jesus said to them, "You don't take a lamp and hide it under a bowl or a bed, do you? Of course not. You put it on a lampstand. Everything that is hidden will be made clear. Every secret thing will be made known. You people who hear me, listen!"

KEY THOUGHT

Confusion is one of the more frustrating states of mind. Not seeing clearly, not being able to perceive fully, and not being able to understand leave us feeling silly or stupid. Jesus didn't want his followers to feel any of these. He wanted them to know that all will be revealed about the Kingdom at the proper time. He didn't come to hide his message in a darkened room. So our job is to listen and wait, always obeying what we understand and trusting that the confusing matters will be brought to light. We mustn't let our frustrations with what is concealed steal from us the things that we know today and our expectation of more light to come.

TODAY'S PRAYER

O Father, I need patience. I am not good at waiting. I want all the answers right now. However, dear Father, I know that you have revealed what I need to know right now. Lead me to know your will and your truth more fully even as I am fully known by you. I cling to Jesus' promise, trusting that all will be made known. In Jesus' authoritative name I pray. Amen.

CONTEXT: MARK 4:21-25

RELATED PASSAGES: 1 CORINTHIANS 13:11-13; MATTHEW 10:26; EPHESIANS 3:5

Day 66

More for the Listener

Mark 4:23-24

*"You people who hear me, listen! Think carefully about what you
are hearing. God will know how much to give you by how much you
understand now. But he will give you more than you deserve."*

Key Thought

If yesterday's message—that one day we will understand all the truth
about the Kingdom—was intended to comfort us, then today's message is
meant to motivate us. We should earnestly and attentively pursue the truth
of Jesus. The only way to do this is by paying attention to what he says.
That means re-acquainting ourselves with the Gospels and focusing on his
words. Only as we apply ourselves to listening to our Master will we be able
to grow in our ability to perceive, understand, and know the full will of our
Savior. The old RCA Victor logo had a picture of a dog listening attentively
to the "speaker"of a gramophone with the title "His Master's Voice." Jesus
is saying that we must have our ear attuned to Scripture and listen for our
Master's voice!

Today's Prayer

*Father in heaven, help me as I try to be more attentive to the words of your Son and
my Savior. I want to know Jesus' truth by studying his life and words, understanding
them, and putting them into practice. Mold me and make me more into a person
like my Lord as I listen for his voice. In Jesus' gracious name I pray. Amen.*

Context: Mark 4:21-25

Related Passages: John 7:16-17; Matthew 7:21; John 8:31-32

Day 67

THE HARD TRUTH ABOUT HEARING

MARK 4:25

"The people who have some understanding will receive more. But those who do not have much will lose even the small amount they have."

KEY THOUGHT

Jesus wants us to know that as we apply ourselves to listening to him, he is still active in the communication. He will help us understand more! But we must be willing to listen, hear, and apply his message to our lives. If we are sloppy, disinterested, or hard-hearted toward the message of Jesus, what little we understand will be stripped away from us. There is an urgency to our hearing the Master. Two raindrops can land less than an inch apart on either side of the Continental Divide in the U.S. and one will ultimately end up in the Pacific Ocean and the other in the Atlantic Ocean. Listeners to Jesus' message can also end up worlds apart based upon their openness to his teaching. We have a tremendous responsibility and opportunity to listen to Jesus! Our commitment to do so greatly determines the ultimate destination of our lives.

TODAY'S PRAYER

O Father God, Lord of heaven and earth, help me hear. Even more, dear Father, create in me a hunger to hear the truth of Jesus. Open my heart to your Son's message. Strip from me the barriers that would keep me from being attentive. I want my life to be shaped by the words of your Son. In Jesus' name I pray. Amen.

CONTEXT: MARK 4:21-25

RELATED PASSAGES: MATTHEW 10:14-15; MATTHEW 11:15; MATTHEW 12:42

Day 68

THE MYSTERY OF SEEDS

MARK 4:26-29

Then Jesus said, "God's kingdom is like a man who plants seed in the ground. The seed begins to grow. It grows night and day. It doesn't matter whether the man is sleeping or awake, the seed still grows. He doesn't know how it happens. Without any help the ground produces grain. First the plant grows, then the head, and then all the grain in the head. When the grain is ready, the man cuts it. This is the harvest time."

KEY THOUGHT

The Kingdom of God is progressing toward an end. While we may not fully understand all that goes on, we can be sure that it is growing, and when it comes to full maturity the harvest will come. There is movement and mystery, but ultimately there is also harvest. We also need to understand this about the Kingdom: it moves and grows despite our lack of understanding about all that God is doing. One thing is certain, however: when all things are ready, the harvest will come. So will we be a part of this movement and mystery? Will we grow and be ready for the harvest?

TODAY'S PRAYER

LORD God Almighty, God of Abraham, Isaac, and Jacob, God of Deborah, Esther, and Mary, I want you to be Sovereign Lord in my life. Just as clearly as you have worked in the history of Israel, I pray that you will work in your Kingdom to your glory at your time—and that I may be part of this movement of your grace. In Jesus' name. Amen.

CONTEXT: MARK 4:26-34

RELATED PASSAGES: 1 CORINTHIANS 15:21-29; COLOSSIANS 1:13-14; COLOSSIANS 3:1-4

Day 69

MORE THAN A MUSTARD SEED

MARK 4:30-32

Then Jesus said, "What can I use to show you what God's kingdom is like? What story can I use to explain it? God's kingdom is like a mustard seed, which is smaller than any other seed on earth that you can plant. But when you plant it, it grows and becomes the largest of all the plants in your garden. It has branches that are very big. The wild birds can come and make nests there and be protected from the sun."

KEY THOUGHT

If mystery and movement were the heart of Jesus' Kingdom message in our devotional yesterday, today his message is about power and grace. God's Kingdom may appear small in the face of the world's political and military powers. However, the Kingdom we see is only a seed, not the fully mature shelter. But the Kingdom is growing and will be large enough to furnish safety and security for those who live in its branches. Don't be afraid, dear Kingdom seeker; the God who propels the mustard seed to great growth is at work in his Kingdom to do far greater things than we can ask or imagine. So find your shelter in this Kingdom. All others will pass away, but this one will endure—forever.

TODAY'S PRAYER

O LORD my God, how awesome are your works in all the earth. The beauty and diversity of your creation astound me. Yet I realize that as beautiful as this physical world may be, the unseen realm of your Kingdom, majesty, and might are far greater still! Even those bits and glimpses of your Kingdom I experience now are wonderful. I look forward to the day when they are fully visible to all. Until that day, shelter me in the cover of your Kingdom and grace. In Jesus' name. Amen.

CONTEXT: MARK 4:26-34

RELATED PASSAGES: EPHESIANS 1:19-23; EPHESIANS 3:14-21; MATTHEW 6:10

Day 70

LIMITED DOSES AND VISUAL HOOKS

MARK 4:33

Jesus used many stories like these to teach the people.
He taught them all they could understand.

KEY THOUGHT

Jesus was an incredible teacher. In his earthly ministry, he used common, everyday images as hooks on which to hang eternal truth. The people would see these images in their day-to-day lives and then could grasp the eternal truth that Jesus hooked on the image. This was crucial. They couldn't understand everything all at once. Until his death and resurrection and without the work of the Holy Spirit, much of what he said was a mystery. Yet these images allowed him to share messages "pregnant" with meaning. Later, as these disciples learned more about his life and ministry and as the Holy Spirit begin to work in each follower's life, they could see the visual image, take Jesus' message off the visual hook, and more fully understand it. Teaching God's truth is an awesome and humbling responsibility. Jesus is the great reminder that it is also a creative responsibility. More than just communicating a message, we're communicating God's will to people who need to understand, to obey, and to be blessed by this message.

TODAY'S PRAYER

God, my dear Abba Father, please help me to be more creative and effective in my teaching of your will. I want my life to display what I teach so others can know that this message is not only true, but also liveable. Help me convey the power, beauty, mystery, grace, and holiness of your will. I cannot do this on my own, dear Father, so I commit to becoming a good steward of the grace you have given me. However, Father, I ask that your Spirit take what is good and make it better and that your grace take what is bad and remove it so that it will not hinder those eager to know your truth. In Jesus' name. Amen.

CONTEXT: MARK 4:26-34

RELATED PASSAGES: 1 CORINTHIANS 2:12-16; 1 PETER 4:10-11; JAMES 3:1

Day 71

TO HIS OWN

MARK 4:34
*He always used stories to teach them. But when he was alone
with his followers, Jesus explained everything to them.*

KEY THOUGHT

While the parables were a mystery to many, Jesus made sure his closest followers knew what he meant when he spoke them. We too can ask Jesus to make his truth clear to us. He has promised that the Holy Spirit would use the Word and make the necessary impact on our hearts. So when we open the Word, let's not go just to read; let's offer ourselves to the Lord. Let's ask that his Spirit help us understand what we need to know, convict us of where we have fallen short, and equip us to live the kind of life that shows others the character of Jesus.

TODAY'S PRAYER
Holy God, as I open your Word, as I seek to know Jesus, have the Holy Spirit penetrate my heart with your truth, open my eyes to my sins, and equip me to live the life of service that glorifies my Savior. In Jesus' name I pray. Amen.

CONTEXT: MARK 4:26-34

RELATED PASSAGES: EPHESIANS 6:17-18; 2 TIMOTHY 3:14-17; HEBREWS 4:12

Day 72

ALONE TO MENTOR AND EXPLAIN

MARK 4:35-36

That day, at evening, Jesus said to his followers, "Come with me across the lake." So they left the crowd behind and went with Jesus in the boat he was already in. There were also other boats that went with them.

KEY THOUGHT

Some things need to be shared in private. Jesus often withdrew to pray. In addition, he pulled away from the crowds so his apostles could rest and rekindle their spirits. He also left the crowds behind so he could more fully teach these men to continue his work after he was gone. One dimension of teaching is preparing other teachers. That requires us to leave the crowds and spend focused time with those whom the church needs for the future. John the Baptizer, Jesus, Barnabas, and Paul all used this basic method of teaching and training. We ignore their example at our own risk. Even if we are not skilled public teachers, we all have people—friends and family—whom we can teach and train by our words and by our character in our private times with them.

TODAY'S PRAYER

Father in heaven, use my life and my words to prepare others to know your Son and share your truth. In Jesus' name I pray. Amen.

CONTEXT: MARK 4:35-41

RELATED PASSAGES: MARK 6:31; 2 TIMOTHY 2:1-2; PHILIPPIANS 4:9

Day 73

FIERCE STORMS

MARK 4:37

*A very bad wind came up on the lake. The waves were coming over
the sides and into the boat, and it was almost full of water.*

KEY THOUGHT

Storms are a part of life—even for Christians. In fact, storms are a part of
life, *especially* for Christians. While some peddle a "gospel" that proclaims only
wealth, blessing, and happiness, we need to remember that Jesus is our hero
and example. We are his presence in this world. We know what the world did
to him. He warns that if the world would do this to him, imagine what it will
do to us. So while we are blessed and our Kingdom is sure, we need to know
that fierce storms will come. The key is to make sure we're with Jesus every
step of the way!

TODAY'S PRAYER

*Father in heaven, give me faith and strength to stand in the hours of my trial. In
addition, dear Father, please be with my brothers and sisters in Christ the world over
who are facing fierce and violent storms because of their faith. In Jesus' name. Amen.*

CONTEXT: MARK 4:35-41

RELATED PASSAGES: MARK 13:13; JOHN 15:21; 1 PETER 1:5-7

Day 74

ANXIOUS HONESTY

MARK 4:38

Jesus was inside the boat, sleeping with his head on a pillow. The followers went and woke him. They said, "Teacher, don't you care about us? We are going to drown!"

KEY THOUGHT

I am so thankful for the honest portrayal of Jesus' disciples. I can see myself in them and know that God uses flawed people like me. The early followers of Jesus had bouts with panic and fear just as we do. In their fear, they don't pretend to have everything under control. They don't puff out their chests with false bravado and act as if they can handle the situation. Even though their honesty leads to a rebuke, it also leads to a miracle! Why? Because they are willing to take their fears honestly to the Savior. They have much to learn . . . and he will teach them. They also have much to lose . . . and he will protect them. What are we holding back in our conversation with the Savior? What has us panicked, afraid, or anxious that we have not fully shared with the Lord? Storms come and go, but only the Lord stands the test of time. Let's be real about our fears and anxieties and let him care for us. Yes, he will challenge us to greater faith. But that's the point isn't it?

TODAY'S PRAYER

Father, I confess to you now the burdens of my heart, knowing that you will hear them and do what is best for me. In Jesus' gracious name I pray. Amen.

CONTEXT: MARK 4:35-41

RELATED PASSAGES: PHILIPPIANS 4:6-7; 1 PETER 5:7; 2 CORINTHIANS 12:8-10

Day 75

QUIET! WHY SO AFRAID?

MARK 4:39

*Jesus stood up and gave a command to the wind and the water. He said,
"Quiet! Be still!" Then the wind stopped, and the lake became calm.*

KEY THOUGHT

"'Quiet down!' . . . and there was a great calm." This is also Jesus' power
in the heart of one of his followers. When we are caught in the middle of
the storms of life, we can learn to listen for his voice, seek out his words, and
remember the full message of his life. Jesus brings us calm when we know that
he is in ultimate control!

TODAY'S PRAYER

*O God, my Father in heaven, give me faith to believe that Jesus can calm my heart
and help me through my storms. In Jesus' awesome and mighty name I pray. Amen.*

CONTEXT: MARK 4:35-41

RELATED PASSAGES: ISAIAH 26:3-4; PSALM 37:37; PHILIPPIANS 1:2

Day 76

Who Is This Man?

Mark 4:40-41

He said to his followers, "Why are you afraid? Do you still have no faith?"

They were very afraid and asked each other, "What kind of man is this? Even the wind and the water obey him!"

Key Thought

"What kind of man is this?" Ah! That's the real question we need to be asking. He is more than a man, but is yet fully human. He was pre-existent and created all things, yet was hung on a tree that he made and killed by people whom he created in the wombs of their mothers. He has all power, yet withholds it to go to the cross to bear the weight of our sins. What kind of man is this? Better yet, who is this man to me?

Today's Prayer

Holy and Almighty King, thank you for Jesus. I know that I will never in this life fully comprehend who he is; yet for me, dear Father, he is everything. In his name, Jesus of Nazareth the Christ, my Lord, I pray. Amen.

Context: Mark 4:35-41

Related Passages: John 1:1-5; Romans 10:8-13; Philippians 2:5-11

Day 77

On Strange Turf

MARK 5:1-2

Jesus and his followers went across the lake to the area where the Gerasene people lived. When Jesus got out of the boat, a man came to him from the caves where the dead are buried. This man had an evil spirit living inside him.

KEY THOUGHT

Jesus is taking his disciples to strange new places. The "strangeness" had to do with what they would experience—an encounter with a demon-possessed man. Adding to this strangeness is the place they encounter him—near a cemetery where he lived among the tombs. If we watch the story carefully, the disciples appear to remain in the boat during this whole encounter. They weren't quite ready to take on this strange new world. Jesus is trying to teach them that he will go with them and empower them to do quite unbelievable things. This experience will be one of those indelible memories they will carry with them as they face their own challenges orchestrated by the dark lord of demons. As the Lord leads us, he reminds us that we are a pilgrim people, always on the move toward God and away from the familiar. Yet as he leads us into new places, we remember how he has been with us in the past and that he has already conquered the dark lord we so often fear.

TODAY'S PRAYER

Almighty God, my Abba Father, give me the courage and strength to follow you wherever you lead me. I know that you have been at work to prepare me, but help me, dear Lord, to move past preparation into a time of fruitfulness. In Jesus' powerful name I pray. Amen.

CONTEXT: MARK 5:1-20

RELATED PASSAGES: HEBREWS 13:5-6; ROMANS 8:35-39; PHILIPPIANS 3:12-15

Day 78

SATAN'S GOAL

MARK 5:3-5

He lived in the burial caves. No one could keep him tied up, even with chains. Many times people had put chains on his hands and feet, but he broke the chains. No one was strong enough to control him. Day and night he stayed around the burial caves and on the hills. He would scream and cut himself with rocks.

KEY THOUGHT

The power and influence of the Devil is often minimized. Believing in a real being behind evil is ridiculed in many circles. Yet Scripture assumes a belief in a real "evil one". What we witness in Mark 5 with this man possessed by demons is the goal of the Devil's work in human lives. He longs to isolate, degrade, and torture those whom he controls. His power is unrelentingly strong, yet he uses his strength to hold people in fear because of death. Ultimately, when the evil one gains a foothold in our lives, he leads us to self-destructive behavior. We must not minimize the Devil's power or presence. Instead, we need to center our lives on Jesus, the one who conquered the evil one's power and broke his death-grip on us.

TODAY'S PRAYER

Father, forgive me if I have ever minimized evil and the Devil's power exerted through it. Thank you for sending Jesus to destroy the Devil's hold on my life. Give me strength to resist his attacks and to overcome his influence in my life. In the name of Jesus, who came for lost sinners like me, I pray. Amen.

CONTEXT: MARK 5:1-20

RELATED PASSAGES: EPHESIANS 6:10-12; HEBREWS 2:14-15; 1 PETER 5:8

Day 79

POWER OVER DEMONS

MARK 5:6-8

While Jesus was still far away, the man saw him. He ran to Jesus and bowed down before him. As Jesus was saying, "You evil spirit, come out of this man," the man shouted loudly, "What do you want with me, Jesus, Son of the Most High God? I beg you in God's name not to punish me!"

KEY THOUGHT

In the Gospel of Mark, we learn that the demons know Jesus' true identity. They fear Jesus and know he has power over them. The man we meet among the tombs in the cemetery—a man whose name we never know because his identity has been stolen by the demons inhabiting him—does not speak. Instead, the demons speak through his voice. Their terror at their own defeat at Jesus' hands is revealed. As God's presence in human flesh—God's Son— Jesus is superior to all beings, heavenly and earthly, good and evil. While on earth and now at the Father's right hand, Jesus holds power over the demons. They cannot and will not defeat him. Even in the cross he triumphs over them because of his sacrificial obedience which purchases our freedom, pardon, and righteousness.

TODAY'S PRAYER

Holy God, Almighty Abba Father, I praise you for Jesus' power over all things and all beings. Give me faith to believe this and live accordingly. While I know I will struggle against the power of Satan and his angels, I truly believe that through Jesus victory is mine. I praise you and thank you in the mighty name of Jesus. Amen.

CONTEXT: MARK 5:1-20

RELATED PASSAGES: PHILIPPIANS 2:9-11; COLOSSIANS 2:12-15; HEBREWS 1:13

Day 30

IDENTITY THEFT

MARK 5:9

Then Jesus asked the man, "What is your name?"
The man answered, "My name is Legion, because there are many spirits inside me."

KEY THOUGHT

Today, because of all the e-commerce and the widespread use of credit cards, identity theft has become a huge concern. People find our key identification numbers and then take over "our identity," charging up enormous bills in our names, stealing our money using our credit. Satan, however, is the greatest identity thief. When he gains control over a human heart, that heart can lose its identity—the values, commitments, and purposes of that person get lost. For this unfortunate demon-possessed man, identity theft is complete. He lives alone in the place of death spending countless hours in sub-human behavior harming himself. He can't even give his name. His identity has been fused with the evil presences that now live inside him. Let's never forget Satan's intentions for us. He longs to rob us of our character, our will, and our identity. Yet we can resist and overcome him by God's power. The key to doing so is a commitment to vigilance and passion for the Kingdom of God and righteousness.

TODAY'S PRAYER

O LORD, Sovereign God of all the earth, come and rule over my heart and drive out from me the influence of the Deceiver and his demonic angels. Purify my heart and remove from me any residue of sin that would open the door for Satan to invade my heart and influence my life. In Jesus' name I pray. Amen.

CONTEXT: MARK 5:1-20

RELATED PASSAGES: JAMES 4:7; 1 JOHN 3:7-10; EPHESIANS 6:11

Day 81

THEY KNEW THEY WERE WHIPPED

MARK 5:10-12

*The spirits inside the man begged Jesus again and
again not to send them out of that area.*

*A large herd of pigs was eating on a hill near there. The evil spirits
begged Jesus, "Send us to the pigs. Let us go into them."*

KEY THOUGHT

The evil spirits begged! While they overpowered the man and struck
fear in the people who lived nearby, they *begged* Jesus! They knew they were
doomed in the face of Jesus' power. Rather than face Jesus—a legion of
demons versus one man of God—they begged to be sent into unclean pigs.
Reminds me of an old song: "He signed my deed with his atoning blood. He
ever lives to make his promise good. Though all the hosts of hell march in to
make a second claim, they all march out at the mention of his name . . . Jesus!"

TODAY'S PRAYER

*Holy God, forgive me for not drawing near to your Son when I faced temptations
in the past. Please remind me to stay near to him so I will have the needed
strength when I am tempted in the future. Give me the courage, dear Father,
to confess the name of Jesus and to know that even the mention of his name
in faith has great power. In the mighty name of Jesus I pray. Amen.*

CONTEXT: MARK 5:1-20

RELATED PASSAGES: MARK 10:32; JAMES 4:5-8; HEBREWS 2:14

Day 82

POWER OVER SATAN

MARK 5:13

So Jesus allowed them to do this. The evil spirits left the man and went into the pigs. Then the herd of pigs ran down the hill and into the lake. All the pigs were drowned. There were about 2,000 pigs in that herd.

KEY THOUGHT

They begged Jesus (see previous verses) so Jesus gave them permission. He had, and still has, power over the demonic world. In fact, his death and resurrection have made clear that power over Satan and his legions. This is important because we clearly see the result of demonic control in the fate of the pigs: death and destruction. From the very beginning of the story of Scripture, when Satan and his demons are allowed control, they bring death and destruction. Let's never forget that our ultimate enemy, the Devil, seeks to work death and destruction in our lives! Let's resist, oppose, fight, stand up against, and defeat his work with the help of God's Spirit at work in our lives.

TODAY'S PRAYER

O LORD God Almighty, I confess that you alone are Sovereign and all-powerful. Please give me a renewed sense of your presence in my life, especially as I seek to resist the temptations and the attacks of the evil one. I know that through my resistance and opposition to his work in my life and through your power at work within me, I can triumph over him. In Jesus' name I pray. Amen.

CONTEXT: MARK 5:1-20

RELATED PASSAGES: GENESIS 4:2-7; EPHESIANS 6:10-13; JAMES 1:14-18

Day 83

FRIGHTENED?

MARK 5:14-15

The men who had the work of caring for the pigs ran away. The men ran to the town and to the farms and told all the people what happened. The people went out to see. They came to Jesus, and they saw the man who had the many evil spirits. He was sitting down and was wearing clothes. He was in his right mind again. When they saw this, they were afraid.

KEY THOUGHT

Let's be honest. Most people don't believe that an old dog can learn new tricks, that a leopard can change its spots, or that people can really change. When they find someone who has been truly and dramatically changed, they are at first curious and then they are frightened. It's as if each person thought to himself or herself, "If Jesus has the power to change someone so much under the control of evil, what kind of changes might he bring in someone like me?" Jesus does bring change . . . real change, transformational change, good change. So we must ask ourselves, "Do I want to change? Do I want Jesus to have his way with me?" Change is scary! So we need to be assured that if we invite Jesus into our world and offer him control of our lives, change awaits! But we don't need to fear! This change is for our good . . . forever.

TODAY'S PRAYER

O Father in heaven, please unleash Jesus' power in my life to change me in ways that drive out the evil, the bad, and the influence of Satan while unleashing the power of your Holy Spirit that brings about the fruit of your righteousness. In the name of the Lord Jesus I pray. Amen.

CONTEXT: MARK 5:1-20

RELATED PASSAGES: REVELATION 3:14-22; 2 CORINTHIANS 5:17; 2 CORINTHIANS 3:17-18

Day 84

FEAR OF CHANGE

MARK 5:16-17

Those who had seen what Jesus did told the others what happened to the man who had the demons living in him. And they also told about the pigs. Then the people began to beg Jesus to leave their area.

KEY THOUGHT

Most folks are afraid of change and of anyone who has the power to change them. Because the crowd couldn't explain how Jesus had power over the man possessed by a legion of demons, they were afraid and asked him to leave. Unfortunately, we often do the same thing—not so much by overtly saying to Jesus, "Please leave me alone." No, we do it by ignoring his presence, staying away from his Word, and associating with people who help drown out the voice of Jesus in our hearts. We must not turn Jesus away. We must not ask him to leave. Instead, let's draw near to him and seek him and follow him. Let's anticipate what he can do in each of our lives!

TODAY'S PRAYER

Sovereign God of all creation, please make me more aware of the nearness of Jesus. Help me to see the changes he is making in my heart and in my life each day. I ask this in his name, Jesus Christ. Amen.

CONTEXT: MARK 5:1-20

RELATED PASSAGES: PHILIPPIANS 4:4-5; 1 TIMOTHY 4:15-16; HEBREWS 10:19-25

Day 85

GO TELL THEM SOMETHING GREAT

MARK 5:18-19

Jesus was preparing to leave in the boat. The man who was now free from the demons begged to go with him. But Jesus did not allow the man to go. He said, "Go home to your family and friends. Tell them about all that the Lord did for you. Tell them how the Lord was good to you."

KEY THOUGHT

"Go . . . tell about all that the Lord did for you." This is not a command just to Legion, but also a command to us! God is merciful! God has saved us! How can we not share this powerful message with others?

TODAY'S PRAYER

O God, give my mouth the words to say and a heart full of joy so that I can be effective in telling others what Jesus has done for me! In Jesus' name I ask for this grace. Amen.

CONTEXT: MARK 5:1-20

RELATED PASSAGES: 1 PETER 3:13-16; COLOSSIANS 1:28-29; ACTS 8:1-4

Day 86

DOING WHAT JESUS ASKS!

MARK 5:20

*So the man left and told the people in the Ten Towns about the
great things Jesus did for him. Everyone was amazed.*

KEY THOUGHT

Amazing things happen when we do what Jesus asks us to do! So what is
Jesus asking you to do today? What is hindering you from obeying him?

TODAY'S PRAYER

*O God, my Abba Father, please give me the courage and the strength to obey what
Jesus has asked me to do. Please use my obedience to bring you glory and to bring
others to know Jesus' saving love. In the name of the amazing Jesus I pray. Amen.*

CONTEXT: MARK 5:1-20

RELATED PASSAGES: JOHN 2:1-5; JOHN 8:51; MATTHEW 7:24

Day 87

WE NEED JESUS!

MARK 5:21-23

Jesus went back to the other side of the lake in the boat. There, a large crowd of people gathered around him on the shore. A leader of the synagogue came. His name was Jairus. He saw Jesus and bowed down before him. He begged Jesus again and again, saying, "My little daughter is dying. Please come and lay your hands on her. Then she will be healed and will live."

KEY THOUGHT

Desperation leads us to do dramatic things! While the people flock to Jesus, the religious leaders are reluctant to put their faith in him and are often hostile to him. Jairus is different. He knows he needs Jesus. He demonstrates his need for Jesus. He pleads with Jesus because of his need. He believes that Jesus can bring the blessing he so desperately needs. In these ways, Jairus serves as a model for us. We know we need Jesus. We are willing to demonstrate our need to Jesus. We are happy to declare our faith in Jesus' power to bring the blessings we most need in our lives.

TODAY'S PRAYER

O God, my Abba Father, I know that I need Jesus and his presence in my life. Please protect me from the things that Satan uses to block my path to your Son and my Savior. In the name of Jesus, my Teacher, Healer, and Lord I pray. Amen.

CONTEXT: MARK 5:21-34

RELATED PASSAGES: MARK 1:40; JOHN 12:42-43; ROMANS 5:6-11

JESUS LOVES US ALL

MARK 5:24

So Jesus went with Jairus. Many people followed Jesus.
They were pushing very close around him.

KEY THOUGHT

We can easily make Jesus into a two-dimensional caricature of himself. He loved the poor, the weak, the downtrodden, the forgotten, and the marginalized and spoke harshly of those in power and of those who were hypocritical in their religion. But Jesus loves all people regardless of their social standing, economic circumstances, religious identity, gender, race, or background. Jesus came looking for those seeking God and recognizing their need for God's work in their lives. So Jesus goes with this man who in many ways is similar to those who will persecute, oppose, and ultimately demand his crucifixion. Why? Because he loves the man and because the man recognizes his need for Jesus' help. This understanding leaves us with three important messages. First, Jesus loves no matter what our background or past may be. Second, he longs for us to admit our need for him and ask for his help. Third, as Jesus' followers, we are called to love all people too!

TODAY'S PRAYER

Lord God, Sovereign over all creation and the Father of all nations, please open my heart and my eyes to love all kinds of people the way your Son demonstrated during his earthly ministry and now does from heaven. In Jesus' name I pray. Amen.

CONTEXT: MARK 5:21-34

RELATED PASSAGES: MATTHEW 28:18-20; LUKE 19:10; GALATIANS 3:26-29

Day 89

HEARD ABOUT JESUS

MARK 5:25-27

There among the people was a woman who had been bleeding for the past twelve years. She had suffered very much. Many doctors had tried to help her, and all the money she had was spent, but she was not improving. In fact, her sickness was getting worse.

The woman heard about Jesus, so she followed him with the other people and touched his coat.

KEY THOUGHT

Jairus (whom we met in the preceding verses) was a man and this is a woman. Jairus was a religious leader and the woman couldn't practice her faith openly because of her problem. He was powerful, but she was poor and destitute because of her illness. While on the opposite end of the spectrum from Jairus, the woman is in the same position: she needs the Lord and the Lord loves her. Both of these very different people demonstrate their faith in the Lord and take risks to get his help. They weren't disappointed in the result. So what makes it so hard for us to demonstrate our need for the Lord and to take risks to draw closer to him? Let's use the example of this woman and of Jairus as our invitation to leave stale and fearful faith behind and reach after the Lord Jesus!

TODAY'S PRAYER

O God, the Almighty, give me courage, strength, and boldness to live my faith in, dependence on, and need for Jesus openly before others. In the name of Jesus, our true hope and great Redeemer, I pray. Amen.

CONTEXT: MARK 5:21-34

RELATED PASSAGES: MATTHEW 11:28; EPHESIANS 2:17-22; COLOSSIANS 1:27

Day 90

TRUST BEYOND HANGING ONTO THREADS

MARK 5:28-29

She thought, "If I can just touch his clothes, that will be enough to heal me." As soon as she touched his coat, her bleeding stopped. She felt that her body was healed from all the suffering.

KEY THOUGHT

Faith is an amazing thing! Jesus said that a faith the size of a mustard seed could move a mountain. It moved more than that for this woman. All she had was a "hem of the garment" sized faith, but it was more than enough. If you struggle with believing, remember: a little faith is a great start. Now act on it. Don't let it sit there and wither, but reach for the "hem of the garment" and begin there. God will grow it as you go.

TODAY'S PRAYER

Father God, please help the following people that I know who are struggling with believing fully in Jesus . . . Please, dear God, use me and others in your family of faith to encourage them to step out on what faith they do have and let you grow it from there. In Jesus' mighty name I pray. Amen.

CONTEXT: MARK 5:21-34

RELATED PASSAGES: MATTHEW 17:20; MARK 10:27; EPHESIANS 3:20-21

Day 91

LOOKING TO BLESS

MARK 5:30-34

Jesus immediately felt power go out from him, so he stopped and turned around. "Who touched my clothes?" he asked.

The followers said to Jesus, "There are so many people pushing against you. But you ask, 'Who touched me?'"

But Jesus continued looking for the one who touched him. The woman knew that she was healed, so she came and bowed at Jesus' feet. She was shaking with fear. She told Jesus the whole story. He said to her, "Dear woman, you are made well because you believed. Go in peace. You will not suffer anymore."

KEY THOUGHT

At first glance, we can misinterpret Jesus' intentions. Some have said that Jesus is just trying to make sure others see that he has done a great miracle. However, if we listen to the Spirit's message in this event, we see that Jesus is looking to bless this woman for her demonstration of faith. Affirmation abounds for major steps taken in faith in the New Testament. Now if we can just let them abound in our churches and families!

TODAY'S PRAYER

Loving God, thank you for adopting me into your family. Use me to welcome others who come to be a part of your people of faith. Use me to bless and affirm their efforts to honor you. In the name of Jesus, my gracious Savior I pray. Amen.

CONTEXT: MARK 5:21-34

RELATED PASSAGES: LUKE 3:21-22; 1 THESSALONIANS 1:2-3; MATTHEW 16:13-17

Day 22

JUST TRUST ME!

MARK 5:35-36

While Jesus was still there speaking, some men came from the house of Jairus, the synagogue leader. They said, "Your daughter is dead. There is no need to bother the Teacher."

But Jesus did not care what the men said. He said to the synagogue leader, "Don't be afraid; just believe."

KEY THOUGHT

When all seems lost, Jesus says, "Just trust me." In the darkest night, Jesus says, "Just trust me." While most of us know these words and find them easy to believe in church services when things are going well, they are much tougher to believe when we find circumstances similar to what Jairus was facing. Fear paralyzes us! Fear controls our thoughts! Fear steals away our faith! So Jesus says, "Don't be afraid. Just trust me!" May God give us the strength to do just that when we face fearful times.

TODAY'S PRAYER

O God, my Abba Father, please help me to trust Jesus and not listen to my fear. I especially need this gracious gift from you when I am struggling with the possible illness and death of a loved one. Come near and fill me, O Holy Spirit. In the name of Jesus, whom I trust. Amen.

CONTEXT: MARK 5:21-43

RELATED PASSAGES: MARK 10:27; MARK 4:35-41; MARK 9:20-24

Day 93

THE INNER THREE

MARK 5:37
Jesus let only Peter, James, and John the brother of James go with him.

KEY THOUGHT

Jesus worked to grow people at all different levels of relationship and maturity. He invested especially in three apostles who would take special leadership in the early church: Peter, James, and John. His work with them reminds us that as important as it is for leaders to help solve problems, to minister to immediate needs, and to encourage all the people of God, they must also set aside time to work with key servant-leaders for the future. With whom are you investing yourself? Who will carry on your ministry after you are no longer here? True leadership invests in the future by investing in future leaders!

TODAY'S PRAYER

Father, give me the wisdom to know those around me with whom I should share my life, my time, and my passion for your work. Use me to call others to serve. In the name of the Lord Jesus Christ, I pray. Amen.

CONTEXT: MARK 5:21-43

RELATED PASSAGES: 2 TIMOTHY 2:1-2; MARK 3:13-15; MARK 9:2-7

Day 94

JUST ASLEEP

MARK 5:38-39

They went to the synagogue leader's house, where Jesus saw many people crying loudly. There was a lot of confusion. He entered the house and said, "Why are you people crying and making so much noise? This child is not dead. She is only sleeping."

KEY THOUGHT

One of the ways early Christians spoke of the death of believers was to say that they had "fallen asleep." While I am not sure they had this encounter with Jesus in mind when they used the term, it is easy to see how they could have made the connection. In the presence of Jesus, death becomes mere sleep as believers await the dawn of their Lord's glorious and triumphant coming.

TODAY'S PRAYER

O LORD God, thank you for sending your Son to destroy the power of death over us. Help me to truly believe that, at its worst, death is no more than a peaceful sleep until we are awakened with the dawn of your Son's return. In Jesus' name. Amen.

CONTEXT: MARK 5:21-43

RELATED PASSAGES: HEBREWS 2:14-15; 1 CORINTHIANS 15:57-58; 1 THESSALONIANS 4:13-18

Day 95

GET UP, LITTLE GIRL!

MARK 5:40-41
But everyone laughed at him.

Jesus told the people to leave the house. Then he went into the room where the child was. He brought the child's father and mother and his three followers into the room with him. Then Jesus held the girl's hand and said to her, "Talitha, koum!" (This means "Little girl, I tell you to stand up!")

KEY THOUGHT

Yes, people laugh at the thought of anyone's being raised from the dead. The thought is ridiculous. The possibility is beyond the realm of our experience. But in this instance, Jesus took those who had faith, or those whom he wanted to have faith, and involved them privately. This was not an attempt to show off or to prove himself to the masses. This was a real need and a real girl and a real time of sorrow. And Jesus changed it all by his word of command, "Get up!" He will one day say the same to those of us who have died before his return and we will rise from death as well.

TODAY'S PRAYER

Gracious God and Almighty Father, thank you for conquering death and bringing us life. I truly believe that you raised Jesus from the dead and I am confident that you will one day raise me if I have died before his return or transform me if I am blessed to be alive at his return. Give me the courage to live boldly for you based upon this conviction. In Jesus' name. Amen.

CONTEXT: MARK 5:21-43

RELATED PASSAGES: JOHN 5:24-30; JOHN 11:25-26; 1 CORINTHIANS 15:42-44

Day 96

ASTOUNDING!

MARK 5:42-43

The girl immediately stood up and began walking. (She was twelve years old.) The father and mother and the followers were amazed. Jesus gave the father and mother very strict orders not to tell people about this. Then he told them to give the girl some food to eat.

KEY THOUGHT

There was an immediate change in the "state" of this girl. One moment she was dead. The next she was alive. Her parents were "absolutely overwhelmed," and how could they not be? There is no place for us to put this in the normal range of human experiences. How does one understand this or even contemplate such an event? Trying to explain it to someone else does not make sense. Jesus' power over death is astounding! Jesus is astounding.

TODAY'S PRAYER

Gracious and Almighty God, your power and grace are astounding. I know that you have power over the physical death that is at work within me. Help me, dear Father, to cling to the memories I have of your gracious love and patience as I try to deal with death personally or confront it through my friendships with others. I pray this in the name of Jesus, who has power over death. Amen.

CONTEXT: MARK 5:21-43

RELATED PASSAGES: MARK 4:41; EPHESIANS 3:14-16;
1 THESSALONIANS 5:10-11

Day 97

Refusing to Believe

MARK 6:1-3

Jesus left there and went back to his hometown. His followers went with him. On the Sabbath day Jesus taught in the synagogue, and many people heard him. They were amazed and said, "Where did this man get this teaching? How did he get such wisdom? Who gave it to him? And where did he get the power to do miracles? Isn't he just the carpenter we know—Mary's son, the brother of James, Joses, Judas, and Simon? And don't his sisters still live here in town." So they had a problem accepting him.

Key Thought

"He's just . . . ." There wasn't anything about Jesus' early life that attracted the attention and fascination of his fellow townspeople. He was just another kid from their town. They knew his family. They expected no great thing out of him. In fact, they were offended by his actions and refused to believe what so many called compelling evidence of his divinity. Despite thousands of years of witnesses, the faith of many in the scientific community, and the testimony of their close friends, many people today refuse to believe. For some, the problem is pride. For others, it is a lifestyle they don't want to change. For others, it is a lack of interest. For others, there are some intellectual hang-ups. But underneath it all, there is a refusal to believe. So which are you: one who refuses to believe and denies faith or one who seeks after truth and finds faith?

Today's Prayer

O Holy and compassionate Father, stir my heart to seek after you. I want to know truth—physical truth and spiritual truth. Correct me in my wrong-headedness and beckon me in my truth-seeking. I ask this in Jesus' name. Amen.

Context: Mark 6:1-13

Related Passages: John 7:16-17; John 12:37-43; Colossians 1:19-21

Day 98

BLOCKING MIRACLES

MARK 6:4-6

Then Jesus said to them, "People everywhere give honor to a prophet, except in his own town, with his own people, or in his home." Jesus was not able to do any miracles there except the healing of some sick people by laying his hands on them. He was surprised that the people there had no faith. Then he went to other villages in that area and taught.

KEY THOUGHT

Jesus is in an important religious place with people who know him well. His intentions are good and he has great power to heal and to help. Yet in this place, he couldn't do nearly as much as he wanted because the people refused to believe and didn't expect him to be able to act. How often have well-intentioned religious people blocked the power of God to work among them because they have refused to believe in Jesus' power? More often than it ever should have!

TODAY'S PRAYER

Father, forgive us, forgive me, for not expecting you to act in powerful ways to bring deliverance, healing and blessing in the lives of your people. I pray this in the name of the one to whom all honor is due, Jesus my Lord. Amen.

CONTEXT: MARK 6:1-13

RELATED PASSAGES: EPHESIANS 1:15-20; EPHESIANS 3:14-19; 2 TIMOTHY 3:5

Day 99

Shake Off the Dust

Mark 6:6-11

*He was surprised that the people there had no faith. Then he
went to other villages in that area and taught.*

*Jesus called his twelve apostles together. He sent them out in groups of two and
gave them power over evil spirits. This is what he told them: "Take nothing for
your trip except a stick for walking. Take no bread, no bag, and no money. You can
wear sandals, but don't take extra clothes. When you enter a house, stay there until
you leave that town. If any town refuses to accept you or refuses to listen to you,
then leave that town and shake the dust off your feet as a warning to them."*

Key Thought

After witnessing Jesus' experience in Nazareth, his disciples knew that
not everyone would welcome their Master. If they had any remaining doubts
that they would meet resistance and rejection, his directions to them made
it clear that they would. He told them what they were to take with them on
their mission, how they were to conduct themselves, and what they were to
do when their message was not received. They would warn people about the
importance of turning from their sins. They would display Jesus' power over
the demonic world. They would bless many with healing. In other words, they
would extend their Master's message to many more people than Jesus could
reach by himself. However, when they were rejected, they were to move on
and do God's work where it would be more warmly received, not wasting their
time trying to convince those who would not believe.

Today's Prayer

*O LORD God Almighty, thank you for your grace. Thank you for your mercy. Thank
you for your gospel. Please help me to not take others' rejection of your message
personally. Instead, dear Father, use me to help others understand that they are
making a decision about their lives, their eternal destiny, and the source of their
grace. When rejection comes, help me to move on, trusting that the seeds of grace that
have been planted may germinate at some later time. In Jesus' name I pray. Amen.*

Context: Mark 6:1-13

Related Passages: Acts 13:48-52; Acts 18:6; 1 Thessalonians 4:8

Day 100

Ministry to All

Mark 6:12-13

The apostles left there and went to other places. They talked to the people and told them to change their hearts and lives. They forced many demons out of people and put olive oil on many who were sick people and healed them.

Key Thought

The disciples told the message to all they met. They didn't try to predict who would welcome the message and who wouldn't. They spread their ministry net over a wide area, expanding Jesus' ministry. They did many good things in the name of Jesus. We *must* learn from them. The old hymn says, "The blessed Gospel is for all; the Gospel is for all." It must be. It is not for a select few—our friends, those we deem most likely to respond, or those with whom we feel most comfortable sharing the message. We must tell all who do not know God to turn their lives to him and find the blessings of knowing Jesus.

Today's Prayer

Father, please forgive any latent prejudice that lingers in my heart without my awareness. I never want my preconceptions to keep me from sharing your good news with people. Use my efforts to expand your Kingdom and reach more people with your saving grace. I pray this in the name of Jesus, who died for all so that we all might be whole. Amen.

Context: Mark 6:1-13

Related Passages: Matthew 28:18-20; 1 Corinthians 9:20-23; Colossians 1:28-29

Day 101

WILD SPECULATIONS

MARK 6:14-16

King Herod heard about Jesus, because Jesus was now famous.
Some people said, "He is John the Baptizer. He must have risen
from death, and that is why he can do these miracles."

Other people said, "He is Elijah."

And others said, "He is like the prophets who lived long ago."

Herod heard these things about Jesus. He said, "I killed John by
cutting off his head. Now John has been raised from death!"

KEY THOUGHT

Jesus' ministry was effective, powerful, and rumor-worthy! In addition
to the effective ministry of Jesus himself, Jesus' followers were spreading his
reputation, his teachings, and his blessings. They were trying to understand
just who this powerful miracle-worker and truth-teacher actually might be.
Wild speculations were made, but no one could speculate wildly enough to
recognize his true identity . . . at least not yet! Our job is to help others know
about Jesus and spread his reputation far and wide and get them asking
questions about Jesus. Then, as we are given the opportunity, help them
understand more fully just who Jesus is—the Christ, the Son of God.

TODAY'S PRAYER

Father, please use the events, rumors, movies, and speculations about your Son to your
glory. Please open doors of opportunity for your children, and especially me, to share
the message of Jesus more effectively. In the saving name of Jesus' I pray. Amen.

CONTEXT: MARK 6:14-29

RELATED PASSAGES: ACTS 4:12; 1 CORINTHIANS 16:8-9; EPHESIANS 6:19-20

Day 102

COURAGE TO TELL THE TRUTH

MARK 6:17-20

Herod himself had ordered his soldiers to arrest John and put him in prison. Herod did this to please his wife Herodias. She had been married to Herod's brother Philip, but then Herod married her. John told Herod, "It is not right for you to be married to your brother's wife." So Herodias hated John. She wanted him dead, but she was not able to persuade Herod to kill him. Herod was afraid to kill John, because he knew that he was a good and holy man. So he protected him. He liked listening to John, although what John said left him with so many questions.

KEY THOUGHT

Unfortunately, over the years, way too many of Jesus' followers have lost their courage to tell the truth and have become puppets of political correctness—either the "correctness" of the popular culture or of the religious culture in which they found themselves. John spoke the truth. He spoke the same truth no matter the power of the person listening to his message and the potential danger he might encounter for his proclamation. I cannot think of many things more needed in our time than this kind of courage.

TODAY'S PRAYER

O Father in heaven, give all of us the courage as Christian witnesses to tell your truth in love no matter the circumstances in which we find ourselves and regardless of the consequences we may encounter for declaring your message. I ask this in Jesus' name. Amen.

CONTEXT: MARK 6:14-29

RELATED PASSAGES: JOHN 7:16-19; GALATIANS 1:10; 1 THESSALONIANS 1:4-6

Day 103

SHAMEFUL

MARK 6:21-26

Then the right time came for Herodias to cause John's death. It happened on Herod's birthday. Herod gave a dinner party for the most important government leaders, the commanders of his army, and the most important people in Galilee. The daughter of Herodias came to the party and danced. When she danced, Herod and the people eating with him were very pleased.

So King Herod said to the girl, "I will give you anything you want." He promised her, "Anything you ask for I will give to you—even half of my kingdom."

The girl went to her mother and asked, "What should I ask King Herod to give me?"

Her mother answered, "Ask for the head of John the Baptizer."

So right then the girl went back in to the king. She said to him, "Please give me the head of John the Baptizer. Bring it to me now on a plate."

King Herod was very sad, but he didn't want to break the promise he had made to her in front of his guests.

KEY THOUGHT

This horrible story is a reminder that proclaiming truth does not necessarily lead to pleasant short-term results for God's truth-telling people. John loses his life because of the unscrupulous desires of an immoral Herodias and the political cowardice of Herod—who added incest to his adultery by taking Herodias (his half-brother's wife and the daughter of another half-brother) as his own wife. People entrenched in sin often hate truth-telling and will do whatever is necessary to hide the truth, sometimes even killing the truth-teller. So we shouldn't be surprised in our day when the truth is opposed by those who choose the way of immorality. Let's pray for truth-tellers!

TODAY'S PRAYER

O God, please protect and empower your truth-tellers. Make their voices effective. Keep their political enemies from silencing them. When their ministry is complete, please bring them home to you with great joy. In Jesus' name. Amen.

CONTEXT: MARK 6:14-29

RELATED PASSAGES: JOHN 3:16-21; JOHN 15:21; MATTHEW 5:43-48

Day 104

Brutality and Grief

Mark 6:27-29

So he sent a soldier to cut off John's head and bring it to him. The soldier went and cut off John's head in the prison. He brought the head back on a plate and gave it to the girl, and the girl gave it to her mother. John's followers heard about what happened, so they came and got John's body and put it in a tomb.

Key Thought

We often forget that we have brothers and sisters in Christ who have to face incredible inhumanity and brutality because of their faith, righteousness, and unwavering loyalty to Jesus. Let's use this gruesome reminder of John the Baptizer's death to jar us into an acute awareness of our fellow believers worldwide who are suffering and dying for the cause of Christ.

Today's Prayer

O God, my Abba Father, it pains me deeply to think about your precious children who are facing horribly brutal times because of their faith. Please work in the affairs of our world to bring an end to the regimes and conditions that allow such inhumanity and brutality to have power. In Jesus' name I pray. Amen.

Context: Mark 6:14-29

Related Passages: 1 Timothy 2:1-6; Matthew 25:34-40; Hebrews 10:32-34

Day 105
A Quieter Spot

Mark 6:30-32

The apostles Jesus had sent out came back to him. They gathered around him and told him about all they had done and taught. Jesus and his followers were in a very busy place. There were so many people that he and his followers did not even have time to eat. He said to them, "Come with me. We will go to a quiet place to be alone. There we will get some rest."

So Jesus and his followers went away alone. They went in a boat to a place where no one lived.

Key Thought

The good we do for the Kingdom occurs because of God's work through us. Yes, we offer ourselves to be used by God as his vessels, but the power and effectiveness come from our obedient submission and God's glorious work through us. To God belongs all the glory! But, being used by God is tiring work no matter how exciting it may be. God's servants need periods of rest and renewal. This means getting away from the rush of ministry and rekindling our passions, energy, and focus in the presence of other devoted servants and in the presence of Jesus as we honor God. Humility has two faces: first, humility is seen in the life of a person who serves God for the Father's glory; and second, it is seen when those who serve God acknowledge their need for rest and time away from the rush to be with God.

Today's Prayer

Father, please give me the right heart to be a humble servant. Remove from me the desire to accomplish great things so my name is known or my actions are praised. I want you to be glorified. In addition, dear Father, please gently humble me when I try to depend upon my own energies rather than spending time resting in your presence and letting you re-kindle my spirit and re-energize my body. I ask this in Jesus' gracious name. Amen.

Context: Mark 6:30-44

Related Passages: Luke 5:15-16; 1 Peter 4:10-11; Acts 14:26-28

Day 106

COMPASSIONATE TEACHING

MARK 6:33-34

But many people saw them leave and knew who they were. So people from every town ran to the place where they were going and got there before Jesus. As Jesus stepped out of the boat, he saw a large crowd waiting. He felt sorry for them, because they were like sheep without a shepherd to care for them. So he taught the people many things.

KEY THOUGHT

Jesus was tired and the people were spiritually lost and in danger—"sheep without a shepherd." So Jesus gave them what they needed most: "He taught them many things." A "shepherd and teacher" from a Christian point of view is redundant. A shepherd teaches by guiding, leading, protecting, correcting, and caring. Let's call our modern Christian teachers to that high standard! They must be more than a classroom lecturer. They must live the message they teach and love the people with whom they share it.

TODAY'S PRAYER

O dear Father, please give your people, your church, more genuine shepherds and teachers. So often your people are like sheep without a shepherd. Please raise up more godly and faithful shepherds among us. In the name of Jesus, the great Shepherd of the sheep, I fervently ask this. Amen.

CONTEXT: MARK 6:30-44

RELATED PASSAGES: JOHN 10:11-15; ACTS 20:28-29; EPHESIANS 4:11-13

Day 107

CONCERN FOR THE CROWDS

MARK 6:35-36

It was now very late in the day. Jesus' followers came to him and said, "No one lives around here, and it is already very late. So send the people away. They need to go to the farms and towns around here to buy some food to eat."

KEY THOUGHT

At first glance, and because we know the outcome of the story, we might miss the concern the disciples have for the crowd. They are genuinely concerned for the physical well being of the people who are following Jesus. Sometimes we get so caught up in the spiritual talk and show of church that we forget the very real physical needs of each other. However, being a follower of the Christ is not just about talk and intentions. It is offering genuine care and concern. Little do the disciples know that Jesus will raise their expectations of what that means before this incident is over!

TODAY'S PRAYER

Father, open my heart to the physical needs around me and help me to do something to help the people with those needs. I ask this in the name of my kind and compassionate Savior. Amen.

CONTEXT: MARK 6:30-44

RELATED PASSAGES: 1 JOHN 3:16-18; JAMES 2:14-17; MATTHEW 25:31-36

Day 108

LIMITED RESOURCES?

MARK 6:37-38

But Jesus answered, "You give them some food to eat."

They said to Jesus, "We can't buy enough bread to feed all these people. We would all have to work a month to earn enough to buy that much bread!"

Jesus asked them, "How many loaves of bread do you have now? Go and see."

They counted their loaves of bread. They came to Jesus and said, "We have five loaves of bread and two fish."

KEY THOUGHT

In the previous verses, Jesus' disciples expressed their concern for the crowds following Jesus. Now Jesus challenges them to do the impossible: "You feed them!" At first, they don't get the impossibility of his command. They are still locked into their normal ways of handling need. So Jesus tells them to check their available resources—five loaves and two fish. Now they can be certain that the task they face is impossible for them. At one time or another, nearly every one of us is called upon to serve others in an impossible situation: during the illness of a family member or in a time of real financial pinch or when we're facing a difficult ministry challenge or in an unfamiliar environment or . . . . No matter what the challenge may be, we realize that we cannot accomplish our tasks through our own strength. Jesus wants us to see exactly where we are: in an impossible situation unless his provision, his guidance, and his providence carry us through. Jesus wants us to know that our resources are limited . . . but his are unlimited.

TODAY'S PRAYER

Father in heaven, I realize that I am not sufficient for the challenges I face. I confess that my personal resources are limited and that without your mercy, grace, and power I cannot do what I need to do. Please help me! In Jesus name I pray. Amen.

CONTEXT: MARK 6:30-44

RELATED PASSAGES: ZECHARIAH 8:6; MARK 10:27; ROMANS 11:33

Day 109

Unlimited Resources!

Mark 6:39-42

Then Jesus said to them, "Tell everyone to sit in groups on the green grass." So all the people sat in groups. There were about 50 or 100 people in each group.

Jesus took the five loaves and two fish. He looked up to the sky and thanked God for the food. Then he broke the bread into pieces, which he gave to his followers to distribute to the people. Then he divided the two fish among everyone there.

They all ate until they were full.

Key Thought

Jesus' disciples were concerned about the physical needs of the crowd following Jesus and realized they didn't have the resources to meet those needs. (See the previous verses.) Now, however, Jesus shows them the unlimited resources of God when they place what is available into the hands of the Lord. Jesus took their meager meal of five loaves and two fish and made it more than sufficient; he made it ample. Now the Lord looks to you and me and asks us to offer our resources to him so that he can bring us the blessing and provision of God.

Today's Prayer

O glorious Father in heaven, I believe, but help my unbelief. Help me offer my limited resources to you so that they will be made more than sufficient to do your work and minister to those in need. I pray in the name of Jesus, who is able to do more through me than I can ask or imagine. Amen.

Context: Mark 6:30-44

Related Passages: 2 Corinthians 3:4-5; 2 Corinthians 12:7-10; Ephesians 3:20-21

Day 110

HANDS-ON PROVISION

MARK 6:42-44

*They all ate until they were full. After they finished eating, the
followers filled twelve baskets with the pieces of bread and fish
that were left. There were about 5000 men there who ate.*

KEY THOUGHT

Mark makes it clear that this was an incredible miracle of provision.
People were satisfied. Five thousand ate. Bread and fish were left over even
though they started with only five loaves and two fish. However, we may miss
the most important part of the story if we do not pay attention. There are
twelve baskets of leftovers, one basket for each apostle. Each of them was able
to touch this miracle with his own hands. When we offer Jesus our meager
resources, he enables us to use those resources to bless others and we get to
have a hands-on experience of his grace.

TODAY'S PRAYER

*Father, please give me faith to trust that Jesus can make my feeble
resources, skills, and intellect more than sufficient to meet the needs
of those you want me to serve. In Jesus' name I pray. Amen.*

CONTEXT: MARK 6:30-44

RELATED PASSAGES: 2 CORINTHIANS 9:6-8; PHILIPPIANS 4:13, 18-20;
MATTHEW 6:24-34

Day 111

COMPONENTS OF JESUS' MINISTRY

MARK 6:45-46

Then Jesus told the followers to get into the boat. He told them to go to the other side of the lake to Bethsaida. He said he would come later. He stayed there to tell everyone they could go home. After he said goodbye to them, he went up into the hills to pray.

KEY THOUGHT

This whole episode began with Jesus sensing that he and his disciples needed rest. However, the people found them and came to them for help and teaching. Jesus provided for them. Then Jesus, like any great leader sometimes has to do, protected his disciples and sent them away while he dealt with the crowds. Yet Jesus knew he needed to get away and be alone with his Father, so he sends the crowds away. Ministry is exhausting. Dealing with people and their issues takes a toll. Being used by God can be physically taxing. So Jesus seeks rest, especially in the middle of high ministry demands. Let's learn from the Master.

TODAY'S PRAYER

O Abba Father, please correct me for not resting in your presence and not spending enough time in prayer. Help me stay on track with my commitment to properly rest, and to also stay on track in my prayer life. In Jesus' name I pray. Amen.

CONTEXT: MARK 6:45-56

RELATED PASSAGES: 1 THESSALONIANS 4:16-18; PSALM 23:1-6; ACTS 3:19-20

Day 112

I AM HERE!

MARK 6:47-50

That night, the boat was still in the middle of the lake. Jesus was alone on the land. He saw the boat far away on the lake. And he saw the followers working hard to row the boat. The wind was blowing against them. Sometime between three and six o'clock in the morning, Jesus went out to the boat, walking on the water. He continued walking until he was almost past the boat. But the followers saw Jesus walking on the water. They thought he was a ghost, and they started screaming. It scared them all to see him. But he spoke to them and said, "Don't worry! It's me! Don't be afraid."

KEY THOUGHT

Where do we most fear being abandoned? Jesus will be there! Jesus comes to us in the middle of the storm. If we will call out to him and trust his desire to come to us and to help us, we can see him there. We don't need to fear the storm! We don't have to be disconsolate because of the fear in the eyes of those around us. Jesus will meet us in our storms and bring us safely to our home.

TODAY'S PRAYER

O Abba Father, help me believe that I will never be abandoned or left alone—not even in my worst and most fearful times. In Jesus' name I ask for this faith. Amen.

CONTEXT: MARK 6:45-56

RELATED PASSAGES: MATTHEW 28:20B; ROMANS 8:35-39; HEBREWS 13:5-6

Day 113

Astonished Misunderstanding

Mark 6:51-52

When he got into the boat with the followers, the wind stopped. The followers were completely amazed. They could not believe what happened. It was like the miracle he did with the bread. They still didn't understand what that meant.

Key Thought

They couldn't get it! Maybe they *wouldn't* get it! Only God could feed a multitude out of such a small collection of bread and fish. Only God could still a storm and bring the boat to immediate safety at the intended destination. Jesus was God with them. Faith in him opened the door to what is not humanly possible. Yet even with what they saw, they found it hard to really believe in Jesus as the Son of God. He seemed simply too good to be true.

Today's Prayer

O LORD God, my righteous Father, please help me overcome my pockets of weak faith and my areas of lacking belief. In the name of Jesus, who will never forsake me, I pray. Amen.

Context: Mark 6:45-56

Related Passages: Mark 6:1-6; John 14:28; Ephesians 3:20-21

Day 114

JUST TO TOUCH THE FRINGE

MARK 6:53-56

Jesus and his followers went across the lake and came to shore at Gennesaret. They tied the boat there. When they were out of the boat, the people there saw Jesus. They knew who he was, so they ran to tell others throughout that area. They brought sick people on mats to every place Jesus went. Jesus went into towns, cities, and farms around that area. And every place he went, the people brought sick people to the marketplaces. They begged him to let them touch any part of his coat. And all those who touched him were healed.

KEY THOUGHT

Jesus' power is fully displayed through a whole series of ministry moments in this context. However, many more people than just the disciples realized Jesus had great power to heal, bless, and deliver from Satan. The crowds knew. They swarmed him. They anticipated his next move. They dogged his steps. They brought their sick to him. Jesus was the one who had the power and they knew it. The real question is whether we know it. Do we trust he has the power to help us in our time of need? Do we believe that his power is real or just a figment of an overactive religious imagination? I don't know about you, but I believe!

TODAY'S PRAYER

Lord God Almighty, thank you for giving Jesus all power and authority. I believe he is glorious, almighty, and powerful! May Jesus' power be displayed in my heart, my words, and my life. In Jesus' name. Amen.

CONTEXT: MARK 6:45-56

RELATED PASSAGES: EPHESIANS 1:19-23; HEBREWS 4:14-16; EPHESIANS 3:20-21

Day 115

RITUALLY CLEAN?

MARK 7:1-5

Some Pharisees and some teachers of the law came from Jerusalem and gathered around Jesus. They saw that some of his followers ate food with hands that were not clean, meaning that they did not wash their hands in a special way. The Pharisees and all the other Jews never eat before washing their hands in this special way. They do this to follow the traditions they have from their great leaders who lived long ago. And when these Jews buy something in the market, they never eat it until they wash it in a special way. They also follow other rules from their people who lived before them. They follow rules like the washing of cups, pitchers, and pots.

The Pharisees and teachers of the law said to Jesus, "Your followers don't follow the traditions we have from our great leaders who lived long ago. They eat their food with hands that are not clean. Why do they do this?"

KEY THOUGHT

Wouldn't it be nice if we could be spiritually clean simply by being physically and ritually clean? Unfortunately, we can't. Only God can make us truly clean. So while observing local customs about cleanliness can be helpful in winning our acceptance by others, only Jesus can win their hearts for God. Unfortunately, many folks simply take the physical shortcut hoping to achieve spiritual goals but come up empty because they have not fully submitted themselves to God.

TODAY'S PRAYER

O LORD, only you can make me clean. Please cleanse me; don't just forgive me, but make me new, dear Lord. In Jesus' holy name I pray. Amen.

CONTEXT: MARK 7:1-23

RELATED PASSAGES: PSALM 9:12-14; PROVERBS 20:9; 1 JOHN 1:7

Day 116

Spiritually Unclean!

Mark 7:6-8

Jesus answered, "You are all hypocrites. Isaiah was right when he wrote these words from God about you: 'These people honor me with their words, but I am not really important to them. Their worship of me is worthless. The things they teach are only human rules.' You have stopped following God's commands, preferring instead the man-made rules you got from others."

Key Thought

We try to be nice in today's politically correct environment. However, some truth—God's truth—is just simply the real truth. When people fake their religious devotion or when they bend God's word to justify the way they want to live, then it is hypocrisy no matter who they are. Jesus hates hypocrisy. When folks sink into hypocrisy, Jesus will not pretend that they are righteous. So what do we do with these harsh words from Jesus? First, let's ask ourselves if we are guilty of the sin Jesus condemns. If we are, then let's change and put our lives where our mouths are! Second, we need not to be so bashful with each other when hypocrisy creeps into our lives. Let's lovingly and humbly help each other identify and correct any hypocrisy. Hypocrisy destroys our hearts and ruins the influence of Jesus' people on the world.

Today's Prayer

O God, always righteous and yet boundlessly merciful, I confess that I have sometimes sinned because I'm weak and have stumbled. But there have been times when I've been criticizing others for their sin yet allowed myself to do what I know was not right. Correct me gently and humble me tenderly so I can serve you without hypocrisy. In Jesus' name I humbly ask for this grace. Amen.

Context: Mark 7:1-23

Related Passages: Ezekiel 14:10; Mark 12:13-17; 1 Peter 2:1

Day 117

TWISTING THE MOST BASIC TRUTHS

MARK 7:9-13

Then he said, "You show great skill in avoiding the commands of God so that you can follow your own teachings! Moses said, 'You must respect your father and mother.' He also said, 'Whoever says anything bad to their father or mother must be killed.' But you teach that people can say to their father or mother, 'I have something I could use to help you, but I will not use it for you. I will give it to God.' You are telling people that they do not have to do anything for their father or mother. So you are teaching that it is not important to do what God said. You think it is more important to follow those traditions you have, which you pass on to others. And you do many things like that."

KEY THOUGHT

Jesus gives an example of the teachers' and Pharisees' hypocrisy. In this case, the hypocrisy was finding a legalistic rationale to withhold support from parents, thus disobeying one of the Ten Commandments. The brazenness of such rationalization of one of the ten bedrock truths of their existence just proves how entrenched the practice of hypocrisy can become. Legalistic hypocrisy abounds in all sorts of religious groups and religious experiences. Let's obey, not rationalize. Let's respond graciously to God's grace and not seek to work our way out of our responsibilities to each other and to God.

TODAY'S PRAYER

O God, thank you for such clear examples of legalistic hypocrisy. I hate that Jesus had to see this in his day, but it helps me see what I need to avoid and what your heart hates. Purify my heart and keep a right attitude in me through your Holy Spirit. I pray this in Jesus' holy name. Amen.

CONTEXT: MARK 7:1-23

RELATED PASSAGES: PSALM 51:2, 7; ZEPHANIAH 3:9-13; JAMES 4:8

Day 118

WHAT TRULY DEFILES

MARK 7:14-16

Jesus called the people to him again. He said, "Everyone should listen to me and understand what I am saying. There is nothing people can put in their mouth that will make them wrong. People are made wrong by what comes from inside them."

KEY THOUGHT

Our words and our actions say it all, don't they! So let's take seriously our use of language—both what we say and how we say it. Let's also look at our lives and see what our actions say about our loyalty to God. Our intentions matter for good only if we follow through on them! Repentance that is only a change of heart and not also a change in actions is not really repentance at all.

TODAY'S PRAYER

Bless me, LORD God Almighty, that by the power of your Spirit I can change my behavior and my values to more perfectly reflect your holiness, mercy, and righteousness. I ask for this grace and power in Jesus' name. Amen.

CONTEXT: MARK 7:1-23

RELATED PASSAGES: GALATIANS 2:22-26; 1 JOHN 3:7-8; PSALM 19:12-14

Day 119

FOOD WON'T DEFILE

MARK 7:17-19

*Then Jesus left the people and went into the house. The followers asked
Jesus about what he had told the people. He said, "Do you still have trouble
understanding? Surely you know that nothing that enters the mouth from
the outside can make people unacceptable to God. Food does not go into a
person's mind. It goes into the stomach. Then it goes out of the body." (When
Jesus said this, he meant there is no food that is wrong for people to eat.)*

KEY THOUGHT

Once again Jesus wants his closest followers to know that the issues of
genuine faith focus on our heart-driven actions and not on the cosmetic ones.
Luke and Mark add the powerful commentary that "there is no food that is
wrong for people to eat," a truth that took some time to sink in among Jesus'
early followers. The declaration is radical, not just because he declared all
food clean, but because he wanted us to look in our hearts instead of having
a perfunctory religious check list of good deeds that do not demand much of
our hearts.

TODAY'S PRAYER

*O God, please make my deeds helpful and genuine and my heart pure.
I want to love you, and I want to love others, in deeds and truth as
well as in words and speech. In Jesus' name I pray. Amen.*

CONTEXT: MARK 7:1-23

RELATED PASSAGES: 1 JOHN 3:16-18; 1 SAMUEL 6:16-17; MATTHEW 15:15-20

Day 120

FROM WITHIN: THE HEART INSIDE

MARK 7:20

*And Jesus said, "The things that make people wrong
are the things that come from the inside."*

KEY THOUGHT

Wow! What a powerful message in today's world where we deliberately
expose ourselves to so many forms of hurtful images and thoughts. Jesus
stressed the importance of being pure—not just in our actions, but especially
in our hearts and minds! Let's hear clearly Jesus' demand that we be righteous
in body, soul, and spirit!

TODAY'S PRAYER

*Holy Father, my loving God, please forgive me of secret sin. Especially
forgive and strengthen me so that I can throw off any influence that
would pull me away from you and the holiness that you long to share
with me. Help me keep my thoughts pure. In Jesus' name. Amen.*

CONTEXT: MARK 7:1-23

RELATED PASSAGES: 1 CHRONICLES 28:9; PSALM 7:9; MARK 12:30

Day 121

DEFILED!

MARK 7:21-23

*"All these bad things begin inside a person, in the mind: bad thoughts,
sexual sins, stealing, murder, adultery, greed, doing bad things to people,
lying, doing things that are morally wrong, jealousy, insulting people, proud
talking, and foolish living. These evil things come from inside a person.
And these are the things that make people unacceptable to God."*

KEY THOUGHT

Sometimes in our quest to emphasize Jesus' concern about our inner
being, we accidentally let go of any sense of holy standards. Jesus did not.
Jesus' followers were instructed not to do so. Morality was stressed as a
response to God's grace. This morality was the product of a life empowered
by the Holy Spirit and was the demonstration that one had died to the old
life of sin upon being baptized with Christ into his death. Immorality was
condemned in specific and strong terms. The observable immorality and
corruption, however, found its origin in Satan's influence on the inner being
of a person. Externals were simply the way a person's inner life became
exposed.

TODAY'S PRAYER

*Father in heaven, please work on my heart. Purify my motives and my
desires. Make me your person, holy and pure. In Jesus' name. Amen.*

CONTEXT: MARK 7:1-23

RELATED PASSAGES: GALATIANS 5:19-21; PSALM 139:23-24; JAMES 1:13-15

Day 122

COULDN'T KEEP IT QUIET

MARK 7:24-25

Jesus went from there to the area around Tyre. He did not want the people in that area to know he was there, so he went into a house. But he could not stay hidden. A woman heard that he was there. Her little daughter had an evil spirit inside her. So the woman came to Jesus and bowed down near his feet.

KEY THOUGHT

Jesus and his leading followers are still in need of rest. The crowds have pressed upon them repeatedly. Jesus' reputation has grown and he is well known even far away from his home and center of ministry. Gentiles, people who were not Jews, have heard of his power and know their need for help. So a Gentile woman comes to Jesus with a deep concern on her heart. Her daughter is possessed by an evil spirit. The Phoenician people had a proud but very pagan heritage (from a Jewish point of view). They had often been bitter enemies with the children of Israel. For this woman to fall at the feet of a Jew, especially one of "no noble rank," was indeed a sign of desperation and humility. No distance—geographical, religious, or racial—could keep Jesus' saving power from becoming known!

TODAY'S PRAYER

O God, please awaken us to realize that what we have to share with the world is Jesus—not our technology, our culture, our knowledge. While many other things are good to share and I know we need to be generous in sharing them, please give us more passion about sharing Jesus both in our teaching and in our conduct. In Jesus' powerful name I pray. Amen.

CONTEXT: MARK 7:24-37

RELATED PASSAGES: ACTS 4:10-12; JOHN 4:39-42; 1 JOHN 4:11-14

Day 123

BEGGING THE LORD

MARK 7:26

*She was not a Jew. She was born in Phoenicia, an area in Syria.
She begged Jesus to force the demon out of her daughter.*

KEY THOUGHT

Are we too proud to beg? Do we have such an elevated view of ourselves that falling on our knees and begging seem beneath us? Are our spiritual issues any less in need of Jesus than this woman's concern for her daughter? What would we *not* do to place ourselves before the Lord and his grace? This woman would not let anything separate her from Jesus' power to deliver her girl. She was willing to beg! Incredibly, we don't have to . . . even though we often need to!

TODAY'S PRAYER

O gracious Father, full of mercy and compassion, forgive me when I am arrogant and proud. Gently humble me and craft me into a vessel fit for your use in your work for your glory. In Jesus' gracious name I pray. Amen.

CONTEXT: MARK 7:24-37

RELATED PASSAGES: ROMANS 5:6-11; COLOSSIANS 1:19-22; LUKE 16:3

Day 124

EVEN THE PUPPIES GET SOME CRUMBS

MARK 7:27-28

Jesus told the woman, "It is not right to take the children's bread and give it to the dogs. First let the children eat all they want."

She answered, "That is true, Lord. But the dogs under the table can eat the pieces of food that the children don't eat."

KEY THOUGHT

Wow! Think how this would come off in our racially charged world of political correctness. Now double that and you get the impact of this exchange in Jesus' time of extreme racial tension between Jews and Gentiles. Even though Jesus' statement about dogs (or puppies) might seem insensitive, he was undoubtedly testing this woman's faith. But this woman will not let anything keep her from her goal. She wants Jesus to cure her daughter. Jesus' earthly ministry may have been directed only to the children of Israel, but even in Israel the puppies, that is, the Gentiles in this case, get the scraps. What humility and commitment not to lose sight of her goal! I'm afraid my pride might have gotten in the way. I'm afraid my anger would have bubbled to the surface. But not this woman! Her passion did not go unnoticed.

TODAY'S PRAYER

LORD God Almighty, I'm not sure I would have handled this situation as well as the woman in the story. Thank you for her faith and for her tenacity. Please give me more of both and help me be less reactive to language that is insensitively directed toward me. I ask for this grace in Jesus' name. Amen.

CONTEXT: MARK 7:24-37

RELATED PASSAGES: GALATIANS 5:22-26; PHILIPPIANS 3:6-14; PROVERBS 11:2

Day 125

THE DEMON WAS GONE

MARK 7:29-30

*Then he told her, "That is a very good answer.
You may go. The demon has left your daughter."*

The woman went home and found her daughter lying on the bed. The demon was gone.

KEY THOUGHT

The woman's answer was good, not just because it was clever but also because she showed her humble faith. She received the goal of her heart: her daughter was delivered from the power of the evil spirit. Let's remember that nothing, absolutely *nothing*, is more important in our daily lives than deliverance from evil's powerful grip, impact, and control. Let's not let anything take our hearts off that goal in our lives. We must want deliverance from evil and its power in every form. This kind of deliverance can only come from Jesus. Finally, we must use this deliverance as an opportunity to be used in the work of God.

TODAY'S PRAYER

Father, dear Abba the Almighty, please remove my sin from me. Help me see any stumbling block that I might be placing in my own path or in the paths of those I love. Use me to bring others to your grace and holiness so they can find deliverance from evil in any of its forms. In the name of Jesus, the great deliverer, I pray. Amen.

CONTEXT: MARK 7:24-37

RELATED PASSAGES: MATTHEW 6:9-13; COLOSSIANS 1:11-14; EPHESIANS 2:1-6

Day 126

THE TOUCH OF HIS HAND

MARK 7:31-32

Then Jesus left the area around Tyre and went through Sidon. On his way
to Lake Galilee he went through the area of the Ten Towns. While he was
there, some people brought a man to him who was deaf and could not talk
clearly. The people begged Jesus to put his hand on the man to heal him.

KEY THOUGHT

Jesus' reputation as a miracle worker is now driving people's reaction to
his ministry. He is well known as a healer in Galilee, the region of Tyre and
Sidon, and also Decapolis (the area of Ten Towns). Jesus can no longer operate
in secrecy. It seems as if everyone has heard of him. However, as Mark will
show in subsequent verses, Jesus' concern has to do with the perception of
the people. How can he call them to deeper discipleship if they see him only
as a personal miracle worker? Jesus will re-assert his concern that people
get to know him as he wants to be known. This will mean conflict and
misunderstanding in the following episodes in which we find Jesus. Yet despite
this concern, he consistently shows tender and compassionate concern for the
individuals in need while keeping his ministry from becoming just a traveling
healing show.

TODAY'S PRAYER

Father, with so many demands on my time, please help me not to cave into the
demands of others to be the person they want me to be. I want to please you. At the
same time, dear Father, I want to deal personally and compassionately with people
as your Son did. In the name of Jesus, your Son and my Savior, I pray. Amen.

CONTEXT: MARK 7:24-37

RELATED PASSAGES: MARK 1:35-42; JOHN 2:23-25; JOHN 6:22-27

Day 127

AWAY FROM THE CROWD

MARK 7:32-35

While he was there, some people brought a man to him who was deaf and could not talk clearly. The people begged Jesus to put his hand on the man to heal him.

Jesus led the man away from the people to be alone with him. He put his fingers in the man's ears. Then he spit on a finger and put it on the man's tongue. Jesus looked up to the sky and with a loud sigh he said, "Ephphatha!" (This means "Open!") As soon as Jesus did this, the man was able to hear. He was able to use his tongue, and he began to speak clearly.

KEY THOUGHT

Jesus concern is clearly to bless and heal this man. He has power over disease as well as demons. His desire is to use that power to bless and deliver, not to amaze or bewilder the crowds. As God's Son among us, Jesus is personal and intentional with his care. He will not exploit another's misfortune to receive praise from the crowd or to gain a following as a miracle worker. What a powerful lesson for all of us who call him our Lord and example!

TODAY'S PRAYER

Father, thank you for the powerful example of Jesus. He is not trying to grow a bigger reputation or just please the crowd, but to bless the broken and train his followers to be compassionate. Please give me this same balance in my life and in my ministry. In Jesus' mighty name I pray. Amen.

CONTEXT: MARK 7:24-37

RELATED PASSAGES: MATTHEW 6:1-4; MARK 5:37-43; JOHN 8:3-11

Day 128

Everything Well!

Mark 7:36-37

Jesus told the people not to tell anyone about this. But the more he told them not to say anything, the more people they told. They were all completely amazed. They said, "Look at what he has done. It's all good. He makes deaf people able to hear and gives a new voice to people who could not talk."

Key Thought

Despite Jesus' intentions to keep things quiet about his miraculous power to heal, the healing miracle in the previous verses became known and his reputation only spread faster and farther. The people were amazed and wanted others to know. And yes, his deeds were wonderful, but Jesus was so much more than a miracle worker. With popularity often comes misunderstanding. Some of that misunderstanding can actually inhibit us from fulfilling our mission from God. So as we look at our churches and ministries, let's pray for true success—an impact on the broken world for Jesus and faithfulness to the mission God has given us.

Today's Prayer

O Father, I know that the good things that I am able to do to bless others is because of your grace and power. I do want my influence for you to expand and impact others. As that happens, dear LORD, please keep my heart pure, my mission in focus, and your glory uppermost on my heart. In Jesus' name and for your glory I pray. Amen.

Context: Mark 7:24-37

Related Passages: John 7:12, 31; Luke 7:16-17; Matthew 15:31

Day 129

CONCERNED ABOUT THE HUNGER

MARK 8:1-3

Another time there were many people with Jesus. The people had nothing to eat.

So he called his followers to him and said, "I feel sorry for these people. They have been with me for three days, and now they have nothing to eat. I should not send them home hungry. If they leave without eating, they will faint on the way home. Some of them live a long way from here."

KEY THOUGHT

Two concerns are on Jesus' heart. First, he cares about the physical needs, especially the hunger, of the crowd that has been following him. Second, how can he help his disciples learn to trust that he will help them minister in situations beyond their ability? In this story, Jesus will help make sure both concerns are addressed. For me, this story is a reminder that ministry needs to occur on two fronts. First, we need to be raising up people to minister to others, using the gifts that God has given them. That means involving them in ministry and helping them learn to depend upon the Christ they serve. If you have a ministry in which you now serve, then get others involved with you. If you do not have a ministry, find someone working in an area in which you are interested and ask to go along and learn to minister with them. Second, we must care for the needs of others—and not just their spiritual needs, but also their physical needs. Jesus shows us a powerful way to do both things at once in this story.

TODAY'S PRAYER

Father, I pray that you will use me to serve others and to train others to serve. Please lead me to people I can effectively serve with your grace and help me to not only see the opportunity to serve, but to follow through on that opportunity as well. In Jesus' name I pray. Amen.

CONTEXT: MARK 8:1-10

RELATED PASSAGES: MARK 3:13-15; MARK 6:6-7; JOHN 20:19-21

Day 130

RESOURCES?

MARK 8:4

Jesus' followers answered, "But we are far away from any towns.
Where can we get enough bread to feed all these people?"

KEY THOUGHT

Jesus' followers were basically saying that they didn't have the resources to meet the needs of the people around them. Sound familiar? Often we don't pursue opportunities to serve others because we lack the resources. Clearly, we should count the cost before we begin a ministry so we won't have to pull back half way through our commitment. However, we must minister in situations that extend beyond our ability to meet people's needs. This allows us the opportunity to see the Lord at work as he displays his power where our strength, resources, and insight are limited. In our time of weakness and insufficiency, we realize again that all effective service is done by the Lord's power and grace.

TODAY'S PRAYER

Father, please forgive me for having such small dreams of serving others. Open my eyes to the needs around me. Please show me the proper balance between responsible planning and having the courage to step out in faith trusting you to provide the resources needed to bless those in need. In the name of the Lord Jesus Christ I pray. Amen.

CONTEXT: MARK 8:1-10

RELATED PASSAGES: 2 CORINTHIANS 3:4-6; 2 CORINTHIANS 12:6-10; EPHESIANS 3:20-21

Day 131

THE RESOURCE MAKER

MARK 8:5-7

Then Jesus asked them, "How many loaves of bread do you have?"

They answered, "We have seven loaves of bread."

Jesus told the people to sit on the ground. Then he took the seven loaves and gave thanks to God. He broke the bread into pieces and gave them to his followers. He told them to give the bread to the people, and they did as he said. The followers also had a few small fish. Jesus gave thanks for the fish and told them to give the fish to the people.

KEY THOUGHT

Jesus does not need our resources. He does, however, call us to use our resources to bless others. When we bring those resources to him, and offer ourselves to him, he will make them more than what they are and help us be better than we can be on our own. Jesus is the Resource Maker and the Resource Stretcher.

TODAY'S PRAYER

Holy Father, take me and use me. Take my resources and use them. Make them more than they are and use them for your glory. In Jesus' name. Amen.

CONTEXT: MARK 8:1-10

RELATED PASSAGES: 2 CORINTHIANS 9:10-15; PSALM 50:7-15; DEUTERONOMY 15:11

Day 132

SENT HOME SATISFIED

MARK 8:8-10

They all ate until they were full. Then the followers filled seven baskets with the pieces of food that were left. There were about 4000 men who ate. After they ate, Jesus told them to go home. Then he went in a boat with his followers to the area of Dalmanutha.

KEY THOUGHT

Wouldn't it be great if everyone could go home from church satisfied—both physically and spiritually? That is not going to happen unless we let Jesus be the center of what we do!

TODAY'S PRAYER

Holy God, help me, and help us, to understand that it's not about me and not about us, but about the sufficiency of your Son and his power to provide all we need. In the name of Jesus, our Lord and Christ, I pray. Amen.

CONTEXT: MARK 8:1-10

RELATED PASSAGES: 1 TIMOTHY 6:6-10; PHILIPPIANS 4:19-20; MATTHEW 6:19-21

Day 133

Changing Regions

MARK 8:10
Then he went in a boat with his followers to the area of Dalmanutha.

Key Thought

Sometimes God's truths need to be heard with finality and without a lot of discussion. The starkness or challenge of the truth sometimes needs to be left in the hands of the hearers and the messenger needs to move on to the next group of people who need God's truth, grace, and hope. May God give us the wisdom to know when to stay and when to go! May God's grace give us the love to stay in tough circumstances when it is his will and the courage to leave when we need to move on to other places! May the Father give us the courage to leave and allow time for the Word to convict and germinate in the hearts of men and women who are not ready to respond immediately!

Today's Prayer

Father in heaven, I cannot read the hearts of people very well. I know that you know them. I know that you know what is best for them at any given moment. Please, dear Father, help me know when to move on to other people and other fields of service that are ready for truth, love, and grace. However, dear Father, help me know when to stay and keep loving and serving people as well. Please give me this wisdom in Jesus' name. Amen.

Context: Mark 8:1-10

RELATED PASSAGES: MARK 1:35-39; 1 CORINTHIANS 16:5-9; JAMES 4:8

Day 134

PROVE YOURSELF

MARK 8:11

The Pharisees came to Jesus and asked him questions. They wanted to test him. So they asked him to do a miracle as a sign from God.

KEY THOUGHT

Seeking hearts in Jesus' day could see proof of his divinity by honest observation. Some who were not seeking saw Jesus as God's Son as well. However, those who came to ask him questions only to test him could not see this truth. One more miracle, yet another sign, and still another display of power would never be enough for them to believe. So much of our faith is tied to our own hearts. Are we seeking for truth? Are we seeking God? Do we yearn for what is really life? These are the first crucial questions for us as we seek not only to know, but also to believe, in Jesus.

TODAY'S PRAYER

Father, I believe, but I want to believe more strongly and more completely. I don't want my faith to be shallow—just a mere emotional cloud that is here today and gone tomorrow. Guide my heart and my mind as I seek to know truth, your truth, about who you are and what you want of me. In Jesus' name I pray. Amen.

CONTEXT: MARK 8:11-21

RELATED PASSAGES: MARK 15:25-30; JOHN 7:17; JOHN 8:31-32

Day 135

LEAVING THE CYNICS BEHIND

MARK 8:12-13

Jesus sighed deeply and said, "Why do you people ask to see a miracle as a sign? I want you to know that no miracle will be done to prove anything to you." Then Jesus left them and went in the boat to the other side of the lake.

KEY THOUGHT

Sometimes we just have to say, "No!" Jesus would not let his ministry become a sideshow. He would not pander to an audience that was important, but which was determined not to believe. There are times when we need to recognize that the people are not going to believe and move on to others who are looking for God and his grace in Jesus.

TODAY'S PRAYER

O Father, help me know when to move on! I know I have prayed this prayer several times within the week, but it is so important to me. I don't want to give up on someone seeking you, but I also know that I can get so caught up trying to reach one specific person that I fail to see the many around me who are seeking but have no one to share your grace with them. In the name of Jesus of Nazareth I ask for wisdom. Amen.

CONTEXT: MARK 8:11-21

RELATED PASSAGES: MARK 6:6-13; JOHN 6:22-30; ACTS 13:48-51

Day 136

WATCH OUT FOR BAD BREAD!

MARK 8:14-15

The followers had only one loaf of bread with them in the boat. They forgot to bring more bread. Jesus warned them, "Be careful! Guard against the yeast of the Pharisees and the yeast of Herod."

KEY THOUGHT

Don't you just love the way Jesus helps his disciples move from temporal concerns and physical needs to spiritual and eternal issues? How often do we get so bogged down in the physical details that we lose sight of spiritual truths? Let's ask Jesus to take us deeper into what is truly life, what is genuine spirituality. Let's not settle for worrying about temporal "stuff" God has already promised to take care of for us!

TODAY'S PRAYER

O God, I confess that I sometimes get anxious about things that don't really matter. I sometimes get hung up on concerns that are not spiritual matters. Help me see the issues, needs, and concerns that are truly important. Help me focus on them! In Jesus' name I ask this. Amen.

CONTEXT: MARK 8:11-21

RELATED PASSAGES: MATTHEW 6:24-27; JAMES 1:5-11; MATTHEW 6:31-34

Day 137

OPEN YOUR EYES!

MARK 8:14-18

The followers had only one loaf of bread with them in the boat. They forgot to bring more bread. Jesus warned them, "Be careful! Guard against the yeast of the Pharisees and the yeast of Herod."

The followers discussed the meaning of this. They said, "He said this because we have no bread."

Jesus knew that the followers were talking about this. So he asked them, "Why are you talking about having no bread? Do you still not see or understand? Are you not able to understand? Do you have eyes that can't see? Do you have ears that can't hear? Remember what I did before, when we did not have enough bread?"

KEY THOUGHT

Worry is a sign we've forgotten the great blessings and providence of God in our past. That is why the praise we offer to God for what he has done for us is so important. In praise we rehearse and remember the great things God has done and remember the great God he has been in the past and has promised to be in our future. It helps us acknowledge that God is and was and will be the great provider and Shepherd for his sheep.

TODAY'S PRAYER

O LORD God, you are my Great Shepherd. I recognize that every good thing I have comes from you. Forgive me for the times in the past when I have doubted your active providence in my life and worried about your sustaining grace for the future. I know that you can bless, support, and sustain. Thank you. In Jesus' name. Amen.

CONTEXT: MARK 8:11-21

RELATED PASSAGES: PSALM 23:1-3; PSALM 34:10; JAMES 1:17-18

How Many?

Mark 8:19-21

"I divided five loaves of bread for 5000 people. Remember how many baskets you filled with pieces of food that were not eaten?"

The followers answered, "We filled twelve baskets."

"And when I divided seven loaves of bread for 4000 people, how many baskets did you fill with the leftover pieces?"

They answered, "We filled seven baskets."

Then he said to them, "You remember these things I did, but you still don't understand?"

Key Thought

Jesus is trying to help his closest followers remember with the eyes of faith. This means more than merely recalling what has occurred; they must recall what the events had meant based upon their faith in Jesus and their past experiences with the power of God. Lest we are tempted to look down on them for their forgetfulness, let's remember all the times and ways that God has blessed, rescued, and provided for us. Let's also remember how often that we find ourselves needlessly worrying about our future and wondering if God is going to help us!

Today's Prayer

Heavenly Father, I'm so very sorry for the many times that I've failed to remember your tremendous care, provision, rescue, comfort, and protection. Use your Holy Spirit to help me remember through the eyes of faith and to take comfort in your constant presence and care in my life. In Jesus' mighty name I ask for this grace. Amen.

Context: Mark 8:11-21

Related Passages: Hebrews 13:5-6; Romans 8:28-29; Matthew 6:31-33

Day 139

PLEASE OPEN HIS EYES!

MARK 8:22

*Jesus and his followers came to Bethsaida. Some people brought
a blind man to him and begged him to touch the man.*

KEY THOUGHT

Who do you know who faces great difficulty in his or her life and
who needs friends like the ones we find in today's verse? The real test of
our discipleship is not just our feelings of compassion; instead, genuine
compassion is displayed by what we do to act on our feelings of concern for
those in need and bless them. Let's get off our backsides and into the lives of
those who truly need to experience Jesus' love!

TODAY'S PRAYER

*Father, help me show your Son's love and my empathy to those in need by my actions
and not just by my talk. In the name of Jesus, your compassionate Son, I pray. Amen.*

CONTEXT: MARK 8:22-26

RELATED PASSAGES: 1 JOHN 3:16-18; JAMES 2:14-17; MATTHEW 25:41-46

Day 140

CAN YOU SEE?

MARK 8:23-26

So Jesus held the blind man's hand and led him out of the village. Then he spit on the man's eyes. He laid his hands on him and asked, "Can you see now?"

The man looked up and said, "Yes, I see people. They look like trees walking around."

Again Jesus laid his hands on the man's eyes, and the man opened them wide. His eyes were healed, and he was able to see everything clearly. Jesus told him to go home. He said, "Don't go into the town."

KEY THOUGHT

For those who are familiar with Jesus' other miracles, this seems bizarre! When Jesus heals, people are healed immediately and completely. Not this time! So why not? Jesus is still trying to get his followers to understand through the eyes of faith. This blind man becomes the mirror for them to see themselves. While they can see partially who Jesus is because of their previous involvement with him, they must come to him and let him fully reveal his true identity. Like the blind man in the story, they need Jesus to complete his work of helping them see who he really is! Their confusion should remind us to keep coming back to the Bible and to keep asking Jesus to make himself more fully known to us.

TODAY'S PRAYER

O Father, I want to truly know your Son, the Lord Jesus. I don't want a partial, lopsided view of him, but I want to know him fully even as I am fully known. Please remove the blind spots in my understanding of your Son. In Jesus' name I ask for this grace. Amen.

CONTEXT: MARK 8:22-26

RELATED PASSAGES: JOHN 4:39-42; JOHN 5:39-49; JOHN 14:20-23

Day 141

WHO DO THEY SAY I AM?

MARK 8:27

Jesus and his followers went to the towns in the area of Caesarea Philippi. While they were traveling, Jesus asked the followers, "Who do people say I am?"

KEY THOUGHT

If you ask people today who Jesus is, you will get a myriad of answers. Many folks don't know and quite a few don't care. The lost world's greatest need is for Jesus' followers to both know who he really is and demonstrate it in our lives!

TODAY'S PRAYER

O Father in heaven please help us—and especially help me—better demonstrate who Jesus is to those around us. In Jesus' name I pray. Amen.

CONTEXT: MARK 8:27-33

RELATED PASSAGES: ACTS 4:12; ROMANS 10:14-15; ACTS 8:1-4

Day 142

ONE OF THE PROPHETS?

MARK 8:27-28

Jesus and his followers went to the towns in the area of Caesarea Philippi. While they were traveling, Jesus asked the followers, "Who do people say I am?"

They answered, "Some people say you are John the Baptizer. Others say you are Elijah. And others say you are one of the prophets."

KEY THOUGHT

Jesus is recognized as a significant religious leader and a powerful teacher by many of the world's religions. However, Christians see Jesus as much more than a prophet, a great teacher, or the founder of a new religion. He is the Christ, the unique Son of the Living God. He is Lord. He is the Savior of the world, the only true way to God. Let's help the world know just who Jesus truly is!

TODAY'S PRAYER

O God, please bless the efforts of your children who are trying to let the world know who Jesus is. I pray this in the name above all names, Jesus Christ the Lord. Amen

CONTEXT: MARK 8:27-33

RELATED PASSAGES: ACTS 2:36; JOHN 14:6-7; 2 JOHN 7-11

Day 143

YOU ARE THE MESSIAH!

MARK 8:29

Then Jesus asked, "Who do you say I am?"
Peter answered, "You are the Christ."

KEY THOUGHT

This is the key question that Jesus asks each of us: "Who do you say I am?" Our answer is crucial! Our eternal destinies hang in the balance as we answer this question. Yes, Peter says, "You are the Messiah." However, Jesus is much more than the Messiah; he is our Lord; he is our Savior; he is our brother; he is our King; he is our High Priest; and he is so much more! So who do you say that Jesus is? (Today, especially, please read the Related Passages listed below this devotional and see how important Jesus is to each of us!)

TODAY'S PRAYER

O LORD God Almighty, my Heavenly Father, thank you for Jesus. He is so much more than words can capture. He exhausts the meaning of every title. I praise you for your plan and purpose in sending him. In Jesus' name I offer my prayer and my life to you. Amen.

CONTEXT: MARK 8:27-33

RELATED PASSAGES: ROMANS 10:8-13; COLOSSIANS 1:15-22; HEBREWS 2:13-18

Day 144

DON'T TELL!

MARK 8:29-30

Then Jesus asked, "Who do you say I am?"
Peter answered, "You are the Christ."
Jesus told the followers, "Don't tell anyone who I am."

KEY THOUGHT

Jesus' warning seems bizarre to many readers today. However, if we follow the story of Jesus in the Gospel of Mark, we realize that the people who hear him want to define what it means for Jesus to be Messiah and Son of God rather than letting God define it. So Jesus warns those who catch a glimpse of his identity not to tell. He wants to define what it means to be Messiah (the Christ) and Son of God. That means going to a cross, something that was beyond their comprehension. (Notice Peter's reaction to this revelation in the verses that follow.) The basic message for you and me is this: we must let Jesus define his messiahship and then re-define our lives as we follow him.

TODAY'S PRAYER

O Father, teach me to understand more fully who your Son is and
to follow him without reservation, no matter what the personal cost
may be. In the name of Jesus, the Messiah, I pray. Amen.

CONTEXT: MARK 8:27-33

RELATED PASSAGES: MARK 1:21-28; MARK 5:35-43; 7:31-37

Day 145

JESUS' CENTER

MARK 8:31

Then Jesus began to teach his followers that the Son of Man must suffer many things. He taught that the Son of Man would not be accepted by the older Jewish leaders, the leading priests, and the teachers of the law. He said that the Son of Man must be killed and then rise from death after three days.

KEY THOUGHT

Jesus knew his mission. It was a hard mission: he was to die for the sins of the people—including you and me—after being rejected and ridiculed. This sacrificial death, however, was his center. He lived his whole life in the shadow of the cross. He proclaimed this center of his mission several times to his key followers, yet they were not be able to receive that teaching. It was beyond their grasp. (See the verses that follow.) Jesus, however, did not deviate from it. He obeyed and pleased his Father no matter the cost. The challenge for you and me is the same: to obey the Father no matter the cost and to be willing to lay down our lives for him.

TODAY'S PRAYER

O dear Father in heaven, stir my heart and increase my courage so that I am truly willing to follow you no matter the cost. I pray this in the name of Jesus, the Son of Man who died for me. Amen.

CONTEXT: MARK 8:27-33

RELATED PASSAGES: MARK 10:42-45; PHILIPPIANS 2:5-11; MARK 9:30-32

Day 146

Rebuke from Ignorance

Mark 8:31-32

Then Jesus began to teach his followers that the Son of Man must suffer many things. He taught that the Son of Man would not be accepted by the older Jewish leaders, the leading priests, and the teachers of the law. He said that the Son of Man must be killed and then rise from death after three days. Jesus told them everything that would happen. He did not keep anything secret.

Key Thought

Peter had his own conceptions of what it meant for Jesus to be Messiah. For him, God's Messiah wouldn't go to a cross. Such an idea was an outrage. It was impossible. So Peter rebukes Jesus out of his own bias and ignorance. Rather than letting Jesus define his own messiahship, Peter wanted Jesus to conform to what he wanted from him rather than allowing Jesus to follow God's plan. We need to ask ourselves how we have tried to tell Jesus what it means for him to be our Lord, Savior, and Messiah? What are our expectations of Jesus? Are we willing to live our lives, like he lived his, in the shadow of the cross? Are these expectations getting in the way of following and obeying Jesus as our Lord?

Today's Prayer

God, I confess that I find myself selfishly wanting to determine what it means for Jesus to be my Messiah, Savior, and Lord. Rather than following obediently, I want to be blessed and protected rather than facing my own cross. Father, please use your Spirit to conform me into a true follower of your Son, in whose name I pray. Amen.

Context: Mark 8:27-33

Related Passages: Mark 8:34-38; Luke 14:25-33; John 21:15-19

Day 147

REBUKED!

MARK 8:31-33

Then Jesus began to teach his followers that the Son of Man must suffer many things. He taught that the Son of Man would not be accepted by the older Jewish leaders, the leading priests, and the teachers of the law. He said that the Son of Man must be killed and then rise from death after three days. Jesus told them everything that would happen. He did not keep anything secret.

Peter took Jesus away from the other followers to talk to him alone. Peter criticized him for saying these things. But Jesus turned and looked at his followers. Then he criticized Peter. He said to Peter, "Get away from me, Satan! You don't care about the same things God does. You care only about things that people think are important."

KEY THOUGHT

Peter tried to rebuke Jesus. Jesus then shows how important this matter is to him. He calls Peter Satan. Ouch! What a stern rebuke! However, the orientation of Scripture is clear: without the grace that comes from Jesus' sacrificial death, men and women are under the influence and control of Satan. The majority rule of humanity is never going to be the will of God. The will of the Lord will always be a "minority opinion" among people even though it is God's truth and God's standard! We must open our eyes and ask the Lord to open our hearts to know his truth, his will, and his way.

TODAY'S PRAYER

Teach me, O God, to know your truth. Open my heart to follow your will. Don't let Satan blind me to your way, your truth, and your light. In Jesus' name, the name above all names, I pray. Amen.

CONTEXT: MARK 8:27-33

RELATED PASSAGES: EPHESIANS 2:1-3; JOHN 14:28-31; EPHESIANS 6:10-12

PICK UP YOUR CROSS

MARK 8:34

Then Jesus called the crowd and his followers to him. He said, "Any of you who want to be my follower must stop thinking about yourself and what you want. You must be willing to carry the cross that is given to you for following me."

KEY THOUGHT

For Jesus' true followers, the cross is not a piece of jewelry or even a symbol; it is a lifestyle. It is the willingness to follow Jesus in every way, including the way of the cross. To do that we must surrender our selfishness and lay down our lives for the needs of others. We must show unflinching loyalty to God no matter the cost. More than just a burden to bear, "our cross to bear" is a total "buy-in" to the life, character, and way of Jesus. We are called to live our lives in the shadow of the cross!

TODAY'S PRAYER

O Father, form me more perfectly into the nature, character, and lifestyle of Jesus. In the name of Jesus, who was crucified for my sins and raised by your power, I pray. Amen.

CONTEXT: MARK 8:34-38

RELATED PASSAGES: PHILIPPIANS 2:5-11; JOHN 15:9-13; 1 JOHN 4:9-10

Day 149

GET LIFE!

MARK 8:35

"Any of you who try to save the life you have will lose it. But you who give up your life for me and for the Good News will save it."

KEY THOUGHT

So often what we most passionately pursue because of our earthly perspective of things is what we cannot achieve, purchase, or find on our own. Life is found in Jesus. Life is found in obeying Jesus. Life is found in living for Jesus. Anything else is lost in death.

TODAY'S PRAYER

O Father, help me refine my focus so that I find my life built and centered in your Son as my Lord. This I pray in the name of the Lord Jesus. Amen.

CONTEXT: MARK 8:34-38

RELATED PASSAGES: JOHN 1:1-5; JOHN 5:26; JOHN 10:10B

Day 150

TRUE WORTH

MARK 8:36-37
*"It is worth nothing for you to have the whole world if you yourself
are lost. You could never pay enough to buy back your life."*

KEY THOUGHT
So much of life gets lost in the pursuit of things we incorrectly think are important. We trade our time for that which does not matter. We trade our energy for gains never realized. We trade our hopes for what winds up as wrecked dreams. Our very lives, our souls, can find their true resource only in the Lord. He must remain the center, the goal, and the purpose of our lives or we lose ourselves in our pursuit of things that don't really matter.

TODAY'S PRAYER
*O God, please forgive me for the times when my priorities and my pursuits have been
focused on things that really didn't matter. Please help me to focus my priorities
on Jesus and his priorities. In Jesus' name, and for Jesus' glory, I pray. Amen.*

CONTEXT: MARK 8:34-38

RELATED PASSAGES: HAGGAI 1:3-6; MATTHEW 6:19-27; LUKE 15:11-16

Day 151

ASHAMED?

MARK 8:38

"People today are so sinful. They have not been faithful to God. As you live among them, don't be ashamed of me and my teaching. If that happens, I will be ashamed of you when I come with the glory of my Father and the holy angels."

KEY THOUGHT

Like many others before us, we find ourselves in a time when believers are ridiculed. In some places, they are openly persecuted—their property is confiscated and they suffer violent attacks. In such times as these, it is easy to be a "closet Christian" and never do anything to show ourselves as believers or to stand up for our Lord. Jesus wants us to do more than just hold the truth; he wants us to live it and share it openly and boldly.

TODAY'S PRAYER

Father, open my heart and strengthen my courage so that I will not act in ways that bring you dishonor. I don't want to say or do anything that suggests to anyone that I'm not your loyal and devoted child. Please strengthen me and guide me as I try to show your Son's love in everything I do. In the powerful name of Jesus' I ask for this grace. Amen.

CONTEXT: MARK 8:34-38

RELATED PASSAGES: ACTS 5:38-42; ROMANS 1:16-17; 2 TIMOTHY 1:5-8

Day 152

KINGDOM PREVIEW

MARK 9:1

Then Jesus said, "Believe me when I say that some of you people standing here will see God's kingdom come with power before you die."

KEY THOUGHT

Kingdom and power belong to our God and to his Son. Those who belong to Jesus will experience this power and belong to this Kingdom. The question is not if God can make this possible; he already has in Jesus. The question is whether or not we have decided to honor God's Kingdom and live for his Son so his "great power" can be at work in us.

TODAY'S PRAYER

Father, I want to see the power of Jesus unfold and to experience the full victory of your Kingdom when he comes. Align my heart with you so that it is fit for your Kingdom. Remove duplicity, dishonesty, and doubt so that I can serve you with an undivided heart. In Jesus' powerful name I pray. Amen.

CONTEXT: MARK 9:1-13

RELATED PASSAGES: LUKE 11:20; 1 CORINTHIANS 4:20; REVELATION 12:10

Day 153

Revealing His Glory to the Three

Mark 9:2-4

Six days later, Jesus took Peter, James, and John and went up on a high mountain.
They were all alone there. While these followers watched him, Jesus was changed.
His clothes became shining white—whiter than anyone on earth could make them.
Then two men were there talking with Jesus. They were Elijah and Moses.

Key Thought

Jesus appears with two groups of "friends." Group one is made up of Jesus' inner circle of three followers, Peter, James, and John. The other is made up of two great figures from Israel's past, Moses and Elijah. Jesus' dazzling white clothing is a powerful symbol of his heavenly origin and superiority. For Jesus to be friends and in conversation with Moses and Elijah is incredible to his three followers. Little do they realize that God will elevate Jesus to a status above these great teachers, leaders, and prophets. Of particular interest to me, Jesus doesn't have all his followers with him—not even all the twelve apostles participate in this moment. Jesus shared in relationships at different levels of closeness. But not everyone was invited into every moment. He invested heavily in twelve apostles and even more heavily in his "inner three" who would each impact the early church in powerful ways. We can't change everyone. We can't change the world alone. We can impact a few, who in turn can impact a few more. Before long, our influence reaches way beyond ourselves. So let's ask ourselves with whom we are investing our lives and to whom are we passing on our faith?

Today's Prayer

Father, please use my life to make an impact for good and spread the
grace and character of your Kingdom. Give me wisdom to know those in
whom I should invest my life. In Jesus' glorious name I pray. Amen.

Context: Mark 9:1-13

Related Passages: Mark 3:13-15; Mark 14:32-38; 2 Timothy 2:1-2

Day 154

Speaking Without Knowing

Mark 9:5-6

Peter said to Jesus, "Teacher, it is good that we are here. We will put three tents here—one for you, one for Moses, and one for Elijah." Peter did not know what to say, because he and the other two followers were so afraid.

Key Thought

Peter's words, though well intentioned, are ludicrous. Some moments need to be held in silent awe. Words shouldn't desecrate the moment. Rather than trying to be the wise one, the outspoken one, and the one who leads the pack, sometimes we need to be silent and let God reveal the meaning and the power of the moment. Peter couldn't grasp that Jesus was so far superior to the others. Even with that ignorance, however, he should have waited in awe until God's will was revealed rather than trying to speak when he didn't know what to say.

Today's Prayer

O God, forgive me for trying to always have words when my awe-filled and reverent silence should be the gift I offer in the presence of your glory. In Jesus' name. Amen.

Context: Mark 9:1-13

Related Passages: Ecclesiastes 5:1-2; Habakkuk 2:18-20; Isaiah 6:1-5

Day 155

LISTEN TO HIM!

MARK 9:7

*Then a cloud came and covered them. A voice came from the cloud
and said, "This is my Son, the one I love. Obey him!"*

KEY THOUGHT

God is very clear to the amazed followers of Jesus. As important as
Elijah and Moses are to the Jewish people, among them stands one who is
far superior, Jesus Christ, God's Son and their Lord. They should listen to
Jesus. Jesus is the supreme teacher. Jesus is the supreme prophet. Jesus is the
supreme hope and Messiah of God's people. Listen to him!

TODAY'S PRAYER

*Father, thank you for speaking to us fully and definitively through your Son—both
while he was on earth and as he continues to provide guidance and strength for us now.
May I not only listen and know your Son's words, but help me obediently live them out
in my daily life. In Jesus' name I offer you my thanks, praise, and obedience. Amen.*

CONTEXT: MARK 9:1-13

RELATED PASSAGES: JOHN 1:14-18; ACTS 4:12; HEBREWS 1:1-2

Day 156

ONLY JESUS!

MARK 9:8
The followers looked, but they saw only Jesus there alone with them.

KEY THOUGHT

If God's message to Jesus' followers in the previous verse about listening to Jesus as their primary source of God's revelation was ignored, then the disappearance of Moses and Elijah made God's point clear. The Father wanted Jesus to be honored, revered, followed, and obeyed. Jesus is the one to whom they and we must listen! Jesus is God's fullest and most complete message to us (Hebrews 1:1-3). We must listen to him!

TODAY'S PRAYER

O Father, open my heart as well as my ears to the message of your Son, who uniquely has brought your message to life in our world. In Jesus' name I pray. Amen.

CONTEXT: MARK 9:1-13

RELATED PASSAGES: MATTHEW 13:16-17; MARK 4:9; MARK 7:14

Day 157

WAITING BEFORE WITNESSING

MARK 9:9-10

As Jesus and the followers were walking back down the mountain, he gave them these instructions: "Don't tell anyone about what you saw on the mountain. Wait until after the Son of Man rises from death. Then you can tell people what you saw."

So the followers waited to say anything about what they saw. But they discussed among themselves what Jesus meant about rising from death.

KEY THOUGHT

Jesus didn't want his three key followers telling others about what had happened on the mountain when he spoke with Moses and Elijah. Why? There are many reasons. First, they did not yet fully understand what had happened. Second, they didn't understand what lay ahead for Jesus— his death and resurrection. Third, no one would believe them, much less understand that Jesus was superior to Moses and Elijah. Fourth, those who followed Jesus based on this kind of testimony would have been looking only for a "special effects" Jesus rather than the servant Messiah he chose to be. They needed to wait and let God more fully reveal who Jesus is and then they could share with others what they had seen and heard.

TODAY'S PRAYER

O Father, help me share Jesus properly with others. I want my friends and loved ones to know of his saving grace, his awesome power, and his ultimate triumph over sin and death. Help me know how and when to share these things. In Jesus' name. Amen.

CONTEXT: MARK 9:1-13

RELATED PASSAGES: JUDE 1:25; 2 PETER 1:16-18; 1 PETER 3:15-16

Day 158

Elijah Comes First

Mark 9:11-12

They asked him, "Why do the teachers of the law say that Elijah must come first?"

Jesus answered, "They are right to say that Elijah must come first. Elijah makes all things the way they should be. But why do the Scriptures say that the Son of Man will suffer much and that people will think he is worth nothing?"

Key Thought

The great ending hope of the Old Testament as we now have it is that God will send Elijah to prepare people's hearts for the Messiah. John the Baptizer was identified as this "new" Elijah. He did make a people ready for the Lord. But, this "new" Elijah was treated harshly, unfairly, and eventually murdered by the political establishment. Jesus wants his followers to know that just as John has been rejected and treated harshly, so Jesus will also be treated unfairly and harshly. He wants them to realize what lies ahead for the Son of Man.

Today's Prayer

O God, I am not sure how Jesus endured the unfairness he endured, especially knowing that it was coming and knowing that he had the power to squash anyone or anything that opposed him. Thank you, Lord Jesus, for enduring all the indignities and unfairness that you faced. Thank you for sacrificing yourself for me. To you, O Lord Jesus, and in your name, we offer our thanks, praise, and prayer to the Father. Amen.

Context: Mark 9:1-13

Related Passages: Malachi 4:5-6; Mark 1:1-4; Mark 6:15

Day 159

TREATED WITH CONTEMPT

MARK 9:12-13

*Jesus answered, "They are right to say that Elijah must come first. Elijah makes
all things the way they should be. But why do the Scriptures say that the Son
of Man will suffer much and that people will think he is worth nothing? I tell
you that Elijah has already come. And people did to him all the bad things
they wanted to do. The Scriptures said this would happen to him."*

KEY THOUGHT

John the Baptizer was the Elijah that preceded Jesus. His death helped
indicate how Jesus' ministry would end—a death at the hands of the political
and religious power brokers. Why is it that God's servants are often treated
with contempt by the powers of the world? Both the Bible and secular history
reveal Satan's attempts to thwart any good work from God by attacking those
leading that good work. Opposition, persecution, and martyrdom are not
signs of God's disapproval. In fact, many of God's greatest servants have
faced such challenges and God has used them to advance his work rather than
limit it.

TODAY'S PRAYER

*God, my heavenly Father and LORD Almighty, please give me the courage I need to
endure whatever the world or Satan may direct toward me. I know your servants through
the ages have had to face many difficulties. Give me the strength to honor you no matter
what the circumstances of my life. I ask for this courage and grace in Jesus' name. Amen.*

CONTEXT: MARK 9:1-13

RELATED PASSAGES: ACTS 5:38-42; 2 TIMOTHY 3:10-12; 1 PETER 5:8-9

Day 160

GREETED BY THE CROWD

MARK 9:14-15

*Then Jesus, Peter, James, and John went to the other followers. They saw many
people around them. The teachers of the law were arguing with the followers.
When the people saw Jesus, they were very surprised and ran to welcome him.*

KEY THOUGHT

People were not quite sure what to think or do about Jesus. Some argued
with his disciples about the small points of his ministry. I find it interesting
that those who gave Jesus' disciples the hardest time were the religious
teachers. The regular folks, "the crowd," saw something in Jesus that was
awesome and were drawn to him. I wonder what would happen if we as
"religious people" worried less about pleasing other religious people and
focused more on sharing Jesus with the masses of common folks who do not
really know him?

TODAY'S PRAYER

*O God, forgive me for trying to keep the religious folks around me happy while
ignoring the lost and hungry souls around me. Please help me get my priorities straight
and seek out the people who need to know you. In Jesus' name I pray. Amen.*

CONTEXT: MARK 9:14-29

RELATED PASSAGES: MARK 7:1-8; MARK 8:31; MARK 11:18

Day 161

Unable to Meet the Need

Mark 9:16-18

Jesus asked, "What are you arguing about with the teachers of the law?"

A man answered, "Teacher, I brought my son to you. He is controlled by an evil spirit that keeps him from talking. The spirit attacks him and throws him on the ground. He foams at the mouth, grinds his teeth, and becomes very stiff. I asked your followers to force the evil spirit out, but they could not."

Key Thought

Does this sound familiar to you? "They couldn't do it!" So often we don't find out what is truly possible until we reach the end of our abilities and admit that for us it is impossible unless God works through us.

Today's Prayer

Father, forgive me for my arrogance and thinking that I am somehow necessary in your work. I recognize that my only sufficiency for ministry comes from my weakness being offered to your service and empowered by your grace. In Jesus' name I pray. Amen.

Context: Mark 9:14-29

Related Passages: 2 Corinthians 4:7; 2 Corinthians 12:10; Isaiah 35:1-4

Day 162

Rebuke from Concern

Mark 9:19

Jesus answered, "You people today don't believe! How long must I stay with you? How long must I be patient with you? Bring the boy to me!"

Key Thought

Don't you know that Jesus was really frustrated with his key followers at times? This time he is more than frustrated. He had given them the power to do what needed to be done. But they didn't do it. They even thought they couldn't do it, so of course they couldn't! I appreciate Jesus' honest rebuke. So often we do far less than we are capable of doing because we lack the faith to try and don't pray for God's power to be exerted.

Today's Prayer

O LORD God almighty, you are capable of doing anything your heart desires. I recognize that my lack of faith often inhibits your desire to work in the world through me. Please increase my faith. In Jesus' name I pray. Amen.

Context: Mark 9:14-29

Related Passages: Mark 6:1-6; Mark 10:27; Ephesians 3:20-21

Day 163

HAVE MERCY!

MARK 9:20-22

So the followers brought the boy to Jesus. When the evil spirit saw Jesus, it attacked the boy. The boy fell down and rolled on the ground. He was foaming at the mouth.

Jesus asked the boy's father, "How long has this been happening to him?"

The father answered, "Since he was very young. The spirit often throws him into a fire or into water to kill him. If you can do anything, please have pity on us and help us."

KEY THOUGHT

Have mercy on us! Isn't that our real place before God? Don't we need to come into the holy and awesome presence of God with the cry, "Have mercy on me, O God!" Of course God loves to share mercy and touch us with his grace. He is waiting for us to recognize our need for these. He longs for us to acknowledge that without his grace we have no right, no power, and no place in his presence. Then, when grace and mercy come to us, we can be assured that they are ours because of God's love for us.

TODAY'S PRAYER

Father in heaven, I love you. I thank you. I praise you. There are many reasons why you are worthy of my love, thanks, and praise. One of the foremost reasons is that you have treated me with mercy and welcomed me with love and dealt with my sins graciously. I offer you my thanks and praise in Jesus' name. Amen.

CONTEXT: MARK 9:14-29

RELATED PASSAGES: PSALM 4:1; PSALM 25:16; ISAIAH 55:7

Day 164

ALL THINGS ARE POSSIBLE!

MARK 9:23

Jesus said to the father, "Why did you say 'if you can'? All things are possible for the one who believes."

KEY THOUGHT

"All things are possible for the one who believes!" Enough said. No more words are needed!

TODAY'S PRAYER

Forgive me and forgive us, O God, for doubting your power and might shared with us in your mercy and grace. In Jesus' mighty name I pray. Amen.

CONTEXT: MARK 9:14-29

RELATED PASSAGES: ISAIAH 49:15; ISAIAH 53:11; 1 CORINTHIANS 1:30

Day 165

HELP ME NOT TO DOUBT

MARK 9:24
Immediately the father shouted, "I do believe. Help me to believe more!"

KEY THOUGHT

All through this story, each of the people involved is so genuine about his emotions and faith. Rather than pretending he had full faith, the father acknowledged he believed, but needed help in overcoming his doubt. I don't know about you, but this is where I often find myself during a period of testing in my life. Imagine how powerful this honest prayer can be in our lives!

TODAY'S PRAYER
O Abba Father, I believe, but please help my faith to grow stronger and to become more confident so that I can serve you in more powerful ways . . . to your glory. In Jesus' name. Amen.

CONTEXT: MARK 9:14-29

RELATED PASSAGES: MARK 11:22-24; JAMES 1:5-8; MARK 6:27-52

Day 166

DELIVERED!

MARK 9:25-27

Jesus saw that all the people were running there to see what was happening. So he spoke to the evil spirit. He said, "You evil spirit that makes this boy deaf and stops him from talking—I command you to come out of him and never enter him again!"

The evil spirit screamed. It caused the boy to fall on the ground again, and then it came out. The boy looked as if he was dead. Many people said, "He is dead!" But Jesus took hold of his hand and helped him stand up.

KEY THOUGHT

One of the things I love so much about Jesus is that his miracles were not about him or for him. He cared about the people he healed. He guarded their dignity as well as caring for their physical ailments. Jesus healed the boy before the crowd of onlookers grew too large. When the boy was healed, he took him by the hand and helped him up. The miracle wasn't about Jesus or his dazzling the crowds with his power. No, the miracle was about the love and care of God being shown to someone in deep need.

TODAY'S PRAYER

O Father in heaven, please help me to treat with dignity and grace all those you give me the privilege to serve. In Jesus' name and for his glory I pray. Amen.

CONTEXT: MARK 9:14-29

RELATED PASSAGES: MARK 5:35-43; JOHN 9:1-3; MARK 1:40-41

Day 167

HONEST FRUSTRATION

MARK 9:28

Then Jesus went into the house. His followers were alone with him there.
They said, "Why weren't we able to force that evil spirit out?"

KEY THOUGHT

Many of us who seek to minister in Jesus' name need to ask this question more: "Why couldn't we do it, Lord?" More than just being honest about our lack of power, we also need answers for our failures. While we may not get that question answered as clearly and exhaustively as we would like, we open the door for God to teach us and we regain our place of humility in the presence of the Almighty.

TODAY'S PRAYER

Dear Heavenly Father, I am frustrated about some things that have not turned out as I believed they would. I trust in you. I want to serve you and bring you glory. Yet some things didn't happen how I thought they should have happened and some people weren't touched that need to be touched. Please help me understand why. If part of the problem is me—my faith or my character or my prayer life—please help me come to this understanding and work with you on strengthening my area of weakness. In Jesus' name I request this grace. Amen.

CONTEXT: MARK 9:14-29

RELATED PASSAGES: JUDGES 6:11-14; 1 KINGS 9:6-9; PSALM 44:23

Day 168

ONLY BY PRAYER

MARK 9:29
Jesus answered, "That kind of spirit can be forced out only with prayer."

KEY THOUGHT

So often the reason God's people don't do what we are capable of doing for the Kingdom of God is because we don't pray. Let's rededicate ourselves to prayer. Let's return to God in prayer to ask for his help, power, and mercy. Let us also return to God in prayer to humble ourselves before the mighty hand of our Father so that he will lift us up. Great things for God can be done consistently and effectively only when God's people pray.

TODAY'S PRAYER

Forgive my silence and my sense of self-sufficiency, O God. I know that without your mercy, power, and grace I will fail. Please accept my passionate pleas for your mercy, your grace, your strength, and your direction. In the mighty name of Jesus I pray. Amen.

CONTEXT: MARK 9:14-29

RELATED PASSAGES: JOHN 14:12-14; JAMES 5:13-16; ACTS 4:31

Day 169

PREPARING HIS DISCIPLES

MARK 9:30-31

Then Jesus and his followers left there and went through Galilee. Jesus did not want the people to know where they were. He wanted to teach his followers alone. He said to them, "The Son of Man will be handed over to the control of other men, who will kill him. After three days, he will rise from death."

KEY THOUGHT

Jesus is the Son of Man. He knows that his time is short. He knows that he must invest his time wisely. He knows that he must prepare his key followers for what lies ahead. He must reproduce his influence, teaching, and ministry if the good news of God's Kingdom is going to take hold in peoples' hearts. So Jesus withdraws to teach the closest followers, his key followers, personally.

TODAY'S PRAYER

Father, give me wisdom to know best how to invest my time and in whom I should invest it. Like Jesus, I want to make the most of the time you have given me. For Jesus, and in his name, I ask for your help in this matter. Amen.

CONTEXT: MARK 9:30-37

RELATED PASSAGES: MARK 6:31; MATTHEW 28:18-20; 2 TIMOTHY 2:1-2

Day 170

BLOCKED UNDERSTANDING

MARK 9:30-32

Then Jesus and his followers left there and went through Galilee. Jesus did not want the people to know where they were. He wanted to teach his followers alone. He said to them, "The Son of Man will be handed over to the control of other men, who will kill him. After three days, he will rise from death." But the followers did not understand what he meant, and they were afraid to ask him.

KEY THOUGHT

Despite some of Jesus' own personal teaching, the disciples are having a very difficult time understanding that he must die and be raised from the dead. From their understanding and because of their expectations, the Messiah should be a conquering redeemer. With all the powerful displays they had seen from Jesus, we can understand that it must have been hard for them even to imagine anyone having the power of Jesus. Sometimes our understanding about Jesus' truth is blocked because of our expectations of him. Let's ask God to remove the blindness from our own eyes!

TODAY'S PRAYER

O Father, I confess that what I want from Jesus sometimes blinds me to what I need from him and what he longs to teach me. Please remove my blindness and gently correct me so that I can know and live your truth. In Jesus' name I pray. Amen.

CONTEXT: MARK 9:30-37

RELATED PASSAGES: MARK 8:22-25; JOHN 9:39-41; ACTS 9:17-18

Day 171

THE FALL REVISITED

MARK 9:33-34

Jesus and his followers went to Capernaum. They went into a house, and Jesus said to them, "I heard you arguing on the way here today. What were you arguing about?" But the followers did not answer, because their argument on the road was about which one of them was the greatest.

KEY THOUGHT

Sin entered the world because human beings wanted to be as important as God. Often our sins still center around our desire to be our own little gods. Maybe we don't want to be in charge of the whole universe, but we do want to be the most important and significant person in our own sphere of existence. We want to be the greatest in our own world. This is where being honest with Jesus about our desires is crucial. We can't invite the one who left heaven to serve us into our presence without falling under conviction that our desires for greatness are selfish arrogance and not a desire for excellence. In fact, Jesus personifies excellence and redefines what a life of excellence is all about—self-sacrificing service to others, as the next verses show.

TODAY'S PRAYER

O Father, gently humble me. Remove the dross of my character. Purge out the arrogance and selfishness of my heart so that I can serve you, and others, with Christ-like love and care. In Jesus' name I humbly pray. Amen.

CONTEXT: MARK 9:30-37

RELATED PASSAGES: GENESIS 3:1-10; MARK 8:29-33; 1 SAMUEL 2:3

Day 172

FIRST

MARK 9:35

Jesus sat down and called the twelve apostles to him. He said,
"Whoever wants to be the most important must make others more
important than themselves. They must serve everyone else."

KEY THOUGHT

Jesus' life is a demonstration of what he teaches us in this statement about greatness. As followers of Jesus, we are never greater than when we surrender our rights and our position to serve others. No one demonstrated this better than Jesus Christ, our Lord and teacher.

TODAY'S PRAYER

Father, help me to aspire to greatness as defined by your Son's words and life.
Give me the courage to serve and empower me by your Spirit to become more like
Jesus in my attitude as I serve. In the name of the Lord Jesus I pray. Amen.

CONTEXT: MARK 9:30-37

RELATED PASSAGES: MARK 10:42-45; PHILIPPIANS 2:5-11; 1 PETER 5:1-4

Day 173

WELCOME THE CHILD

MARK 9:36-37

Then Jesus took a small child and stood the child in front of the followers. He held the child in his arms and said, "Whoever accepts children like these in my name is accepting me. And anyone who accepts me is also accepting the one who sent me."

KEY THOUGHT

How we treat those from whom we can receive no boost in earthly status reveals our hearts. In Jesus' day, children were not held to be overly important in the social pecking order. In many ways, that is still true today—consider how day-care workers and teachers are still among the lowest paid professional workers in many modern countries. So Jesus reminds his followers that the way we welcome, treat, and value children reveals a great deal about our hearts.

TODAY'S PRAYER

Father, thank you for challenging me to value people whom others neglect, devalue, and overlook. Help me to follow through on my conviction to love all people, especially those from whom I can receive no monetary, status, or power benefit. In Jesus' name I ask that you help me serve others more like Jesus did. Amen.

CONTEXT: MARK 9:30-37

RELATED PASSAGES: MARK 10:13-16; EPHESIANS 6:4; MATTHEW 21:14-16

NOT ONE OF US!

MARK 9:38

Then John said, "Teacher, we saw a man using your name to force demons out of someone. He is not one of us. So we told him to stop, because he does not belong to our group."

KEY THOUGHT

Isn't it amazing how quickly we can split up into our own little groups and begin to arrogantly do as a group what Jesus had just challenged his disciples not to do as individuals? (Jesus has just told his followers that the greatest among them must be a servant to all! See Mark 9:30-37.) We all want to picture ourselves as "insiders" in the Kingdom of God—those who are righteously superior and correct. When others appear to be doing God's good work, we feel threatened rather than delighted. How shallow, how petty, and how unlike Jesus is such arrogance!

TODAY'S PRAYER

Father in heaven, I love you. But I have to admit that I frustrate myself with my own selfish and petty loyalties and pride. Even though I hate that trait in others, I need your help, Father, to hate it in myself and remove it from my own heart. Help me be more open just as your Son was while on the earth. I ask for this help in Jesus' name. Amen.

CONTEXT: MARK 9:38-50

RELATED PASSAGES: ROMANS 15:5-7; JAMES 3:17; 1 PETER 5:14

Day 175

DON'T STOP HIM!

MARK 9:38-39

Then John said, "Teacher, we saw a man using your name to force demons out of someone. He is not one of us. So we told him to stop, because he does not belong to our group."

Jesus said, "Don't stop him. Whoever uses my name to do powerful things will not soon say bad things about me."

KEY THOUGHT

Good deeds done in the name of Jesus are a blessing no matter which group or what person is doing them. Our goal should be for people to be blessed and Jesus to be praised!

TODAY'S PRAYER

LORD God, my Abba Father, may your name be praised and lost people be reached through the work of others I don't yet know. Help my heart rejoice in that work and those who do it. In Jesus' name I pray. Amen.

CONTEXT: MARK 9:38-50

RELATED PASSAGES: PHILIPPIANS 1:15-18; 1 CORINTHIANS 3:5-9; GALATIANS 2:6-10

Day 176

NOT AGAINST US!

MARK 9:40
"Whoever is not against us is with us."

KEY THOUGHT

Christianity faces enough opposition in the world without its own proponents fighting and devouring each other because they fancy each other as enemies. Jesus' words here are powerfully universal and clear: notice the use of the words "the person" (or "anyone" in other translations) is general. If people don't oppose us, they aren't the enemy! In fact, Jesus says even more than that: they are working to benefit the cause of Jesus and his followers.

TODAY'S PRAYER

Father, I pray that those of us who seek to honor you will quit treating each other as enemies. I also pray that your children can find their unity in Jesus, in whose name I pray. Amen.

CONTEXT: MARK 9:38-50

RELATED PASSAGES: JOHN 17:20-21; ROMANS 12:18; 3 JOHN 1:5-8

Day 177

A Cup of Water

Mark 9:41

"I can assure you that anyone who helps you by giving you a drink of water because you belong to the Christ will definitely get a reward."

Key Thought

God doesn't forget kindness that is demonstrated with actions that are simple and real. In fact, this is the kindness that Jesus expects us to display and promises to reward. When we are kind to other believers or they are kind to us, God sees, remembers, and rewards! Of course Jesus didn't want us to limit kindness to believers; he also wanted us to give unbelievers an opportunity to share their kindness with his followers. Simple acts of kindness may seem simple, but they are a genuine reflection of the Lord's kindness and compassion that were shared with all sorts of people.

Today's Prayer

Father, thank you for sending Jesus who makes your way of life so simple and clear. Thank you for remembering acts of kindness. Thank you for those who have demonstrated that kindness to me and to your Son through their kindness to me. Please bless them. In Jesus' name. Amen.

Context: Mark 9:38-50

Related Passages: Matthew 25:31-40; Hebrews 6:10; Hebrews 13:16

NO STUMBLING BLOCKS ACCEPTED

MARK 9:42

"If one of these little children believes in me, and someone causes that child to sin, it will be very bad for that person. It would be better for them to have a millstone tied around their neck and be drowned in the sea."

KEY THOUGHT

So often in our passion to preserve the purity of the faith, we begin to exclude others. While purity in our faith is important, Jesus reminds us of the other side of the equation: woe to us if we exclude someone who Jesus sees as belonging to him or do anything to cause another to lose faith. New Christians, weak believers, and children are all precious to God. He doesn't want a single one to lose faith because of the hard-headedness, hard-heartedness, or arrogance of another believer.

TODAY'S PRAYER

God, please help me be more careful in what I say and how I act. I don't want to discourage a single believer from following you. Help my life, my words, and my actions to be an encouragement rather than a discouragement to your people. In Jesus' name. Amen.

CONTEXT: MARK 9:38-50

RELATED PASSAGES: HEBREWS 12:13; ROMANS 14:20; 1 CORINTHIANS 8:9

Day 179

THE GREATER PRIORITY

MARK 9:43-48

"If your hand makes you sin, cut it off. It is better for you to lose part of your body and have eternal life than to have two hands and go to hell. There the fire never stops. If your foot makes you sin, cut it off. It is better for you to lose part of your body and have eternal life than to have two feet and be thrown into hell. If your eye makes you sin, take it out. It is better for you to have only one eye and enter God's kingdom than to have two eyes and be thrown into hell. The worms that eat the people in hell never die. The fire there is never stopped."

KEY THOUGHT

Sin, and leading others to sin, should be avoided at all costs. Being God's pure people is vitally important. So Jesus uses very powerful words and imagery to forcefully drive home his point. His point is that we should make every possible effort to avoid sin or causing others to sin.

TODAY'S PRAYER

Father in heaven, I confess that the lack of concern the world around me has about sin sometimes infiltrates my own thinking. Please, dear Father, not only forgive me, but also stir my heart to yearn for holiness. In Jesus' name I ask for this grace. Amen.

CONTEXT: MARK 9:38-50

RELATED PASSAGES: 1 JOHN 2:1-2; JAMES 1:26-27; GALATIANS 5:22-23

PURIFIED

MARK 9:49
"Everyone will be salted with fire."

KEY THOUGHT

Like yesterday's verse, today's words from Jesus are tough and shocking. The Lord reminds us that the real character of our lives will not be left in doubt. Facades will fall. Hidden secrets will be revealed. Well-camouflaged sins will be brought out into the open. Every action will be made clear. Nothing can be hidden from the purifier's fire. All that is dross will be removed. Only what is pure will remain.

TODAY'S PRAYER

O LORD God Almighty, the judge of all people, I pray that the defects, impurities, and dross in my life will be purified now so that you will be glorified in my life both now and in the day of judgment. In Jesus' name and for your glory I pray. Amen.

CONTEXT: MARK 9:38-50

RELATED PASSAGES: 1 CORINTHIANS 3:11-15; 1 CORINTHIANS 5:3-5; HEBREWS 10:1-2

Day 181

A Salty Peace

Mark 9:50

"Salt is good. But if it loses its salty taste, you can't make it good again. So, don't lose that good quality of salt you have. And live in peace with each other."

Key Thought

Jesus wants us to be people of character: the salty taste in Jesus words refers to people who are holy, righteous, pure and redemptive in a world that is none of those things. Jesus wants us to live in peace with each other in our local congregations as well as with other believers even if we do not recognize them as being in "our group." Jesus gives us two clear commands without equivocation: to be at peace and to have a godly influence on those around us. Obedience to these two important commands is needed so very much in the divided culture and fallen world in which believers in Jesus now find themselves.

Today's Prayer

Holy Father, please help me exemplify the desires Jesus has for me; I want to be holy and redemptive as I live before my neighbors and I want to be at peace with those who share faith in Jesus as Lord. In Jesus' name I ask for your help in being fully obedient to you in these matters. Amen.

Context: Mark 9:38-50

Related Passages: 1 Thessalonians 4:1-8; 1 Corinthians 6:19-20; Hebrews 12:14

Day 182

TEACHING THE CROWDS

MARK 10:1

Then Jesus left there and went into the area of Judea and across the Jordan River. Again, many people came to him, and Jesus taught them as he always did.

KEY THOUGHT

Two characteristics marked Jesus' ministry at this stage of his life. First, he was very popular and crowds accompanied him everywhere he went. Second, he taught them God's will and demonstrated a life yielded to the Father's will. Jesus' goal in attracting people was not to gain an earthly following, but to teach and to train a group of people who would change the world. He saw teaching as his task—not his only task, but his primary task during his ministry.

TODAY'S PRAYER

Father God, I thank you for those who have so wonderfully taught me. I realize, dear Father, that these people gave me one of the most wonderful gifts anyone could give. May I never forget their sacrifices, and may I be effective in helping to pass the Good News along to others. In Jesus' name I pray. Amen.

CONTEXT: MARK 10:1-12

RELATED PASSAGES: MATTHEW 9:36; MARK 14:27-30; JOHN 10:14-15

Day 183

THE QUESTION TRAP

MARK 10:2

Some Pharisees came to Jesus and tried to make him say something wrong. They asked him, "Is it right for a man to divorce his wife?"

KEY THOUGHT

Isn't it amazing how religious people can resort to trickery and legalistic debate to try to prove their superiority? Shouldn't we focus on the real issues of God's heart like justice, mercy, and righteous living? Words are important, but religious words become righteous only when they truly come to life in people who are living to honor God.

TODAY'S PRAYER

O Righteous Father, may the words of my mouth, the thoughts of my mind, the motivation of my heart, and the actions of my life be pleasing to you. I pray this in the name of Jesus my Lord. Amen.

CONTEXT: MARK 10:1-12

RELATED PASSAGES: MICAH 6:8; MATTHEW 23:23-24; 2 TIMOTHY 2:22-26

Day 184

MOSES

MARK 10:3-4
Jesus answered, "What did Moses command you to do?"

The Pharisees said, "Moses allowed a man to divorce his wife by writing a certificate of divorce."

KEY THOUGHT

In this Scripture, the Pharisees are able to tell Jesus correctly what Moses said about divorce. In the subsequent verses, Jesus confronts the Pharisees with the truth revealed in their question; they were missing God's central principle about marriage. It is easy to quote Scripture; but living God's truth revealed in that Scripture is much more challenging! Let's not seek just to know the Scriptures, but let's also commit to know the heart and will of God who lies behind the Scriptures.

TODAY'S PRAYER
O God, teach me your way, instruct me in your will, and lead me so that I can walk with you each day. In Jesus' name I ask for help to better know your heart and your truth. Amen.

CONTEXT: MARK 10:1-12

RELATED PASSAGES: MARK 6:6-7; JOHN 5:38-39; 2 TIMOTHY 3:14-17

Day 185

HARD-HEARTEDNESS

MARK 10:5

*Jesus said, "Moses wrote that command for you because
you refused to accept God's teaching."*

KEY THOUGHT

What Moses did in allowing the children of Israel a legal means of divorce
(see the three previous devotionals) was done only as a concession. It was
not God's original plan. It was not what was best for the people involved.
It was allowed only because of the hard hearts of the people who wouldn't
honor their vows to each other and to God. In a world where many people
continue to break their vows, refuse to be faithful to each other, and wound
their spouses and their children, the focus shouldn't become the legality of the
concession, but should become a focus on the prevention of divorce through
healthy and loving marriages and restoration of the people broken by divorce.

TODAY'S PRAYER

*God, I ask first that you help me be a faithful, loyal, and loving person who
lives up the vows and promises that I make. Second, dear Father, I pray that
you use me to encourage others to do the same. Finally, Righteous Father,
I ask that you show me the best ways to help restore and encourage those
who have been wounded by divorce. In Jesus' name I pray. Amen.*

CONTEXT: MARK 10:1-12

RELATED PASSAGES: MALACHI 2:13-16; 1 CORINTHIANS 7:10-11;
ECCLESIASTES 5:1-2

Day 186

GOD'S PLAN

MARK 10:6
"But when God made the world, 'he made people male and female.'"

KEY THOUGHT

God's plan, rooted in the creation story of Genesis 2, is that one woman and one man be married for life. As male and female, they are different, yet each one is created in the image of God. They are different, not just because of the differences in their two lives, with different experiences and different tastes, but also because they are made fundamentally different—different physically and in many other ways. Learning to blend these differences through mutual love and submission reflects the mystery of God himself, who is Father, Son, and Holy Spirit.

TODAY'S PRAYER

O Father in heaven, help the marriages among your people today more fully reflect your divine intention. Teach us to submit to each other out of love and respect—not just love and respect for our marriage partner, but also love and respect for Jesus as our Lord. In his name I pray. Amen.

CONTEXT: MARK 10:1-12

RELATED PASSAGES: GENESIS 1:26-27; EPHESIANS 5:21; GENESIS 2:22-25

Day 187

LEAVING THE NEST

MARK 10:7
"That is why a man will leave his father and mother and be joined to his wife."

KEY THOUGHT

One of the key elements of marriage as God designed it is the transfer of the primary personal relationship from one's parents to one's marriage partner. In the vast majority of cultures, it is assumed that the woman will leave her parents to begin her new family with her husband. Jesus makes clear that the man must leave his parents for his wife as well. They must learn to rely on one another and not their parents. In their differences as male and female, they must learn that the other completes what is lacking as they serve each other and depend upon God.

TODAY'S PRAYER

Father, I pray that I will live to see a deeper appreciation of your plan for marriage in my culture. Until that day, I pray that those in my family will embody your will in our marriage and family relationships. In Jesus' name I pray. Amen.

CONTEXT: MARK 10:1-12

RELATED PASSAGES: MATTHEW 10:37-39; EPHESIANS 5:31-33; RUTH 2:11-12

Day 188

United into One

MARK 10:8
"'And the two people will become one.' So the people are not two, but one."

Key Thought

Marriage is about two people becoming one. Jesus makes this powerfully clear by emphasizing "oneness" four times in the whole passage—vs. 7

"joined"; vs. 8

"two people will become one"; vs. 8 – "not two, but one"; and vs. 9

"God has joined them together." The sexual union between a husband and wife is clearly in view with this context. This is a good and glorious union that is to be enjoyed and celebrated in marriage as part of two lives being joined by God into one.

Today's Prayer

Father, thank you for your plan about the proper place for sexual intimacy within the security and protection of marriage. May I always honor you in handling my sexuality in holiness, righteousness, and love. I pray this in Jesus' name and for his glory. Amen.

Context: Mark 10:1-12

Related Passages: 1 Thessalonians 4:1-5; 1 Corinthians 7:3-4; Proverbs 5:18-20

Day 189

GOD JOINED

MARK 10:9
"God has joined them together, so no one should separate them."

KEY THOUGHT

God has the power to make two people one. Marriage is not about a wedding, but about a man and a woman entering into a special covenant relationship with God and with each other. The man and the woman should give their highest allegiance and commitment to God when they marry. There will be times when each spouse will disappoint the other or let them down. However, God wants each of them to remember that the highest priority must be treating the other as God would have them be treated. Honoring God in this way is the key to marriage. God hates covenants made with him to be broken because it not only dishonors him, but also wounds others as well.

TODAY'S PRAYER

O God, please give your people a deeper appreciation of what it means to enter into covenant with you when they marry. I am concerned about all the money we spend on wedding ceremonies when there is often so little appreciation for the covenant relationship that begins when a couple is married. Help me, O God, to be a covenant-keeper and a person who encourages others to be loyal to you and the covenants they make with each other. In Jesus' name I pray. Amen.

CONTEXT: MARK 10:1-12

RELATED PASSAGES: MALACHI 2:13-15; EXODUS 19:5-6; PSALM 25:10

Day 190

DIVORCE AND ADULTERY

MARK 10:10-12

*Later, when the followers and Jesus were in the house, they asked him again about
the question of divorce. He said, "Whoever divorces his wife and marries another
woman has sinned against his wife. He is guilty of adultery. And the woman who
divorces her husband and marries another man is also guilty of adultery."*

KEY THOUGHT

In a world that takes divorce lightly despite the carnage left in the lives
of the people involved and their children, Jesus reminds his followers that
God takes divorce seriously. He views unscriptural divorce and remarriage
as adultery—the betrayal of the marriage covenant that was made with him
and between them. God hates divorce and doesn't want it to happen among
his people. Why? Because of the damage done to each of the people involved
and the damage to their families, their children, and their faith. As far as it is
possible, let's work to prevent divorce and learn to make homes full of love,
joy, and peace through the power of the Holy Spirit.

TODAY'S PRAYER

*O Father, forgive us and help us. So many people in our time feel the pain of
abandonment and loss because a spouse has left them. Others have grown up
wondering what they did wrong because a parent abandoned them and their
family. Heal our wounds. Heal our land. Pour out your Spirit and restore
our love for each other in our homes. Help us, O Lord, find the way back to
your grace and power so that we can be a people of solid marriages, loving
families, and compassionate ministry. In Jesus' name I pray. Amen.*

CONTEXT: MARK 10:1-12

RELATED PASSAGES: MALACHI 2:15-16; 1 CORINTHIANS 7:10-11; JOHN 8:1-11

Day 191

PLEASE BLESS THEM

MARK 10:13

People brought their small children to Jesus, so that he could lay his hands on them to bless them. But the followers told the people to stop bringing their children to him.

KEY THOUGHT

We can never seem to find enough time to do the things we need to do. So who gets left out in the "busy-ness" of life? Children tend to be forgotten, neglected, ignored, or left out when schedules get crunched—and this is true even in our child-dominated cultures. Even when children are a key part of adult schedules, the time is often centered on the children performing or competing against other children. We sometimes take such little amounts of time just to be with our children and let them just be with us. Jesus had many important things to do. The disciples just didn't realize children should be viewed as very important. Jesus did. Now so should we!

TODAY'S PRAYER

O Father in heaven, thank you for the gift of children. Thank you for the gift of future. Thank you for the gift of wild-eyed wonder. Help me to show the children around me that they are special and important—not only to me, but also to you. I pray this in the name of your Son, Jesus. Amen.

CONTEXT: MARK 10:13-25

RELATED PASSAGES: MARK 10:46-52; LUKE 22:24-27; JOHN 3:3-7

Day 192

LET THEM COME TO ME!

MARK 10:14

Jesus saw what happened. He did not like his followers telling the children not to come. So he said to them, "Let the little children come to me. Don't stop them, because God's kingdom belongs to people who are like these little children."

KEY THOUGHT

Let's not do anything to keep "little ones"—whether that means new baby followers of Jesus or young children—from knowing the grace and power of Jesus! Even more than that, let's actively encourage and help the Lord's "little ones" to find their place in Jesus' family, have their needs fulfilled by Jesus' grace, and use their gifts as part of Jesus' Body.

TODAY'S PRAYER

O Father, please help me to never put off a child who needs to know your love. Help me and use me, O God, to show children your love and help them serve to your glory. In Jesus' name. Amen.

CONTEXT: MARK 10:13-25

RELATED PASSAGES: MATTHEW 18:1-6; MALACHI 2:13-16; JOHN 12:23-24

Day 193

A CHILD KIND OF FAITH

MARK 10:14B-15

So he said to them, "Let the little children come to me. Don't stop them, because God's kingdom belongs to people who are like these little children. The truth is, you must accept God's kingdom like a little child accepts things, or you will never enter it."

KEY THOUGHT

We must have child-like faith to be a part of God's Kingdom. So many things about the Kingdom require of us a "dangerous innocence" and genuine humility. Yet Jesus demonstrated these child-like qualities. He wants us to travel along our journey as God's trusting children, not necessarily as worldly-wise, theologically astute scholars. Now don't take me wrong on this; we are not told to throw away our brains to become Christians. However, we are taught to live in a way that is often upside down to the world and its conventional wisdom. To do that, we need to go back and experience the gift of salvation, the magnificence of God, and the wonders of grace as wide-eyed, excitable children who trust in God's ways, God's love, and God's care.

TODAY'S PRAYER

O God, make my heart child-like and my faith fresh and new each day. In Jesus' name. Amen.

CONTEXT: MARK 10:13-25

RELATED PASSAGES: 2 CORINTHIANS 5:16-17; GALATIANS 4:4-7; 1 PETER 2:1-3

Day 194

A HANDFUL OF BLESSING

MARK 10:16

Then Jesus held the children in his arms. He laid his hands on them and blessed them.

KEY THOUGHT

Jesus frequently touched people. So must we. In a world so devoid of human contact—especially genuinely affectionate, loving, and supportive non-sexual contact—many people ache just to be touched. Jesus reminds us how important and powerful touch can be. He shows us that we can communicate God's love and acceptance through touch. So let's reach out and touch someone today as an expression of God's love in ways that are appropriate and appreciated by those who need his love.

TODAY'S PRAYER

O God, thank you for the gift of touch. To receive the affectionate, loving, and supportive touch of a friend or loved one is precious. To be able to share my loving touch with another person is such a great gift. Help me to use this gift generously and wisely I pray. In Jesus' name. Amen.

CONTEXT: MARK 10:13-25

RELATED PASSAGES: MARK 1:40-42; MARK 5:38-43; 1 CORINTHIANS 16:20

Day 195

ENTRANCE REQUIREMENTS?

MARK 10:17

Jesus started to leave, but a man ran to him and bowed down on his knees before him.
The man asked, "Good Teacher, what must I do to get the life that never ends?"

KEY THOUGHT

This is a great question if it comes from a genuine heart. Each of us will have to read the following verses for ourselves to decide if we think this man's heart was genuine. Better yet, each of us should look at our own heart and ask the Lord Jesus this same question. I bet if we listen this week, he will make clear to us if our hearts are genuinely seeking to honor him or simply trying selfishly to get something for ourselves.

TODAY'S PRAYER

O God, please help me be confident of my future with you. May that confidence be based on your gracious gift of salvation. I trust that by the power of the Holy Spirit, you will empower me to be and to do what pleases you. In Jesus' name I ask for this grace. Amen.

CONTEXT: MARK 10:13-25

RELATED PASSAGES: ACTS 16:29; ACTS 2:36-41; JOHN 3:1-7

Day 196

ONLY GOD IS GOOD

MARK 10:18
Jesus answered, "Why do you call me good? Only God is good."

KEY THOUGHT

Yes, only God is good. But then that is the point, isn't it? Jesus is God with us and we must put our faith in him and listen to him and obey just as we must with God. If the man who asked the question in the previous verse can't see that Jesus has God's authority as well as God's goodness, he will never relinquish complete control of his heart, his life, and his future. Come to think of it, neither will we. Only God is good! So then, Lord Jesus, you have our attention as God speaking to us!

TODAY'S PRAYER

O Father in heaven, hallowed is your mighty name. I recognize that your Son, Jesus, is God come in the flesh, your very presence with us. Thank you for becoming one of us and living among us and showing us what true goodness looks like. In Jesus' name I pray. Amen.

CONTEXT: MARK 10:13-25

RELATED PASSAGES: JOHN 1:17-18; MARK 9:1-7; TITUS 2:11-14

Day 197

YOU KNOW THE COMMANDMENTS!

MARK 10:19

"And you know his commands: 'You must not murder anyone, you must not commit adultery, you must not steal, you must not lie, you must not cheat, you must respect your father and mother . . . .'"

KEY THOUGHT

Do you know the commandments? Do you know the core teachings of God's morality? If not, why not review them today. They can be found in Exodus 20. As followers of Jesus, we are not justified by law, but by God's grace given us in Jesus. God's grace and the power of the Holy Spirit help us to be what we could never be under law—people who live morally pleasing lives to God. God wants his holy character, revealed by his commands and empowered by his Holy Spirit, to be seen in us.

TODAY'S PRAYER

O holy and righteous Father, conform me to your character and write your moral will on my heart so that I can display it in my daily life. In Jesus' name I pray. Amen.

CONTEXT: MARK 10:13-25

RELATED PASSAGES: EXODUS 20:1-17; ROMANS 8:1-4; JEREMIAH 31:33

Day 198

I'M PERFECT!

MARK 10:19-20

"And you know his commands: 'You must not murder anyone, you must not commit adultery, you must not steal, you must not lie, you must not cheat, you must respect your father and mother . . . .'"

The man said, "Teacher, I have obeyed all these commands since I was a boy."

KEY THOUGHT

Here's a guy pretty sure that he has mastered it all . . . and he even began as a child. Oops! This is where his spiritual "heart problems" begin to show through his veneer of legalistic righteousness. Instead of keeping the law to honor God, this fellow was using his law-keeping as leverage to exalt his status before God. The pride of law-keeping has become the false god that blinds this man to his own failures in living up to God's holiness.

TODAY'S PRAYER

Father in heaven, you are holy and majestic. I know that my attempts to be holy are oftentimes going to be met with failure. I commit to being a holy person, but I know that my own efforts, even on my best days, are going to fall short. I thank you for giving me righteousness beyond my abilities, works, and efforts. Thank you for Jesus, whose sacrifice for me makes me righteous, and thank you for the Holy Spirit whose power transforms me into your character and holiness. In Jesus' name I pray. Amen.

CONTEXT: MARK 10:13-25

RELATED PASSAGES: GALATIANS 5:22-27; 1 CORINTHIANS 6:18-20; COLOSSIANS 1:18-23

Day 199

Then Come!

Mark 10:21

Jesus looked at the man in a way that showed how much he cared for him. He said, "There is still one thing you need to do. Go and sell everything you have. Give the money to those who are poor, and you will have riches in heaven. Then come and follow me."

Key Thought

Jesus had genuine love and compassion for this man. He was so close. He was headed in the right direction. But Jesus wanted his heart to yield and not just his actions. So he called him to do what is hardest—the "one thing" he lacked. Shouldn't each of us ask ourselves two important questions? "Could I do this?" "Jesus, what is the 'one thing' I lack?"

Today's Prayer

O Father, please don't let greed, love for money, or my desire for things block me from totally surrendering my heart to you. I want to be yours, heart, soul, mind, and strength. I want to be like you, holy, righteous, compassionate, and generous. Humble me gently and conform me completely so that my stubborn will is completely yielded to your will. In Jesus' name I ask you to revel to me the "one thing" I lack in surrendering my heart to you. Amen.

Context: Mark 10:13-27

Related Passages: Luke 14:33-35; Matthew 6:19-21; 1 Timothy 6:17-19

Day 200

SADLY AWAY

MARK 10:21-22

Jesus looked at the man in a way that showed how much he cared for him. He said, "There is still one thing you need to do. Go and sell everything you have. Give the money to those who are poor, and you will have riches in heaven. Then come and follow me."

The man was upset when Jesus told him to give away his money. He didn't want to do this, because he was very rich. So he went away sad.

KEY THOUGHT

The Bible has heart-wrenching stories of men and women who came to know the will of the Lord and yet were not willing to respond because something was holding them back. I'm sure you know someone—that someone may even be you—who has something holding him or her back from totally surrendering to the will and grace of God. Please pray for that person today. While we cannot ensure he or she will ever respond to God's offer of grace, at least we can pray that they will be lovingly confronted with the decision to accept or reject the will of the Lord.

TODAY'S PRAYER

O LORD God Almighty, I confess that there are times when I want you to more forcefully reveal yourself to friends of mine who will not surrender to your grace. I know that you will not overpower their wills. I know that you want our hearts and not a forced, coerced, or manipulated response to your offer of salvation in Jesus. So please use me and my influence to be a helpful, tender, and clear example to my friends who have not decided to follow your Son. In Jesus' name I pray. Amen.

CONTEXT: MARK 10:13-25

RELATED PASSAGES: ROMANS 12:1-2; ACTS 26:24-29; JOHN 5:35-40

Day 201

SO HARD

MARK 10:23-25

Then Jesus looked at his followers and said to them, "It will be very hard for a rich person to enter God's kingdom!"

The followers were amazed at what Jesus said. But he said again, "My children, it is very hard to enter God's kingdom! It is easier for a camel to go through the eye of a needle than for a rich person to enter God's kingdom!"

KEY THOUGHT

As the disciples processed the information they had seen and heard in Jesus' interchange with the young man who went away sorrowfully (see the previous verses), they were shocked. Being on the poorer end of the economic scale, they assumed that the richer folks would have a better chance of making it into heaven. Jesus told them the exact opposite was true: it would be hard for those who were rich to enter the Kingdom of God. This must be a sober warning to us. Most of us with access to a computer are much better off financially than the majority of the world's population. Yet we often focus on what we lack rather than what God has given us. We must not let ourselves become possessed by our possessions and our desire for them. They turn our hearts away from God and become idols that replace God in our lives.

TODAY'S PRAYER

O Father, bless me with wisdom, generosity, and a passion for your work as I seek to use "my" financial and material blessings to honor you and bring others closer to you. In Jesus' name I pray. Amen.

CONTEXT: MARK 10:13-27

RELATED PASSAGES: 1 TIMOTHY 6:6-10; 1 TIMOTHY 6:17-19; LUKE 16:13

Day 202

WHO CAN BE SAVED?

MARK 10:25-26

The followers were amazed at what Jesus said. But he said again, "My children, it is very hard to enter God's kingdom! It is easier for a camel to go through the eye of a needle than for a rich person to enter God's kingdom!"

The followers were even more amazed and said to each other, "Then who can be saved?"

KEY THOUGHT

If we are talking about meeting a legal requirement to be saved, we're all doomed. God is holy and we are not. God is pure and we are not. God is generous and we struggle to be. God is genuine and we struggle with hypocrisy. God is gracious and we are often petty and grudging. And . . . when it comes to money, the vast majority of people are selfish or fearful or miserly or faithless. So who can be saved? Ah, God has already provided for our shortcomings and rebellious moments, as long as they are moments and not a way of life. That is why Jesus came and called us to follow him. Otherwise, who could be saved?

TODAY'S PRAYER

O Father, I recognize salvation as a gift from your grace. I do not deserve it. I did not earn it. However, dear Father, please know I cherish this gift of grace and I praise you for your loving and sacrificial generosity shown me in Jesus. Amen.

CONTEXT: MARK 10:13-27

RELATED PASSAGES: ROMANS 3:21-25; EPHESIANS 2:1-10; ACTS 2:36-40

Day 203

EVERYTHING IS POSSIBLE

MARK 10:26-27

The followers were even more amazed and said to each other, "Then who can be saved?"

Jesus looked at them and said, "That is something people cannot do, but God can. He can do anything."

KEY THOUGHT

This is true or our faith is really in vain. We have strength beyond human willpower, knowledge, or ability. Even more importantly, God through Jesus has covered all of the shortcomings and sins that we have. God is . . . and was . . . and will be . . . God. Nothing is impossible with him. Our God can do anything!

TODAY'S PRAYER

O Father, please make this truth that nothing is impossible with you self-evident to those who lead in your churches. Please remind me of this each day as I seek to live for you. I trust that everything is possible with you! In Jesus' powerful name I pray. Amen.

CONTEXT: MARK 10:13-27

RELATED PASSAGES: PHILIPPIANS 4:13; EPHESIANS 3:20-21; MARK 9:23

Day 204

GOD WON'T FORGET

MARK 10:28-30

Peter said to Jesus, "We left everything to follow you!"

Jesus said, "I can promise that everyone who has left their home, brothers, sisters, mother, father, children, or farm for me and for the Good News about me will get a hundred times more than they left. Here in this world they will get more homes, brothers, sisters, mothers, children, and farms. And with these things they will have persecutions. But in the world that is coming they will also get the reward of eternal life."

KEY THOUGHT

Jesus is basically promising three things in this Scripture. First, he is saying that the disciples—and we who follow Jesus today—can't out give God. God will bless them and us far more than we could ever give up for him. Second, that doesn't mean that followers of Jesus will have easy lives on this side of eternity—there will be persecutions. Finally, he promises eternal life. In other words, his followers' sacrifices for their faith will be far overshadowed by the blessings they will receive from their Father in heaven.

TODAY'S PRAYER

O Father, thank you for being so generous. I know that I will be blessed far more than I can imagine as one of your children. Help me not to lose that hope in the face of hardship, discouragement, and persecution. In Jesus' name I pray. Amen.

CONTEXT: MARK 10:28-34

RELATED PASSAGES: ROMANS 8:18-25; PHILIPPIANS 2:5-11; HEBREWS 6:10

Day 205

LEAST AND GREATEST

MARK 10:31

"Many people who have the highest place now will have the lowest place in the future. And the people who have the lowest place now will have the highest place then."

KEY THOUGHT

God evaluates people differently than most earthly judges, critics, and cultures do. Those who appear to be lowly, unimportant, backward, impoverished, broken, and meek will be valued as precious by God. Is it because he favors the poor and the weak over the strong and the rich? Not necessarily. God does cherish the person who serves others regardless of his or her station in life. He does care deeply for the person who recognizes her or his need for God's love, mercy, and grace. God does recognize the genuine humility of a person who has suffered because he or she would not compromise on integrity issues. So those who have cheated their way to the top and thereby gained fame and recognition will not be the ones God honors. No, it will be the people they stepped on but who refused to give up on faith, morality, integrity, honesty, and compassion. It will be the people who serve others in the name of Christ—even serving those who abuse them—that God will honor.

TODAY'S PRAYER

Father, help me value others by your standards. Help me see the value of others through your eyes. Confound my intentions when I choose the wrong path and go the way of fame and fortune rather than faith and service. In Jesus' name and for his glory I ask this. Amen.

CONTEXT: MARK 10:28-34

RELATED PASSAGES: MATTHEW 5:1-12; 1 CORINTHIANS 1:26-29; MATTHEW 23:11

Day 206

FEARFUL FOLLOWING

MARK 10:32

Jesus and those with him were on their way to Jerusalem. He was at the front of the group. His followers were wondering what was happening, and the people who followed behind them were feeling afraid. Jesus gathered the twelve apostles again and talked with them alone. He told them what would happen in Jerusalem.

KEY THOUGHT

Two things strike me powerfully about these verses and the people they describe. First, Jesus' followers still followed him even though they didn't know what was about to happen. We know that Jesus and his followers are moving to Jerusalem and that the shadow of the cross falls across all that Jesus is doing. They do not. Their willingness to follow is a great reminder that faith can lead us to face life's biggest challenges even when we can't understand exactly what is going on and when we're not really ready for the challenges. Second, Jesus knew what lay ahead for himself, but rather than looking after his own needs, he was busy preparing his followers for what lay ahead. Jesus was a servant to his followers even to the very end when he displayed the ultimate act of service and gave his life for them.

TODAY'S PRAYER

O God, give those of us who follow Jesus faith that can inspire our courage and keep us following even when we can't understand. To face life's biggest challenges with question marks and confusion is very difficult for us, but we do trust that you will lead us through. In Jesus' name, we ask that our faith not fail us! Amen.

CONTEXT: MARK 10:28-34

RELATED PASSAGES: PSALM 91:1-6; HEBREWS 12:1-3; JOHN 12:42

Day 207

TERRORS AHEAD

MARK 10:33-34

He said, "We are going to Jerusalem. The Son of Man will be handed over to the leading priests and teachers of the law. They will say that he must die and will hand him over to the foreigners, who will laugh at him and spit on him. They will beat him with whips and kill him. But on the third day after his death, he will rise to life again."

KEY THOUGHT

Jesus knew what lay ahead: a journey to Jerusalem with the shadow of the cross on his heart. While he warned his followers, he was also emphasizing his own awareness of the horrible price his gift of love would cost him. Yet he did this for you and me. He did it knowingly. He did it sacrificially; he deliberately held back his own power to stop what was going to happen to him. He knew and accepted the cross that awaited him, the mockery that lay ahead, and the ugliness that would be heaped upon him by those who hated him. Why? Because a ransom had to be paid and sin had to be atoned. His wounds, the very wounds he was anticipating, were necessary for each of us to be spiritually healed.

TODAY'S PRAYER

O God, what thanks can I offer? What words are adequate to say thank you for the price that was paid for my sins? While my words are inadequate, I trust that the Holy Spirit will present the yearnings of my thankful heart to you with my deepest appreciation for your sacrifice of your Son. In Jesus' name I thank you. Amen.

CONTEXT: MARK 10:28-34

RELATED PASSAGES: 2 CORINTHIANS 5:19-21; ISAIAH 53:3-12; 1 JOHN 2:1-2

Day 208

A FAVOR PLEASE

MARK 10:35-37

*Then James and John, sons of Zebedee, came to Jesus and said,
"Teacher, we want to ask you to do something for us."*

Jesus asked, "What do you want me to do for you?"

*The sons answered, "Let us share the great honor you will have as king.
Let one of us sit at your right side and the other at your left."*

KEY THOUGHT

Sometimes the Scriptures are just too honest. I'm being a little sarcastic . . .
but just a little. Jesus' closest followers reveal that they don't really understand
what he has just said to them and what his life, ministry, and purpose are.
They've told Jesus a few verses earlier what they gave up to follow him. They
seem to ignore what he has just told them in the previous verse that he will
pay a horrible price for them. They can think only of their own glory. So while
they courageously follow him to Jerusalem, they also have a great desire to get
the big pay off from their association with him. Their lack of understanding
and their glory-seeking become the opportunity for us to ask ourselves
a crucial question: "Will I follow Jesus even if the costs are high and the
appearances suggest that there is no earthly pay off?"

TODAY'S PRAYER

*O glorious Father, please forgive my selfishness and for seeking my own glory.
I confess that I want to be treated favorably and be blessed for following you.
Please give me the courage to follow no matter the cost in this life as I reach in
faith for what is life indeed! In Jesus' name and for his glory I pray. Amen.*

CONTEXT: MARK 10:35-45

RELATED PASSAGES: MARK 8:34-37; JOHN 21:15-19; ACTS 20:22-24

Day 209

ARE YOU ABLE!

MARK 10:37-38

*The sons answered, "Let us share the great honor you will have as king.
Let one of us sit at your right side and the other at your left."*

*Jesus said, "You don't understand what you are asking. Can you drink from the cup that
I must drink from? Can you be baptized with the same baptism that I must go through?"*

KEY THOUGHT

Before we overestimate what we would actually do to serve the Lord, we
had better look at some who failed him miserably. This is not to discourage us,
but to humble us and remind us of how difficult it is to let faith triumph over
fear and trust win over trial. We will not make it on our own, but with the help
of the Lord and the encouragement of each other we can remain faithful even
unto the point of death.

TODAY'S PRAYER

*O God, I confess that I cannot do it alone. My strength is not sufficient. Even
looking at the great heroes of faith who have paid the ultimate price before me, I'm
sure that I don't have the strength to pay the ultimate price on my own. So, dear
Father, I turn to you and the power of the Holy Spirit to sustain me. I ask that the
encouragement and support of your people can uphold me. I promise to do my
best, but I also know that without your grace, my best is not sufficient. So please
strengthen my courage and inspire my strength. In Jesus' name I pray. Amen.*

CONTEXT: MARK 10:35-45

RELATED PASSAGES: MARK 14:37-39; 1 PETER 5:6-11; JOSHUA 2:11

Day 210

YOU WILL SHARE MY CUP!

MARK 10:38-39

Jesus said, "You don't understand what you are asking. Can you drink from the cup that I must drink from? Can you be baptized with the same baptism that I must go through?"

The sons answered, "Yes, we can!"

Jesus said to the sons, "It is true that you will drink from the cup that I drink from. And you will be baptized with the same baptism that I must go through."

KEY THOUGHT

James and John both paid a huge price for their faith in Jesus. James was martyred early in the history of the church. John was exiled to the Island of Patmos where he saw visions of what lay ahead—a time of persecution, apostasy, and challenge for the church in Asia Minor and for believers in every age. Each of these brothers gave his life in a different way to follow the Master who saw greatness in sacrifice and not in human success. O that we might have the courage to do as they both did, faithfully serving the Lord no matter what challenges face us in our lives.

TODAY'S PRAYER

O God, you are worthy of my life. You gave it to me at my conception. I pray that you will use it to your glory. And I trust, dear Father, that you will keep it for eternity. In Jesus' name I confess my trust in you. Amen.

CONTEXT: MARK 10:35-45

RELATED PASSAGES: PHILIPPIANS 1:19-24; ACTS 12:1-4; REVELATION 1:9

Day 211

ONLY GOD DECIDES

MARK 10:39-40

The sons answered, "Yes, we can!"

Jesus said to the sons, "It is true that you will drink from the cup that I drink from. And you will be baptized with the same baptism that I must go through. But it is not for me to say who will sit at my right or my left. God has prepared those places for the ones he chooses."

KEY THOUGHT

God the Father holds some things in his hands alone. The Son, in his earthly ministry, will not decide the importance or place of his followers before their lives are finished. Only God will. The point from this seems to be that we are not to live for the place of honor, but for the person of honor—Jesus, the Son of God—and have our lives shaped as his was, by the shadow of the cross.

TODAY'S PRAYER

God, calm my restless and selfish spirit from its striving. To be loved, honored, and welcomed by you and to know that you will dry every tear from my eyes and give me a home with you are far more than I can rightfully ask. Calm me, O Lord, and help me trust that your place for me will be far more glorious than I have a right to expect because your grace is more than sufficient for me. In Jesus' name I ask for this grace. Amen.

CONTEXT: MARK 10:35-45

RELATED PASSAGES: MATTHEW 25:31-40; MARK 13:32; HEBREWS 6:10

Day 212

PETTY PARTNERS

MARK 10:41
When the other ten followers heard this, they were angry with James and John.

KEY THOUGHT
Lest we think that James and John were selfish in their requests, we need to realize they were not alone. Envy and greed, the need for attention and honor, are beastly stumbling blocks for followers of Jesus. Yes, we can be sickened and disheartened by self-avowed followers of Jesus who are jockeying for attention, prominence, and importance, but we also should see in them a warning: we will all find ourselves there but for the grace of God.

TODAY'S PRAYER
Humble me gently, O Father in heaven. Lead me to follow you with honor, integrity, humility, courage, and faithfulness and to trust you for the outcome. Father, I ask for your grace in all of these things in Jesus' name. Amen.

CONTEXT: MARK 10:35-45

RELATED PASSAGES: COLOSSIANS 3:12; TITUS 3:1-2; PSALM 69:32

Day 213

AMONG YOU, IT SHOULD BE QUITE DIFFERENT

MARK 10:42-44

Jesus called all the followers together. He said, "The non-Jewish people have men they call rulers. You know that those rulers love to show their power over the people. And their important leaders love to use all their authority over the people. But it should not be that way with you. Whoever wants to be your leader must be your servant. Whoever wants to be first must serve the rest of you like a slave."

KEY THOUGHT

Jesus' followers have heard a different tune than the world hears. They have a different reason to live in this world. So naturally—or should we say, supernaturally?—we are to live very differently in the world. One of the places this shows up is in those in whom we place value. Our ultimate hero is a servant who washed his followers' feet and then gave up his life for them as he lived out his life faithfully in the shadow of the cross. Shouldn't our everyday heroes follow that same example? The greatest in Jesus' Kingdom *is* a servant. Let's not wait until we are in heaven to recognize this value system; let's display it in our communities today.

TODAY'S PRAYER

O Father, help us—help me—to be quite different from the world in what we value, honor, and hold dear. In the name of Jesus, your Son and the greatest person who ever lived, I ask this. Amen.

CONTEXT: MARK 10:35-45

RELATED PASSAGES: PHILIPPIANS 2:5-11; ROMANS 12:1-2; 1 PETER 2:9-12

Day 214

I Came to Serve and to Give

Mark 10:45

"Follow my example: Even the Son of Man did not come for people to serve him. He came to serve others and to give his life to save many people."

Key Thought

Here is the heart of our Hero given in one simple statement. This is what it means to live in the shadow of the cross put into one short paragraph. We are to serve and sacrifice for others. It is our legacy. It is our life. It is our Lord's example. We were bought and brought to freedom by the ransom price he paid—the giving of his life in big and small ways. We are now called to follow his example and live his life in our world.

Today's Prayer

O Father in heaven, please use my life to your glory and to the blessing of others. In Jesus' name I pray. Amen.

Context: Mark 10:35-45

Related Passages: Psalm 111:9; 1 Peter 4:10-11; 1 Peter 1:18-20

Day 215

HAVE MERCY ON ME!

MARK 10:46-47

Then they came to the town of Jericho. When Jesus left there with his followers, a large crowd was with them. A blind man named Bartimaeus (meaning "son of Timaeus") was sitting by the road. He was always begging for money. He heard that Jesus from Nazareth was walking by. So he began shouting, "Jesus, Son of David, please help me!"

KEY THOUGHT

Often we let pride and social convention keep us from asking from God for what we most need and what he is often most willing to give us: mercy. Let's not be shamed into silence. When we realize we need mercy, grace, and forgiveness, let's not be shy about humbly asking for it from our generous and loving Father.

TODAY'S PRAYER

O Father, without your mercy and grace I would surely fail to find my way into your holy presence. Thank you for lavishing your gifts of grace and the Holy Spirit upon me. Let me never forget your mercy, love, and grace. In Jesus' name. Amen.

CONTEXT: MARK 10:46-52

RELATED PASSAGES: PSALM 4:1; PSALM 30:8-12; PSALM 51:1

Day 216

SHOUTING LOUDER

MARK 10:48

Many people criticized the blind man and told him to be quiet. But he shouted more and more, "Son of David, please help me!"

KEY THOUGHT

While we are not told to be quiet as Jesus physically passes by us, peer pressure and social agendas antagonistic to faith work to keep us away from Jesus. Sometimes people claiming to be Christians push us away from finding Jesus. Let's learn from the blind man not to give up in our quest to find and know Jesus so that we can receive his blessings. Jesus is near. Let's not let anyone silence our voices or push us away from boldly seeking the Lord.

TODAY'S PRAYER

O Father in heaven, help me never give up in my pursuit of your Son and my Lord. In Jesus' name I pray. Amen.

CONTEXT: MARK 10:46-52

RELATED PASSAGES: 1 CORINTHIANS 15:57-58; COLOSSIANS 1:23; JOHN 12:42-43

Day 217

HE'S CALLING YOU!

MARK 10:49-50

Jesus stopped and said, "Tell him to come here."

So they called the blind man and said, "You can be happy now. Stand up! Jesus is calling you." The blind man stood up quickly. He left his coat there and went to Jesus.

KEY THOUGHT

Jesus still calls to us! He wants us to hear the message of his life: you can come to me and receive life, he says to us. He wants us to hear the message of his teaching: you who are heavy burdened come to me and learn from me and find rest with me, he tells us. He wants us to hear the message of his resurrection: you can come to me and find rest, safety, and joy in my presence, he wants us to know. Jesus is calling to you. Will you follow him?

TODAY'S PRAYER

O Father in heaven, help me hear the voice of Jesus calling me to follow, to find rest, and to focus on the glorious future that I have in him. Give me courage to keep hearing his voice and following him faithfully. In Jesus' name I ask for your help. Amen.

CONTEXT: MARK 10:46-52

RELATED PASSAGES: JOHN 4:10-14; MATTHEW 11:28; REVELATION 22:16-17

Day 218

WHAT DO YOU WANT ME TO DO?

MARK 10:51-52

Jesus asked the man, "What do you want me to do for you?"

He answered, "Teacher, I want to see again."

Jesus said, "Go. You are healed because you believed." Immediately the man was able to see again. He followed Jesus down the road.

KEY THOUGHT

Isn't that such a simple question? Wouldn't we better serve others if we asked them questions, listened to their answers, honored their requests, and then affirmed their commitment and faith? We often think we know best how to help people, so we do what we think best rather than asking them what they need. While we can't honor every wish and sometimes people's needs seem self-evident and straightforward, asking them for input gives them the opportunity to share what's on their hearts and to express their needs. At the same time, it affirms their dignity at a time when they may feel as if they have lost every shred of dignity.

TODAY'S PRAYER

O Father, help me patiently wait and look for ways to help and serve others in your name. Give me the wisdom to do what they need, the patience to listen to them as they express that need, and the tenderness to invite them to let me share their burden. In Jesus' name I ask for this help. Amen.

CONTEXT: MARK 10:46-52

RELATED PASSAGES: JOHN 5:1-6; MARK 1:40-42; COLOSSIANS 4:2

Day 219

Embracing the Future

Mark 11:1-3

*Jesus and his followers were coming closer to Jerusalem. They came to the
towns of Bethphage and Bethany at the Mount of Olives. There Jesus sent two
of his followers to do something. He said to them, "Go to the town you can see
there. When you enter it, you will find a young donkey that no one has ever
ridden. Untie it and bring it here to me. If anyone asks you why you are taking
the donkey, tell them, 'The Master needs it. He will send it back soon.'"*

Key Thought

Jesus knows what awaits him in Jerusalem: reception, rejection, and
resurrection. He walks in the shadow of the cross as he faces his future.
He has repeatedly warned his followers. Now he sets the plan in motion.
He sends his followers to get the colt that begins his journey of sacrifice.
He knows the cost. He will have opportunities to turn away from it—he
can choose not to ride into Jerusalem on the donkey's colt; he can avoid
confrontations with the leaders; he can opt out in the Garden of Gethsemane;
he can call down angels to save him; and he can come down from the cross
to prove his identity. Yet at each crossroad of decision, Jesus chooses the will
of God. The cross will be no accident. Jesus chooses this path as he sends his
followers for the colt and begins the journey that will take him to the cross
and bring God's grace upon us.

Today's Prayer

*O Father, I am overwhelmed with the love that Jesus has for me. I know that
as he sends for the donkey's colt, he knows the journey to the cross has begun in
earnest. He knows he will pay for my sins with his life, his dignity, his agony,
and his blood. All I can do is bow in humble appreciation, adoration, and awe.
As the old hymn reminds me, "Love so amazing, so divine, demands my life, my
soul, my all." These I offer to you with all my heart, in Jesus' name. Amen.*

Context: Mark 11:1-11

Related Passages: 8:31-32a; 9:30-34, 45

Day 220

PERMITTED

MARK 11:4-6

The followers went into the town. They found a young donkey tied in the street near the door of a house, and they untied it. Some people were standing there and saw this. They asked, "What are you doing? Why are you untying that donkey?" The followers answered the way Jesus told them, and the people let them take the donkey.

KEY THOUGHT

"The Master needs it. He will send it back soon." That's what Jesus' followers told the owners of the colt. They were permitted to take it when they gave these words. What about us? What in our lives does the Lord need to use? Is it our talent, treasure, or time? Is it our family, friends, or future? What in our lives is hardest for us to relinquish to the Lordship of Jesus? Is it some secret place in our hearts where we have let sin take root? Is it some cherished goal? Is it some lazy habit, personal possession, or cherished accomplishment? Like the owner of this colt, the Lord relays his message: "The Master needs it." So will we release our grip and let him have it? If he can let go of heaven for us, then why would we cling to our temporal toys and block his path to the throne of our hearts?

TODAY'S PRAYER

O God, the loving Almighty, I ask for help in opening every area of my heart, every avenue in my life, to your Son. I want him to be Lord of all of me. In the name of the Lord Jesus I pray. Amen.

CONTEXT: MARK 11:1-11

RELATED PASSAGES: 2 CORINTHIANS 5:21; 2 CORINTHIANS 8:9; PHILIPPIANS 2:5-11

Day 221

WORSHIP AND HONOR IN THE REAL WORLD

MARK 11:7-8

The followers brought the donkey to Jesus. They put their coats on it, and Jesus sat on it. Many people spread their coats on the road for Jesus. Others cut branches in the fields and spread the branches on the road.

KEY THOUGHT

While an unknown owner supplied the young donkey on which Jesus rode, many in the crowd offered their coats to welcome and honor Jesus as he came into town. Others spread branches showing their respect for the Christ. It is a great moment of worship, celebration, and joy. But the real test of the crowd's loyalty will come in the days that lie ahead. Like Christians who celebrate God's grace, Jesus' love, and the Spirit's power on Sunday, the real heart of worship will not be found in the crowds who share the same faith and look on Jesus with joyous admiration. No, the real test will come in the dark hours of trial when our faith is confronted by another, more hostile, crowd. Should we share in the joy of Jesus' glory with those who share our faith? Absolutely! However, we must realize the real test of that faith and the authenticity of our worship will be determined by what we do when confronted by the darkness and the hostile crowd!

TODAY'S PRAYER

O LORD God Almighty, may my life during the week match my worship words on Sunday. Help me in my heart to realize that what I do each day is an integral part of my worship. I want to honor you with my heart, soul, mind, and strength every day of my life. In Jesus' name I pray. Amen.

CONTEXT: MARK 11:1-11

RELATED PASSAGES: ROMANS 12:1-2; HEBREWS 13:11-16; ISAIAH 6:1-8

Day 222

CENTER OF THE PROCESSION

MARK 11:9-10

Some of them were walking ahead of Jesus. Others were walking behind him. Everyone shouted, "'Praise Him!' 'Welcome! God bless the one who comes in the name of the Lord!' God bless the kingdom of our father David. That kingdom is coming! Praise to God in heaven!"

KEY THOUGHT

In the center of all of our worship we will find Jesus. He is God who has come among us to reveal the Father's grace and truth. He is the one who pours out the Spirit who fills us when we praise. His sacrifice and victory over death are at the center of our forgiveness and victorious future. Jesus, Christ our Lord, is the center.

TODAY'S PRAYER

O Father, thank you for your grace lavished on me through your Son. Thank you for revealing yourself so fully, so intimately, so humanly, in Jesus. Open my eyes and help me see what I need to do to have your Son be the center of my life. In the name of Jesus Christ I pray. Amen.

CONTEXT: MARK 11:1-11

RELATED PASSAGES: COLOSSIANS 1:15-23; COLOSSIANS 2:6-10; COLOSSIANS 3:16-17

Day 223

LOOKING OVER JERUSALEM

MARK 11:11

Jesus entered Jerusalem and went to the Temple. He looked at everything in the Temple area, but it was already late. So he went to Bethany with the twelve apostles.

KEY THOUGHT

Jerusalem! The Temple! These places formed the center of Israel's religion during Jesus' day. These were the places where Jesus was rejected. In a bittersweet moment of joy and ominous anticipation, Jesus looked over these cherished places of God's chosen people. Little did the people of Jerusalem understand that a mere forty years later, these cherished places would be destroyed. Even less did they realize that this Jesus, the one whom the powerbrokers of Jerusalem tried to destroy, would one day return in glory. This Jesus that Jerusalem rejected is the Son of David. He is God's Messiah, Lord, and King. One day he will return in glory, honor, and power, but not on this late afternoon as he visited Jerusalem. No, Jesus simply turned and went out to Bethany with his twelve closest followers.

TODAY'S PRAYER

O Father, please keep my heart from finding its security in a place—a city, country, or church building. May I find my refuge in you. May I find my hope in your Son. May I find my source of strength in your Spirit. As precious as some places are to me, I know that my only lasting place and lasting peace is in you. In Jesus' name I pray. Amen.

CONTEXT: MARK 11:1-11

RELATED PASSAGES: JEREMIAH 7:1-11; HEBREWS 11:13-16; HEBREWS 13:14

Day 224

THE FIG TREE

MARK 11:12-14

The next day, Jesus was leaving Bethany. He was hungry. He saw a fig tree with leaves. So he went to the tree to see if it had any figs growing on it. But he found no figs on the tree. There were only leaves, because it was not the right time for figs to grow. So Jesus said to the tree, "People will never eat fruit from you again." His followers heard him say this.

KEY THOUGHT

What? What in the world is this about? Yeah, that's most people's response to this story. Jesus uses his miraculous powers to curse the fig tree. Our human viewpoint looks on this as capricious and unfair. It's not even the season for figs and yet Jesus curses the fig tree because it is fruitless. Jesus wants to teach his closest followers something very important. He has come and invested his life in them, in his people, and in the religious structures of his time. But has it produced fruit? Have people been changed? Has the nation been moved toward God? Has religion embraced him? No. Many are fruitless. So he will remove the sham facades of power and religious structure and look for a people who will produce fruit because of his presence among them.

TODAY'S PRAYER

O Father in heaven, I choose to honor Jesus and trust him to be my Savior. I believe he is the Christ, the Messiah your prophets promised would come. I want him to reign as Lord in my life. I open my life for the Holy Spirit to transform me, conforming me into the character of your Son and into a temple where you live. My prayer is that your holy fruit be formed in me. In Jesus' name I pray. Amen.

CONTEXT: MARK 11:12-25

RELATED PASSAGES: MATTHEW 7:20; JOHN 15:1-8; PHILIPPIANS 1:11

Day 225

No More Den of Thieves

Mark 11:15-17

Jesus went to Jerusalem and entered the Temple area. He began driving out the people who were buying and selling things there. He turned over the tables that belonged to those who were exchanging different kinds of money. And he turned over the benches of those who were selling doves. He refused to allow anyone to carry things through the Temple area. Then Jesus began teaching the people and said, "It is written in the Scriptures, 'My Temple will be called a house of prayer for all nations.' But you have changed it into a 'hiding place for thieves.'"

Key Thought

Jesus invades the Temple to restore it to its purpose. This was to be a place of prayer. This place was to be open to all the nations. This place wasn't about making a profit off people seeking God. While Jesus' actions were bold and shocking to those of his day, we have a tendency to let the distance in both time and culture soften the implications. If Jesus invades our hearts, our worship, our religious places and times, what sacred cows will he drive away? Are we open to other nations and cultures? Are we about being a place and people of prayer? How have we sold out our Savior and our worship of him to our over-commercialized culture? How have we let religious charlatans fleece God-seeking people? And since our bodies are God's temple, let's ask God to show us what it means for us and our lives!

Today's Prayer

O God, my heavenly Father, help me see my sacred cows and let Jesus drive them out of my life. Humble me gently as you lovingly remove the idols and vestiges of false religion that inhabit my heart. In Jesus' name I pray. Amen.

Context: Mark 11:12-25

Related Passages: John 2:13-22; Romans 12:1-2; Colossians 3:5

Day 226

FEAR OF THE CHALLENGER

MARK 11:18-19

When the leading priests and the teachers of the law heard what Jesus said, they began trying to find a way to kill him. They were afraid of him because all the people were amazed at his teaching. That night Jesus and his followers left the city.

KEY THOUGHT

We are brought to the great irony of the story that will continue to unfold: those who hate and want to murder Jesus are afraid of him. They won't believe, but they will fear. Are their fears well founded? If they are trying to preserve the status quo, then their fears are well founded. If they are choosing the preservation of their own religious understanding, then their fears are well founded. If they are trying to maintain the facade of self-determination and control, then their fears are well founded. They will not kill Jesus for being a nice guy, a friend to outcasts, a helper to the weak, and a lover of children. They will kill Jesus because he challenges every false thing they hold dear. What will we do with such a Jesus? Let's bring him close to transform us and not push him away in fear!

TODAY'S PRAYER

Almighty God and gracious Father, while I sometimes fear change in my life, your grace and mercy have taught me not to fear Jesus. However, dear Father, I do find in my heart areas of reluctance that I do not want to relinquish to his control. Please help me relinquish control of these areas of my life to your Son. Please use your Spirit to calm me as I learn to walk by faith in areas of my life where I have tried to maintain control. In Jesus' name I ask this. Amen.

CONTEXT: MARK 11:12-25

RELATED PASSAGES: ACTS 9:10-19; 2 TIMOTHY 1:7-8; 1 JOHN 4:16-18

Day 227

The Power of His Word

Mark 11:20-21

The next morning Jesus was walking with his followers. They saw the fig tree that he spoke to the day before. The tree was dry and dead, even the roots. Peter remembered the tree and said to Jesus, "Teacher, look! Yesterday, you told that fig tree to die. Now it is dry and dead!"

Key Thought

God spoke and the world was created. There is great power in the words of God! Jesus comes as God's presence among us. His words have great power. He speaks and the demons are cast out, the leprosy is healed, the storm is stilled, and what is fruitless is cursed and withered. What is the difference between fearing the words of Jesus and embracing them? The answer is in who we believe Jesus is and how much influence we let him have over our lives. Jesus' power to condemn is often forgotten in our desire to have a soft and winsome Savior to offer a hostile and lost world. However, the cross—the awful and hideous cost to God—is not only a symbol of grace, but also a demand for decision. The voice we hear when Jesus speaks will be largely determined by what we do with his words in our lives today. Which voice of Jesus will we hear?

Today's Prayer

O Father, thank you for the confidence I have in Jesus. I am confident that the Lord to whom I have yielded my life will keep and honor all that I have entrusted to his grace. I long to hear his voice of welcome and to see him face-to-face. In Jesus' name I pray. Amen.

Context: Mark 11:12-26

Related Passages: John 5:25-30; Matthew 28:31-46; Revelation 1:7

Day 228

BELIEVE IT!

MARK 11:22-23

*Jesus answered, "Have faith in God. The truth is, you can say to this mountain,
'Go, mountain, fall into the sea.' And if you have no doubts in your mind
and believe that what you say will happen, then God will do it for you."*

KEY THOUGHT

Jesus had done a spectacular nature miracle in withering the fig tree with his command (Mark 11:12-21). Jesus wants his closest followers to understand that they can do amazing things too, if they will truly believe. Bottom line: Jesus wants us to pursue his will without thought of limitations and without fear of asking too much. "Have faith in God!" our Lord tells us; "have no doubts in your heart." Let's do these things!

TODAY'S PRAYER

O Father, today I want to ask you for something that does not seem possible. I know this cannot be accomplished without your power and blessing. So I ask this of you in the name of Jesus my Lord . . . . (Please share with the Father your personal faith request.) Amen.

CONTEXT: MARK 11:12-26

RELATED PASSAGES: EPHESIANS 3:14-21; JOHN 14:12-14; JAMES 1:5-8

Day 229

GET RID OF THE GRUDGES

MARK 11:24-26

"So I tell you to ask for what you want in prayer. And if you believe that you have received those things, then they will be yours. When you are praying, and you remember that you are angry with another person about something, then forgive that person. Forgive them so that your Father in heaven will also forgive your sins."

KEY THOUGHT

God is lavish with his forgiveness! Aren't we glad? However, just as God is lavish with forgiveness, he is also adamant about our forgiving others. What Jesus says should chill us to our soul. We will be forgiven the way we forgive others. (See also Matthew 6:14-15 to have this point reinforced!) Holding grudges blocks the Lord's graciousness from our lives. Let's be children of our Father—lavish in forgiveness, quick to love, and slow to condemn.

TODAY'S PRAYER

O Father, I trust in your forgiveness and grace. I ask that your Spirit work in my heart to release any grudges that I may have against anyone. I also ask that the Holy Spirit will help me to forgive those against whom I have held grudges. Please help me view them in a new and more loving light. In Jesus' name I pray and ask for this help to be more like you. Amen.

CONTEXT: MARK 11:12-26

RELATED PASSAGES: MATTHEW 6:14-15; EPHESIANS 4:30-32; NUMBERS 14:18

Day 230

BY WHOSE AUTHORITY?

MARK 11:27-28

*Jesus and his followers went again to Jerusalem. Jesus was walking in
the Temple area. The leading priests, the teachers of the law, and the
older Jewish leaders came to him. They said, "Tell us! What authority
do you have to do these things? Who gave you this authority?"*

KEY THOUGHT

The apparent religious leaders demanded Jesus, the true spiritual leader,
to answer their questions about his authority. Before Jesus' crucifixion and
resurrection, this was a natural thing to have happen. The Temple and all
things religious were their domains. They were the respected authorities.
Living on this side of Jesus' crucifixion and resurrection, their challenge of
his authority seems silly. How dare they challenge the one who has the power
over life and death? How dare they doubt the religious authority of the one
for whom God demonstrated his approval and love? They have not seen or
heard of Jesus' resurrection yet, but we have. So the real question for you and
me today is this: "On which side of the cross and resurrection do I view Jesus?
Do I recognize that he has authority to work his will in my life?" Have you
responded to that authority with appreciation, admiration, and obedience?

TODAY'S PRAYER

*O Father, I believe that Jesus died and rose again. I believe he has
the authority over life and death. Help me base my choices on that
conviction and live for him. In Jesus' name I ask this. Amen.*

CONTEXT: MARK 11:27-33

RELATED PASSAGES: ACTS 2:36-39; ROMANS 1:2-4; MATTHEW 28:18

Day 231

HEAVENLY OR HUMAN?

MARK 11:29-30

Jesus answered, "I will ask you a question. You answer my question. Then I will tell you whose authority I use to do these things. Tell me: When John baptized people, did his authority come from God or was it only from other people? Answer me."

KEY THOUGHT

Jesus didn't try to defend his authority. It would be amply demonstrated in his crucifixion and resurrection that would follow. In fact, he had already demonstrated it throughout his ministry by casting out demons, healing diseases, and speaking with the power and wisdom of God himself. If his opponents refused to believe, there was nothing he could do or say to change that . . . except to die and to be raised again. Still, he didn't back down at their questions about authority. Rather than argue with them, he challenged them with a question. His question demonstrated what they refused to believe. When they couldn't answer him, they were left with only the bitterest of plans: they must kill him! They couldn't accomplish their mission as the resurrection of Jesus shows. Yet still today, many want to dismiss the authority of Jesus without realizing that they will one day have to answer to him.

TODAY'S PRAYER

Father, I cannot tell you how comforting it is to know that the one to whom you have given authority over my life is also the one who died to save it. Thank you for grace. Thank you for Jesus. Thank you for placing all authority in him. In Jesus' name, and to his glory as Lord, I offer this prayer. Amen.

CONTEXT: MARK 11:27-33

RELATED PASSAGES: MATTHEW 8:5-10, 13; 2 PETER 1:3-4; REVELATION 5:9-14

Day 232

NO WAY!

MARK 11:31-33

These Jewish leaders talked about Jesus' question. They said to each other, "If we answer, 'John's baptism was from God,' then he will say, 'Then why didn't you believe John?' But we can't say that John's baptism was from someone else." (These leaders were afraid of the people, because the people believed that John was a prophet.)

So the leaders answered Jesus, "We don't know the answer."

Jesus said, "Then I will not tell you who gave me the authority to do these things."

KEY THOUGHT

Jesus refused to give the Jewish religious leaders an answer because they wouldn't answer him. In fact, they weren't looking for the truth; they just wanted to trap Jesus in his words. But they failed, just as they failed at stopping his teaching by killing him and failed at stopping his early followers by persecuting his church. Jesus is *the* authority. They couldn't stop him anymore than they could stop the world from turning. There is no real answer to life's problems for those who look at Jesus and his story simply for ammunition to discredit him. Like the opponents of Jesus of old, opponents of Jesus today are not given an answer because they aren't seeking one. We need to ask ourselves, what—or better yet, who—is the authority in our lives?

TODAY'S PRAYER

Father, please help me find my answers in Jesus. I confess that my own wisdom is flawed. Without your help, your guidance, and your grace I would not find your wisdom, a wisdom that the world may deem foolish but that gives me life. In Jesus' name I pray. Amen.

CONTEXT: MARK 11:27-33

RELATED PASSAGES: 1 CORINTHIANS 1:18-28; 1 PETER 3:13-16; JOHN 14:6-7

Day 233

THROUGH STORIES

MARK 12:1

Jesus used stories to teach the people.

He said . . .

KEY THOUGHT

Jesus knew the power of special stories—often called parables. He used them frequently to convey deep messages that he wanted his followers to remember. These stories would lodge in Jesus' listeners' minds. His lessons would be recalled as they saw those images again in everyday lives. Do not underestimate the importance of stories to convey the truth of God. Not only did Jesus use them, but much of the Bible contains them. Let's ask God to help us hear his voice in the stories of Jesus and the stories of the Bible. Let's thank God for giving so much of his message in stories so that we can easily remember them and put them to use in everyday life.

TODAY'S PRAYER

O Father, thank you for the variety of ways you have communicated your message to us. While I know that Jesus is your ultimate message, I also know that you spoke through prophetic oracles, through laws, through wisdom messages, through the Psalms, and through your actions in history interpreted by your messengers. Please guide me as I open your Word and seek your will, especially in the stories of your men and women of faith. Thank you for speaking to us, your human children, in so many ways. In Jesus' name I thank you. Amen.

CONTEXT: MARK 12:1-12

RELATED PASSAGES: MARK 4:2; JOHN 1:1-4; HEBREWS 1:1-3

Day 234

BEATING THE SERVANT

MARK 12:1-3
Jesus used stories to teach the people.

He said, "A man planted a vineyard. He put a wall around the field and dug a hole for a winepress. Then he built a tower. He leased the land to some farmers and left for a trip.

"Later, it was time for the grapes to be picked. So the man sent a servant to the farmers to get his share of the grapes. But the farmers grabbed the servant and beat him. They sent him away with nothing."

KEY THOUGHT
The symbols in this story were familiar for Jesus' audience. The vineyard was recognized as the nation of Israel, God's chosen people. The tenants were the leaders of God's people. They were given a beautiful vineyard to work, but soon forgot it belonged to God, and so they abused the vineyard owner's servants. These servants were recognized from the Old Testament as God's messengers, the prophets. During bad times, the prophets came with God's message and were abused, mistreated, and even killed. While this story had a clear historical connection, it is also a powerful reminder for us. We easily begin to view God's Kingdom, people, and gifts as our own. We forget that they are all "on loan" from God and to be used for him, his purposes, and his glory. They are not ours by right, but by grace. So we must use these blessings to honor God from whom they have come.

TODAY'S PRAYER
O Father, you have blessed me so incredibly. My physical blessings are wonderful. My spiritual blessings in Christ are beyond description. I thank you in Jesus' name. Amen.

CONTEXT: MARK 12:1-12

RELATED PASSAGES: 2 KINGS 9:7; JEREMIAH 35:15; 1 CORINTHIANS 4:7

Day 235

FINALLY THE SON

MARK 12:4-6

*"Then the man sent another servant to the farmers. They hit this servant
on the head, showing no respect for him. So the man sent another servant.
The farmers killed this servant. The man sent many other servants to
the farmers. The farmers beat some of them and killed the others.*

*"The man had only one person left to send to the farmers. It was his son. He loved
his son, but he decided to send him. He said, 'The farmers will respect my son.'"*

KEY THOUGHT

As this story of Jesus unfolds, we begin to get the picture. God (the owner
of the vineyard) had sent servant after servant (all God's prophets) and they
had been abused, battered, and even killed. So surely, if the owner (God)
sent his dearly loved son (Jesus), then he would be respected and loved by
the farmers. However, we know the way this story ends. Those who want to
maintain control of the vineyard kill the son. Suddenly this story of Jesus is
filled with emotion and with warning. For those of us who know the end of
the story, we can only stand in awe of the love of God and fall on our knees
aghast at the short-sighted brutality of petty religious leaders who want to
control the vineyard more than they want to welcome God's Son.

TODAY'S PRAYER

*O Father, my heart breaks at the thought of your gift of love being so
rejected and abused. Forgive me for my petty and selfish ways, and use
me to share the sacrifice of your Son to touch hearts of those around me
with your grace. In Jesus' name and for his glory I pray. Amen.*

CONTEXT: MARK 12:1-12

RELATED PASSAGES: JOHN 3:16-17; MARK 8:31; MARK 12:10

Day 236

KILLING THE SON

MARK 12:7-8

"But the farmers said to each other, 'This is the owner's son, and this vineyard will be his. If we kill him, it will be ours.' So they took the son, threw him out of the vineyard, and killed him."

KEY THOUGHT

"We want it for ourselves!" That's in essence what the farmers in this vineyard parable were saying. It's also what so many others—including most of us at one time or another—have said. We don't want to have to live by God's standards, God's plans, and God's values. We want the blessings of God for ourselves while doing things the way we want to do them. But God sent his Son so we could be his children. Our place in God's family depends upon what we do with the Son—whether we welcome him and follow him, or whether we want to live life our own way and push him out of our lives.

TODAY'S PRAYER

Thank you, Father, for sending your Son to save me. It gives me great pain to see how he was rejected and abused. I pray that I will always welcome him as the Lord of my heart and of my actions. In Jesus' name I thank you and ask for your grace. Amen.

CONTEXT: MARK 12:1-12

RELATED PASSAGES: HEBREWS 13:10-14; JOHN 19:1-7; JOHN 3:36

Day 237

KILLING THE KILLERS

MARK 12:9

"So what will the man who owns the vineyard do? He will go and kill those farmers. Then he will lease the land to others."

KEY THOUGHT

There are consequences for rejecting the Son of God. In this case, the leaders who put the Son to death would find themselves absolutely powerless and defeated. Some of them would die when Jesus' prediction of destruction came true some forty years later. Others would later realize their awful mistake and turn their lives around to follow him. However, we need to realize that those who reject the Son of God today also face dire consequences. While God is supremely gracious, the consequences of rejecting that grace offered to us in Jesus are dire.

TODAY'S PRAYER

Father, please use me to reach out to those who have rejected your Son. I know that you want all people to come to repentance and to receive your grace. Use me as an instrument of your mercy to help those around me come to know your Son as their Lord and Savior. In Jesus' name I pray. Amen.

CONTEXT: MARK 12:1-12

RELATED PASSAGES: JOHN 5:25-29; 1 JOHN 5:11-12; JOHN 3:16-17

Day 238

MARVELOUS DOINGS OF THE LORD

MARK 12:10-11

"Surely you have read this in the Scriptures: 'The stone that the builders refused to accept became the cornerstone. The Lord did this, and it is wonderful to us.'"

KEY THOUGHT

Jesus finishes his story by quoting a Scripture from the Old Testament that will become one of his early followers' favorite passages. The point of the quotation is simple: God can turn things around and do great things with what looks like rejection and disaster. This is precisely what God does. God raised his Son Jesus from the dead and vindicated his life, his ministry, and his teachings. What begins horribly—the Son's being murdered and his body desecrated outside the city—ends in something marvelous: Jesus is raised and death is defeated. While we hate the rejection, the wounds, the humiliation, and the death that Jesus endured, God has made this precious to us. It is marvelous grace.

TODAY'S PRAYER

My Father in heaven, the only one adequate response that I can give to all that you have given me through your Son is thank you! However, dear Lord, I want that "thank you" to be more than words; I want to say thank you with all of my being, showing my appreciation by the way that I live. In Jesus' name and for his glory I pray. Amen.

CONTEXT: MARK 12:1-12

RELATED PASSAGES: 2 CORINTHIANS 9:15; ACTS 2:32-36; 1 PETER 2:4-10

Day 239

Striking the Mark

Mark 12:12

When these Jewish leaders heard this story, they knew it was about them. They wanted to find a way to arrest Jesus, but they were afraid of what the crowd would do. So they left him and went away.

Key Thought

Sadly, rather than repenting when they heard Jesus' story about the vineyard owner's son, the leaders resolved more intently to arrest and kill him. Their problem, however, was that Jesus was incredibly well liked by the people. So they left Jesus and went away. How sad! Salvation, redemption, love, grace, and power were within their grasp and they turned away. Unfortunately many people do the same thing today.

Today's Prayer

God, my Abba Father, I never want to turn away from Jesus. Please help me never to move away from him because I don't want to change my lifestyle, my basic beliefs, or my comforts to follow him. Give me a heart that seeks after you and your truth no matter the costs. In Jesus' name I pray. Amen.

Context: Mark 12:1-12

Related Passages: John 6:66-67; Mark 11:18; John 11:45-52

Day 240

BAITING ANOTHER TRAP?

MARK 12:13

Later, the Jewish leaders sent some Pharisees and some men from the group called Herodians to Jesus. They wanted to catch him saying something wrong.

KEY THOUGHT

Hatred can sometimes turn rivals into allies. The Pharisees normally didn't get along with supporters of Herod. In fact, they distrusted them and believed them to be traitors to God, the Jewish people, and the Law. Their hatred of Jesus was so great that they compromised their principles and partnered with people they couldn't stand. Let's pray that we never find ourselves doing such a thing. When we start making allies out of those who compromise and trade away what we hold dear, the problem does not lie with someone else, but within us.

TODAY'S PRAYER

O God, please help me see my own moral failings, character defects, and compromises of principle more clearly. Give me courage to stand for holiness, especially in those situations when it seems to be the most difficult and painful choice. In Jesus' name I pray. Amen.

CONTEXT: MARK 12:13-17

RELATED PASSAGES: MARK 3:1-6; PROVERBS 25:26; 1 CORINTHIANS 15:33

Day 241

SEEING RIGHT THROUGH THEIR WAYS

MARK 12:14-15

They went to Jesus and said, "Teacher, we know that you are an honest man. You are not afraid of what others think about you. All people are the same to you. And you teach the truth about God's way. Tell us, is it right to pay taxes to Caesar? Should we pay them or not?"

But Jesus knew that these men were really trying to trick him. He said, "Why are you trying to catch me saying something wrong? Bring me a silver coin. Let me see it."

KEY THOUGHT

Jesus saw through the scheme behind the question of the Pharisees and supporters of Herod. He knew their question wasn't an honest one. They weren't looking for God's answer to their question; they were looking for a way to trick Jesus. The followers of Herod would have demanded that people pay the tax to keep the Romans appeased. The Pharisees deeply resented having to pay tax to anyone, especially the Romans. By teaming up, they thought they had Jesus trapped into an answer that would alienate one side or the other. Instead, Jesus confronted them both with the reality of their deception, and then challenged them with the truth he is about to share with them.

TODAY'S PRAYER

O Father, please give me discernment so that I can recognize the intent of people's words when they speak to me. I want to respond to people fairly and honestly. Yet, dear Father, I don't want to get bogged down in meaningless and spiteful arguments about words. Give me wisdom in the use of words and in my ability to hear the true messages that are spoken to me. In Jesus' name I ask this. Amen.

CONTEXT: MARK 12:13-17

RELATED PASSAGES: ROMANS 13:1-7; 1 PETER 2:14-18; PSALM 120:2

Day 242

Seeing Through Hypocrisy

Mark 12:15-16

But Jesus knew that these men were really trying to trick him. He said, "Why are you trying to catch me saying something wrong? Bring me a silver coin. Let me see it." They gave Jesus a coin and he asked, "Whose picture is on the coin? And whose name is written on it?"

They answered, "It is Caesar's picture and Caesar's name."

Key Thought

Jesus' opponents could not successfully play games or trick him. He knew their hearts. He knew what was inside people. He still does! Rather than trying to play games with Jesus and pretend we are something we are not, why not be honest? When we are weak, let's be honest about our weakness and vulnerability. When we are weary, let's go to him for rest. When we are grief-stricken, let's go to him for comfort. When we are confused, let's be honest about our confusion and ask for his wisdom and discernment. When we are angry, let's confess our anger and its source to him. Jesus knows us. Let's be honest and not try to pretend that we are something we are not. Our games may not be based upon the same kind of deceit that his opponents used to try to trick him, but deceit, dishonesty, and pretension are still tools Satan uses to keep our hearts away from the Savior.

Today's Prayer

O God, even though I believe you know me completely, I still sometimes fear bringing you the darker sides of my personality and the most deeply wounded parts of my heart. Please cure me of my pretension and deliver me from deception. I want to be honest as well as reverent in your presence, dear God, my Abba Father. In Jesus' name I pray. Amen.

Context: Mark 12:13-17

Related Passages: Proverbs 15:4; Hebrews 2:14-18; Genesis 3:8-10

Day 243

GIVE GOD WHAT IS HIS

MARK 12:17

Then Jesus said to them, "Give to Caesar what belongs to Caesar, and give to God what belongs to God." The men were amazed at what Jesus said.

KEY THOUGHT

Jesus' answer was as profound as it was simple. Jesus refused to get caught in a debate with the Pharisees and Herodians, but instead placed the responsibility on each of us to decide what is "Caesar's" and what is God's. Jesus spoke with a convicting simplicity that challenged men and women to take responsibility for honoring God, for living responsibly with others, and for honoring our earthly citizenship in holy and honorable ways. Jesus' words still speak to us. Let's each ask ourselves what Jesus' words are challenging us to do!

TODAY'S PRAYER

O Father, the responsibilities of my earthly citizenship and my heavenly one sometimes pull me in different directions. Help me know what is "Caesar's"! I want to live honorably in my earthly homeland and show myself a good citizen. But I never want to do anything that would compromise my clear allegiance to you. Give me wisdom as I seek to live as an example of your grace and your holy character to those around me. In Jesus' name I ask this. Amen.

CONTEXT: MARK 12:13-17

RELATED PASSAGES: PHILIPPIANS 3:20-21; HEBREWS 13:14; 1 PETER 2:11-14

Day 244

SAD YOU SEE!

MARK 12:18

*Then some Sadducees came to Jesus. (Sadducees believe that no
one will rise from death.) They asked him a question . . . .*

KEY THOUGHT

This period of Jesus' ministry is filled with the carefully crafted questions
of his enemies. Pharisees and Sadducees were not good friends normally.
They each had different political, religious, and social agendas. However,
Jesus' popularity with the common people, his willingness to speak the truth
of God boldly, and his acceptance of the titles of Son of God, Son of David,
and King of the Jews as he entered Jerusalem scared them to death. They
were going to do their best to trap him with their questions. The Sadducees
would have very deep differences with Jesus because they did not believe in
angels or the resurrection. As we read the following verses, Jesus will not use
polite or politically correct speech as he rebukes their wrong-headed denial
of the resurrection. Jesus' greatest exclamation mark on the truth of the
resurrection, however, will be his own empty tomb and his appearances to his
disciples after his death and resurrection.

TODAY'S PRAYER

*Father in heaven, you are the eternal God. From everlasting to everlasting you
have been, will be, and are God. While I cannot completely fathom this truth, dear
Father, I do trust it with all my heart. Thank you for such a great hope. May I
never compromise my faith in this glorious truth. In Jesus' name I pray. Amen.*

CONTEXT: MARK 12:18-27

RELATED PASSAGES: COLOSSIANS 3:1-4; 1 THESSALONIANS 4:15-18;
1 CORINTHIANS 15:12-58

Day 245

YOU JUST DON'T KNOW!

MARK 12:19-24

"Teacher, Moses wrote that if a married man dies and had no children, his brother must marry the woman. Then they will have children for the dead brother. There were seven brothers. The first brother married but died. He had no children. So the second brother married the woman. But he also died and had no children. The same thing happened with the third brother. All seven brothers married the woman and died. None of the brothers had any children with her. And she was the last to die. But all seven brothers had married her. So at the time when people rise from death, whose wife will she be?"

Jesus answered, "How could you be so wrong? It's because you don't know what the Scriptures say. And you don't know anything about God's power."

KEY THOUGHT

Isn't it refreshing to hear Jesus tell the simple truth to these manipulative schemers? "How could you be so wrong? It's because you don't know what the Scriptures say. And you don't know anything about God's power." Rather than sitting in judgment over God's Word, shouldn't we look for ways to obey it? Even more, when someone pontificates on a subject trying to sound religious and yet espouses something counter to biblical truth, shouldn't we gently remind them of Jesus' warning? Could it be that we're a little too infatuated with our opinions and our traditions, but not familiar enough with God's truth?

TODAY'S PRAYER

O Father, forgive me when I live with an inflated view of my own understanding of your Word and find ways to rationalize away the sharp edges of your truth. Gently humble me and lead me to a deeper understanding and appreciation for your will. In the name of the Lord Jesus I pray. Amen.

CONTEXT: MARK 12:18-27

RELATED PASSAGES: 1 TIMOTHY 6:2-5; 2 TIMOTHY 3:1-5; ROMANS 16:19

ANGELS IN HEAVEN!

MARK 12:25
"When people rise from death, there will be no marriage. People will not be married to each other. All people will be like angels in heaven."

KEY THOUGHT

With so much fascination about angels over the last couple of decades, this promise should simply astound us. Our being, our relationships, and our lives will be brought to a higher level of existence after the resurrection. Glory awaits those who belong to Christ. Joy is our future. Victory is our destiny. Transformation into perfection lies ahead. Our eyes will behold our Savior and we will be like the angels. Praise God for such a future. Hallelujah!

TODAY'S PRAYER

O Father, give my heart wings to soar on the faith of such wonderful words. Make them more than words to me. Help me believe and embrace my future with you with great and triumphant joy. In Jesus' name I pray. Amen.

CONTEXT: MARK 12:18-27

RELATED PASSAGES: ROMANS 8:15-19; ROMANS 5:3-5;
1 CORINTHIANS 15:43-44

Day 247

GOD OF THE LIVING

MARK 12:26-27

All people will be like angels in heaven. Surely you have read what God said about people rising from death. In the book where Moses wrote about the burning bush, it says that God told Moses this: 'I am the God of Abraham, the God of Isaac, and the God of Jacob.' So they were not still dead, because he is the God only of living people. You Sadducees are so wrong!"

KEY THOUGHT

Jesus uses skill, wit, and cunning to argue with the religious leaders using their own form of logic. "God is the God of the living," Jesus asserts. So if God is the God of Abraham, Isaac, and Jacob (a truth that these people professed every day), Jesus is saying then there has to be a resurrection. Because God is eternal, we will continue to exist because of him. He is God of the living. Death does not have control over us any longer because our resurrection awaits us.

TODAY'S PRAYER

Father, thank you for ensuring that life is eternal and is found in you. In Jesus' name I pray to you, O eternal Father. Amen.

CONTEXT: MARK 12:18-27

RELATED PASSAGES: REVELATION 1:8; 22:13; 1 JOHN 3:1-2; 2 PETER 3:8-9

Day 248

AN HONEST SEEKER

MARK 12:28

One of the teachers of the law came to Jesus. He heard Jesus arguing with the Sadducees and the Pharisees. He saw that Jesus gave good answers to their questions. So he asked him, "Which of the commands is the most important?"

KEY THOUGHT

An honest seeker overhears all the questions intended to trap Jesus and is impressed with Jesus' answers. He asks an honest question: "Which of the commands is the most important?" When Scripture says something is most important, we should pay attention! When Jesus says it, we had better offer obedience! Don't you think we would be better served in our Christian communities if we stopped the arguments over all the peripheral things that divide us and focused on the things that Scripture says are most important? So let's join this teacher each day as we approach Scripture and ask, "O Lord, what is most important?" Then let's commit to be obedient to what the Lord reveals to us!

TODAY'S PRAYER

Father in heaven, I do love you. Help me show that love through a life of obedience that is focused on the things that you value as most important! In Jesus' name I pray. Amen.

CONTEXT: MARK 12:28-34

RELATED PASSAGES: 1 CORINTHIANS 15:1-4; 1 CORINTHIANS 13:13; DEUTERONOMY 6:4-9

Day 249

LOVE THE LORD

MARK 12:29-30

Jesus answered, "The most important command is this: 'People of Israel, listen! The Lord our God is the only Lord. Love the Lord your God with all your heart, all your soul, all your mind, and all your strength.'"

KEY THOUGHT

The essence of our response of faith is pretty straightforward. Love God. It can be said in a number of different ways. Love God above all things. Love God with all that you are. Love God with all that you dream to become. Love God for as long as you have life. What's most important for us? Loving God!

TODAY'S PRAYER

O Father, may my every word, my every action, my every thought, and my every emotion be brought under your influence and offered to your glory. While I know such surrender will always be a life-long battle, I do pray that you know that this is what I want to do. In Jesus' name I pray. Amen.

CONTEXT: MARK 12:28-34

RELATED PASSAGES: EXODUS 20:2-6; ROMANS 12:1-2; PSALM 31:23

Day 250

LOVE YOUR NEIGHBOR

MARK 12:31

"The second most important command is this: 'Love your neighbor the same as you love yourself.' These two commands are the most important."

KEY THOUGHT

The second great commandment also deals with love. This time, however, Jesus focuses our attention on our love for all other people—our neighbors. In giving these two commandments—love God and love other people as we love ourselves—Jesus has summed up the heart of the Ten Commandments (Exodus 20), God's blueprint for morality. The first four commandments focus on honoring God. The remaining six focus upon treating our neighbors fairly. However, Jesus takes the Ten Commandments a step deeper and makes them simpler to remember. More than honoring God and treating others honorably, we are called to love them. Our motivation and passion are suddenly at issue and not just our behavior. God made us for relationship with him and with others. Our relationships are to all be marked by love.

TODAY'S PRAYER

Father in Heaven, I do love you and I want that love to be shown through all that I am. I confess, dear God, that loving my neighbor can be much harder than loving you—of course I also know that I can't really love you without loving my neighbor. Please fill my heart with your love as I seek to love my neighbors, both those I like and those I don't. In Jesus' name I pray. Amen.

CONTEXT: MARK 12:28-34

RELATED PASSAGES: EXODUS 20:2-17; LUKE 6:27; ROMANS 5:5

Day 251

I Agree!

Mark 12:32-33

The man answered, "That was a good answer, Teacher. You are right in saying that God is the only Lord and that there is no other God. And you must love God with all your heart, all your mind, and all your strength. And you must love others the same as you love yourself. These commands are more important than all the animals and sacrifices we offer to God."

Key Thought

The man's compliment to Jesus is good. He is close to the kingdom of God. Yet it's not what we think about Jesus, but our obedience to his teachings that is the issue. Jesus' wants us to honor the will of God by obeying what he says, not just to approve and admire what he says. While I hope and trust that everyone who reads this appreciates, agrees, and applauds the teaching of Jesus, it is not our place to sit in judgment on the merit of Jesus' teaching. Instead, you and I are called to obey him as our Lord, and thus honor the Father who sent him.

Today's Prayer

O Father, may my search for truth never end with just admiration for the teachings your Son gave to us. Help me in my resolve not only to know the truth, but also to live it. In the name of the Lord Jesus I pray. Amen.

Context: Mark 12:28-34

Related Passages: Mark 3:33-35; Matthew 7:24-27; 2 Timothy 2:23-26

Day 252

NOT FAR FROM THE KINGDOM

MARK 12:34

Jesus saw that the man answered him wisely. So he said to him, "You are close to God's kingdom." And after that time, no one was brave enough to ask Jesus any more questions.

KEY THOUGHT

Despite the hostile environment in which Jesus faced the tough questions put to him, he appreciated the honest, seeking heart of this expert in the Jewish law. In an atmosphere where most were trying to trap him, Jesus still had time to offer a great compliment to this truth-seeker. While many of Jesus' questioners left embarrassed and afraid to ask him any more questions, this questioner left with an affirmation. Jesus is always happy to receive us with our honest questions. However, as we honestly seek to understand his will, we must be certain that we are living in obedience to that will. As we seek to obey our Lord, our hearts are opened to understand his instruction so that his will becomes clearer.

TODAY'S PRAYER

Gracious Heavenly Father, thank you for sending Jesus to share with us and to show us your truth. Be with me and grant me wisdom as I seek to live for you. In Jesus' name I pray. Amen.

CONTEXT: MARK 12:28-34

RELATED PASSAGES: JOHN 8:31-32; ROMANS 12:1-2; JOHN 14:23

Day 253

DAVID'S LORD?

MARK 12:35-37

Jesus was teaching in the Temple area. He asked, "Why do the teachers of the law say that the Christ is the son of David? With the help of the Holy Spirit, David himself says, 'The Lord God said to my Lord: Sit by me at my right side, and I will put your enemies under your control.' David himself calls the Christ 'Lord.' So how can the Christ be David's son?" Many people listened to Jesus and were very pleased.

KEY THOUGHT

The religious scholars of the day liked to play little games with each other to test the Bible knowledge of one another. This ancient version of "stump the Rabbi" was sometimes done with a good spirit. Other times, like those shown in the preceding verses, the questions were offered from a bitter spirit with no intention of getting to the truth. Jesus' opponents were trying to belittle him and make him look silly, ignorant, and blasphemous. Not only were they incapable of stumping Jesus with their questions, they were left embarrassed by Jesus' answers. So Jesus turns the tables around on them and asks a question that lies at the heart of the issue: is he really the Messiah, the descendant of David, and their Lord? While they could not catch Jesus with a mistake or a bad answer to their questions, Jesus completely stumped them with his. The clear implication in the process was this: Jesus is master of the Scriptures because he is not only a great teacher, he is also the Messiah, Son of David, and Lord.

TODAY'S PRAYER

Father in heaven, I find Jesus' use of the Rabbi's own methods fascinating. I love the way Jesus successfully answered every one of their questions, and then turns things around and asks them a question they cannot answer. I believe that Jesus teaches, demonstrates, and embodies your truth. Help me as I seek to live that truth. In Jesus' name I ask for this grace. Amen.

CONTEXT: MARK 12:35-44

RELATED PASSAGES: MARK 1:22; MARK 1:27; JOHN 6:59-69

Day 254

LOVING THE LIMELIGHT

MARK 12:38-39

Jesus continued teaching. He said, "Be careful of the teachers of the law. They like to walk around wearing clothes that look important. And they love for people to show respect to them in the marketplaces. They love to have the most important seats in the synagogues and the places of honor at banquets."

KEY THOUGHT

Living as a follower of Christ and being a teacher of the Bible are not about prestige, position, or applause. Nearly every great teacher of God has had to endure ridicule, rejection, and possibly even suffering at one time or another. But it is easy to mix a sincere desire to teach with the desire for attention, attire, and adulation. This is not God's plan for a leader or teacher. This is not God's will for a faithful servant. In fact, these kinds of hypocrites are to be avoided and their example is to be rejected. Following Jesus is not about being "showy," but about being a servant.

TODAY'S PRAYER

Father, make my soul blanch at the thought of seizing the limelight for myself and parading around like I'm something important. Make me into a useful servant in your Kingdom who cares more about helping the broken than about being recognized by the crowd. In Jesus' name I pray. Amen.

CONTEXT: MARK 12:35-44

RELATED PASSAGES: 2 TIMOTHY 2:22-26; 2 TIMOTHY 4:1-6; MATTHEW 23:1-5

Day 255

CHEATS WHO ARE NOT CONCERNED

MARK 12:40

*"But they cheat widows and take their homes. Then they try to make themselves
look good by saying long prayers. God will punish them very much."*

KEY THOUGHT

In the previous verses, Jesus described the teachers of the law as wanting
places of honor and loving to be recognized as important. Here he emphasizes
that these "teachers" cheat widows and then act very pious by saying long
prayers in public to cover up their shallowness. Does this sound familiar? TV
preachers who constantly make pleas for money, some of whom have been
caught cheating their contributors , have given Christianity and Christian
ministry a bad name. Jesus makes it clear that not only will such charlatans
and cheats be held accountable, but they also will be punished more severely.
Why? Isn't all sin the same in the sight of God? No! People in position of trust
are held to higher standards. When they abuse the people of God for their
own gain, they face additional judgment from God!

TODAY'S PRAYER

*Father, bless those who sacrifice to lead your people. Protect them from harm.
Don't let Satan's attacks discourage and defeat them. On the other hand,
Father, please defeat and remove any who pretend to lead your people but
are using their position to enrich themselves or cheat those they claim to
serve. Please bring them to repentance, I pray, in Jesus' name. Amen.*

CONTEXT: MARK 12:35-44

RELATED PASSAGES: 1 PETER 5:1-4; JAMES 3:1; LUKE 12:42-48

Day 256

MORE THAN ALL THE REST

MARK 12:41-44

Jesus sat near the Temple collection box and watched as people put money into it. Many rich people put in a lot of money. Then a poor widow came and put in two very small copper coins, worth less than a penny.

Jesus called his followers to him and said, "This poor widow put in only two small coins. But the truth is, she gave more than all those rich people. They have plenty, and they gave only what they did not need. This woman is very poor, but she gave all she had. It was money she needed to live on."

KEY THOUGHT

Just as Jesus sees into the hearts of people and knows their situations, he also sees through their facades. That's why he will do the judging. On the surface, the rich who gave large amounts of money as their offerings appear to be making huge gifts. This can sometimes gain them notoriety and applause. However, the ones who give small amounts may actually be giving a lot more because it costs them so much more to give the smaller amount. God doesn't judge the gift by its size, but by the sincerity and generosity of the giver.

TODAY'S PRAYER

O Father in heaven, you have graciously given me everything in Jesus. Please help me as I seek to be a responsible and generous steward of the gracious gifts you have lavished upon me. I pray this in the name of Jesus, my Savior and Lord. Amen.

CONTEXT: MARK 12:35-44

RELATED PASSAGES: 2 CORINTHIANS 8:1-5; 2 CORINTHIANS 9:6-8; 1 TIMOTHY 6:17-19

Day 257

NO NOT ONE

MARK 13:1-2

*Jesus was leaving the Temple area. One of his followers said to him,
"Teacher, look how big those stones are! What beautiful buildings!"*

*Jesus said, "Do you see these great buildings? They will all be destroyed. Every
stone will be thrown down to the ground. Not one stone will be left on another."*

KEY THOUGHT

Many of us today cannot imagine the splendor, the majesty, and the size
of the Temple in Jesus' day. Herod the Great, a ruthless man but a master
builder, had rebuilt the Temple in Jerusalem. It was a holy place, believed to
be protected by God himself and symbolizing all that the Jewish people held
dear. Yet Jesus is clear: the Temple would be destroyed. These words would
seem treasonous as well as bewildering to those who heard them. Who would
destroy it? Why would God let it happen? But it does happen. The strength of
God's people has never been their wealth, their armies, or their buildings; it
has always been the faithfulness of their God and their faithfulness to him. In
a world of economic, religious, racial, and geopolitical tumult, we must invest
our lives in eternal things—spiritual things that cannot be destroyed.

TODAY'S PRAYER

*O Father, help me not glory in the externals of my life, but in you, the Father
and sustainer of all things. I pray for this grace in Jesus' name. Amen.*

CONTEXT: MARK 13:1-13

RELATED PASSAGES: ISAIAH 7:1-11; ISAIAH 31:1; JOHN 2:18-22

Day 258

WHEN?

MARK 13:3-4

Later, Jesus was sitting at a place on the Mount of Olives. He was alone with Peter, James, John, and Andrew. They could all see the Temple, and they said to Jesus, "Tell us when these things will happen. And what will show us it is time for them to happen?"

KEY THOUGHT

We like the "What?" and "When?" questions, don't we? We want to be in the know. So naturally the closest followers of Jesus want to know when this great disaster is going to take place. It is not easy to take the words of anyone, even the Lord of the universe, at face value. Yet Jesus says it, and they are challenged to believe it. We need to ask ourselves which of the biblical promises (including those with dire consequences) we have trouble trusting to be true. We should share those doubts, concerns, and worries with the Lord.

TODAY'S PRAYER

O LORD God Almighty, I trust you in many areas of my life. Yet I confess that there are some things that are difficult for me to release fully to you and take you at your word. I seek to increase my trust in your promises even when I don't have answers to my "What?" and "When?" questions. In Jesus' authoritative name I pray. Amen.

CONTEXT: MARK 13:1-13

RELATED PASSAGES: PSALM 6:3; PSALM 13:1-6; 1 THESSALONIANS 5:1-3

Day 259

MISLEADING TIMES

MARK 13:5-6

*Jesus said to them, "Be careful! Don't let anyone fool you. Many people will come
and use my name. They will say, 'I am the one' and will fool many people."*

KEY THOUGHT

False messiahs will be plentiful! That's Jesus' message. Many people will be
hoodwinked by them and led away from the true faith. Unfortunately, Jesus'
words have been profoundly true through the ages. Good people have been
led astray by evil or deluded leaders. Jesus doesn't want us to focus our eyes on
anyone but him. All others are false.

TODAY'S PRAYER

*Righteous Father, please help me see through the deception and
charisma of false religious leaders. Keep my heart reserved only
for your Son as my Lord. In Jesus' name I pray. Amen.*

CONTEXT: MARK 13:1-13

RELATED PASSAGES: MARK 13:22; 2 CORINTHIANS 11:13-15; 1 JOHN 4:1

Day 260

LED ASTRAY

MARK 13:5-6

Jesus said to them, "Be careful! Don't let anyone fool you. Many people will come and use my name. They will say, 'I am the one' and will fool many people."

KEY THOUGHT

Jesus was concerned that his precious followers could be led astray. He still is today. As Jesus' followers, it is not enough for us to defend the truth; we must go in search of those that have been led astray by false teachers and false messiahs as well as those who become entangled in sin. Let's make a conscious effort to reach out to those who have been led astray and bring them back to the joy of our Father's house.

TODAY'S PRAYER

Gracious and loving Father, please give me a heart like yours for lost people. Especially make me aware of those who have drifted away or who have been led astray. In the name of Jesus, the Messiah, I pray. Amen.

CONTEXT: MARK 13:1-13

RELATED PASSAGES: LUKE 15:3-7; JAMES 5:19-20; GALATIANS 6:1

Day 261

THE END IS NOT NEAR

MARK 13:7

"You will hear about wars that are being fought. And you will hear stories about other wars beginning. But don't be afraid. These things must happen before the end comes."

KEY THOUGHT

When wars occur, people panic. That has always been true and it was certainly true in Jesus' day. However, just because numerous wars are occurring simultaneously does not signal that the end of the world is near. These things have happened and will continue to happen in our fallen world. As sad and horrific as war is, we must know that it is not the cause or determinant of the end of the world.

TODAY'S PRAYER

O Father, I am upset that people are killed, maimed, destroyed, and separated from each other by wars and the destruction they cause. I want to stop these problems, but I know I cannot. Help me not become overly distraught at what I cannot change and help me trust you to be at work in our world. In Jesus' name I pray. Amen.

CONTEXT: MARK 13:1-13

RELATED PASSAGES: JAMES 4:1-4; REVELATION 17:14; PSALM 91:1-8

Day 262

WARS, EARTHQUAKES, AND FAMINES

MARK 13:8

"Nations will fight against other nations. Kingdoms will fight against other kingdoms. There will be times when there is no food for people to eat. And there will be earthquakes in different places. These things are only the beginning of troubles, like the first pains of a woman giving birth."

KEY THOUGHT

The sad reality of our fallen world and our sinful state is that our world will always be full of war and human strife as well as natural disasters and the human suffering that accompanies them. We must endure these difficult struggles as part of life in a temporal world. However, when Jesus does return in glory, we will be blessed and our fallen world will be redeemed. Glory waits beyond the gloom of suffering, brutality, and disaster.

TODAY'S PRAYER

O Father, please keep hope alive in those whose lives are overwhelmed with suffering and fear. Help me see beyond my own challenges and problems to realize that these are part of a world that is passing away. Help me hold on in faith, trusting that the dawn is coming and that your glory awaits all those who love your Son and look expectantly for his coming! In Jesus' name I pray. Amen.

CONTEXT: MARK 13:1-13

RELATED PASSAGES: ROMANS 8:15-25; REVELATION 21:1; 1 PETER 5:3-10

Day 263

USING MISFORTUNE FOR GOOD NEWS

MARK 13:9

"You must be careful! There are people who will arrest you and take you to be judged for being my followers. They will beat you in their synagogues. You will be forced to stand before kings and governors. You will tell them about me."

KEY THOUGHT

Another part of the believer's future is harsh, in addition to the natural disasters and wars mentioned in previous verses. Not everyone will like Christians. Just as Jesus was hated, so also will his followers be hated. Some will be persecuted and even martyred. This is not only to be expected, it is promised before the return of Jesus. How many years the persecution will continue, we don't know. But they are an expected evil that we will endure before the end. But in the process of facing these hardships we will have the opportunity to share our faith in places we might otherwise be denied a voice—like the apostle Paul (Acts 9, 22, 26) and others who had the opportunity to speak about Jesus to high government officials. So we should tell people about Jesus whether our audience is favorable or hostile. This is a part of the plan. This is our opportunity to demonstrate our faith and share our hope with a fallen world.

TODAY'S PRAYER

O God my Heavenly Father, please give me the courage to stand my ground for my faith and not compromise. Please strengthen me through the power of the Holy Spirit to give my testimony to those who doubt, persecute, or hate me. Use me to share the hope of your Son with those in darkness. In Jesus' name I pray. Amen.

CONTEXT: MARK 13:1-13

RELATED PASSAGES: ACTS 8:1-5; 1 PETER 3:13-17; MARK 13:11

Day 264

TO EVERY NATION

MARK 13:10

"Before the end comes, the Good News must be told to all nations. Even when you are arrested and put on trial, don't worry about what you will say. Say whatever God tells you at the time. It will not really be you speaking. It will be the Holy Spirit."

KEY THOUGHT

Before the return of Jesus, the Good News about Jesus and his Kingdom will be preached to every nation. We can do that better today than ever before. So let's make sure we are sharing that Gospel with others around the world and speed the coming of the Lord!

TODAY'S PRAYER

Father, may your message of hope in Jesus be shared with every nation in my generation. In Jesus' name I pray. Amen.

CONTEXT: MARK 13:1-13

RELATED PASSAGES: MATTHEW 28:18-20; REVELATION 7:9-10; COLOSSIANS 1:3-6

Day 265

DON'T WORRY WHAT TO SAY

MARK 13:11

*"Even when you are arrested and put on trial, don't worry about
what you will say. Say whatever God tells you at the time. It will
not really be you speaking. It will be the Holy Spirit."*

KEY THOUGHT

Our witness before unbelievers will not be our wisdom, but the courage
and the powerful guidance we will receive from the Holy Spirit in the dark
days of persecution and trial. Our ultimate testimony will not be of our own
making, but from the Spirit's inspiration.

TODAY'S PRAYER

*O Father, please make me courageously bold by the power of
your Holy Spirit. In Jesus' mighty name I pray. Amen.*

CONTEXT: MARK 13:1-13

RELATED PASSAGES: LUKE 11:11-13; ACTS 4:27-31; ACTS 4:13

Day 266

FAMILY BETRAYAL

MARK 13:12

"Brothers will turn against their own brothers and hand them over to be killed. Fathers will hand over their own children to be killed. Children will fight against their own parents and have them killed."

KEY THOUGHT

Jesus had warned that those loyal to him could find themselves having to choose between their family and their faith, or between their circle of friends and their faith. As the hostility of living in a fallen world breaks upon us, betrayal will strike very close to the hearts of believers just as it did to the Savior. We shouldn't be surprised that some in our own family would betray us if one of Jesus' handpicked apostles did the same to him.

TODAY'S PRAYER

O Master and God, please help me to be strong enough to withstand the betrayal of those close to me and to continue to love them as Jesus loved those who betrayed him. Please let me never outlive my love for your Son. In Jesus' name, and for his glory, I pray. Amen.

CONTEXT: MARK 13:1-13

RELATED PASSAGES: JOHN 15:18-21; 1 JOHN 3:11-13; LUKE 14:25-27

Day 267

SALVATION IN SPITE OF HATE

MARK 13:13
*"All people will hate you because you follow me. But those
who remain faithful to the end will be saved."*

KEY THOUGHT

Even when our situation makes us feel as if everyone is against us, we can endure . . . we must endure . . . we will endure. We can be certain that our future is with the Savior and that great things await us at his return. His sustaining presence through the Holy Spirit will be with us until he returns in power!

TODAY'S PRAYER
*Give me strength, O LORD God Almighty, to endure faithfully to
the end and find your glorious welcome into your eternal Kingdom
of mercy, grace, and joy. In Jesus' name I pray. Amen.*

CONTEXT: MARK 13:1-13

RELATED PASSAGES: REVELATION 2:10; ROMANS 8:35-39; 1 PETER 4:1-4

Day 268

SHORTENING THE DAYS

MARK 13:14-20

"You will see 'the terrible thing that causes destruction.' You will see this thing standing in the place where it should not be." (Reader, I trust you understand what this means.) "Everyone in Judea at that time should run away to the mountains. They should run away without wasting time to stop for anything. If someone is on the roof of their house, they must not go down to take things out of the house. If someone is in the field, they must not go back to get a coat.

"During that time it will be hard for women who are pregnant or have small babies. Pray that these things will not happen in winter, because those days will be full of trouble. There will be more trouble than has ever happened since the beginning, when God made the world. And nothing that bad will ever happen again. But the Lord has decided to make that terrible time short. If it were not made short, no one could survive. But the Lord will make that time short to help the special people he has chosen."

KEY THOUGHT

The troubles and tumult of the end time prior to Jesus' return will be great. Yet despite all outward appearances, God will remain in control and will protect and bring deliverance for his people during these distressing times. As God's children, those whose allegiance is to the Lord Jesus and whose lives are focused on his Kingdom, our triumph is secure. It cannot be taken from us—not by Satan's power, not by evil times, and not by death itself. Our God is in control and our Lord is on the horizon to usher us into his eternal presence. Our task is to remain faithful and be ready for his deliverance.

TODAY'S PRAYER

O Father, empower me to remain faithful to you no matter the times or my current circumstance. In Jesus' name I ask for your sustaining grace. Amen.

CONTEXT: MARK 13:14-27

RELATED PASSAGES: COLOSSIANS 3:1-4; HEBREWS 3:12-13;
1 THESSALONIANS 5:1-11

Day 269

FALSE MESSIAHS

MARK 13:21-23

"Someone might say to you at that time, 'Look, there is the Christ!' Or another person might say, 'There he is!' But don't believe them. False Christs and false prophets will come and do miracles and wonders, trying to fool the people God has chosen, if that is possible. So be careful. Now I have warned you about all this before it happens."

KEY THOUGHT

Since Jesus' return to heaven, many false messiahs have come and tried to present themselves as the one true Messiah of God's people. Jesus is warning us this would be true. When he returns, there will be no doubt about his return. Everyone will know. So we must not let fakes and deceivers create doubt in us, no matter how well intentioned or how deeply deluded they may be.

TODAY'S PRAYER

O Father in heaven, please keep my eyes open to your truth and keep my spiritual discernment sharp so that I will not be deceived by anyone or anything regarding your Son's will for my life or his glorious return. In the name of Jesus, my returning Lord, I pray. Amen.

CONTEXT: MARK 13:14-27

RELATED PASSAGES: 2 CORINTHIANS 12:13-15; ROMANS 16:17-18; LUKE 21:8

Day 270

EVERYONE WILL SEE

MARK 13:24-26

"But in those days, following that distress, 'the sun will be darkened, and the moon will not give its light; the stars will fall from the sky, and the heavenly bodies will be shaken.'

"At that time people will see the Son of Man coming in clouds with great power and glory."

KEY THOUGHT

When Jesus returns in glory, no one will doubt his arrival. His return will be triumphant, glorious, and universally acknowledged—"coming in the clouds with great power." Won't that day be fantastic for those of us who eagerly await his return?

TODAY'S PRAYER

O Father all glorious, we look forward to the return of our Lord and Savior when your reign will be universally recognized and the faithful endurance of your children will be rewarded. In Jesus' name I await this day with the joy of anticipation and praise. Amen.

CONTEXT: MARK 13:14-27

RELATED PASSAGES: REVELATION 1:4B-7; PHILIPPIANS 2:5-11; MATTHEW 16:27

Day 271

GATHERING THE CHOSEN

MARK 13:27
"He will send his angels all around the earth. They will gather his chosen people from every part of the earth."

KEY THOUGHT

Those who belong to the Lord will be gathered to meet him. Those who belong to the Lord will join this celebration whether they are physically alive or dead. All who belong to him will be gathered together for the great reunion of the children of God. What a day of celebration and joy for those who love the Lord! No wonder God's children have looked forward to this day with great anticipation and joy.

TODAY'S PRAYER

O Father, I can't even begin to imagine how glorious the day of Jesus' return will actually be. I look forward to being reunited with those who have gone before me to be with Christ. I look forward to being with those whose language I cannot now speak, but with whom I will enjoy the praise and celebration of heaven. Thank you for such a great hope for my future that rests in Jesus, in whose name I pray. Amen.

CONTEXT: MARK 13:14-27

RELATED PASSAGES: 1 THESSALONIANS 4:14-17;
1 CORINTHIANS 15:51-52; 2 TIMOTHY 4:8

Day 272

RIGHT AT THE DOOR

MARK 13:28-29

"The fig tree teaches us a lesson: When its branches become green and soft, and new leaves begin to grow, then you know that summer is near. In the same way, when you see all these things happening, you will know that the time is near, ready to come."

KEY THOUGHT

Jesus does stand right at the door and waits to enter our world and bring us home. While we cannot know the exact time of his arrival, the events that have been mentioned have been occurring since the days of that first Pentecost and that first generation of believers. Jesus is near. The barrier that separates him from our world and the next is paper-thin. Our call is to be ready, always living in expectation of his imminent coming.

TODAY'S PRAYER

Father, make me ready—ready in my heart, my soul, my mind, and my strength—for the return of your Son. Please use me to help prepare others for this day so that they can join in the victorious celebration of your people. In Jesus' name I pray. Amen.

CONTEXT: MARK 13:28-37

RELATED PASSAGES: MATTHEW 24:36; 1 THESSALONIANS 5:1-3;
1 THESSALONIANS 5:4-11

Day 273

THIS GENERATION

MARK 13:30
*"I assure you that all these things will happen while some
of the people of this time are still living."*

KEY THOUGHT

This statement has been interpreted in numerous ways: (1) Some
understand it to mean that all of Mark 13 is referring to the destruction of
Jerusalem, which occurred in the Jewish war with Rome in A.D. 66-70. (2)
Others believe it means that all these events happened in the first generation
of believers and that we have been on the edge of Jesus' return ever since. (3)
Some even declare that Jesus was wrong and this promise wasn't fulfilled.
(4) Others even claim that Jesus returned and many Christians missed him.
While I believe the second is the more probable (and the third and fourth
are declared to be false elsewhere in the New Testament), the point is that
Jesus' own word stands behind his promised return (1 Thess. 4:15-17). He
has triumphed over death once through his resurrection. He will triumph a
second and final time completely, when he returns and destroys death and
brings immortality to life. And the unfolding of this promise will begin at
any moment!

TODAY'S PRAYER
*Father, give me faith to believe that your Son's return is
always imminent! In Jesus' name I pray. Amen.*

CONTEXT: MARK 13:28-37

RELATED PASSAGES: PHILIPPIANS 1:4-5; REVELATION 1:3, 7; 2 PETER 3:3-10

Day 274

LASTING WORDS

MARK 13:31
"The whole world, earth and sky, will be destroyed, but my words will last forever."

KEY THOUGHT

While heaven and earth will pass away, Jesus' words—his promise to return along with all of his other promises—will be fulfilled. We can count on it because he is faithful and because we can see the track record of God in keeping his promises in the Old Testament. Jesus' words are sure and can be trusted!

TODAY'S PRAYER

Father, in a world of so many words that are used to "spin" so many answers and aid in so much manipulation, I thank you for Jesus' promises that are sure and trustworthy. Help me as I seek to build my life on your Son's promises. In Jesus' name I pray. Amen.

CONTEXT: MARK 13:28-37

RELATED PASSAGES: 1 PETER 1:21-25; 2 CORINTHIANS 1:20-22;
1 THESSALONIANS 4:15

Day 275

No One Knows

MARK 13:32

"No one knows when that day or time will be. The Son and the angels in heaven don't know when that day or time will be. Only the Father knows."

KEY THOUGHT

The greatest secret of all time is the exact day and hour of the Lord's return. So if no one knows, what should our response be to this lack of knowledge? Doubt? Frustration? Disappointment? No! We know the heart of God because we have seen his heart revealed to us by Jesus. We know he desires us to be saved and come to him through Jesus. We know that he spared no sacrifice necessary to redeem us and adopt us into his family. So knowing what we know about God, we can be sure that his promises can always be trusted and that our future is secure. Our task is to live for God and be ready for his Son's return, whenever the Father deems that time has come.

TODAY'S PRAYER

Father, please help me remain diligent in my faith and welcome Jesus when he returns. Thank you for the great price you paid to redeem and adopt me into your family through Jesus, in whose name I pray. Amen.

CONTEXT: MARK 13:28-37

RELATED PASSAGES: 1 THESSALONIANS 5:1-2; ROMANS 13:11-14; 1 PETER 3:8-13

Day 276

STAY ALERT

MARK 13:33
"Be careful! Always be ready. You don't know when that time will be."

KEY THOUGHT

Since we cannot know for certain the exact time of the Lord's return, our approach should be clear and without distraction. We are to stay alert and keep watch so that we are ready for the Lord's return whenever it occurs—ready with constant vigilance, constant anticipation, and constant moral preparedness.

TODAY'S PRAYER

O Father, I want to be ready when Jesus comes. Keep my eyes open, my heart pure, and my hands ready to do your will as I expect the glorious arrival of my victorious Lord. In his name, the mighty name of Jesus Christ, I pray. Amen.

CONTEXT: MARK 13:28-37

RELATED PASSAGES: MATTHEW 26:41; EPHESIANS 6:18;
1 THESSALONIANS 5:6-10

Day 277

DON'T GET CAUGHT SLEEPING

MARK 13:34-36

"It's like a man who goes on a trip and leaves his house in the care of his servants. He gives each one a special job to do. He tells the servant guarding the door to always be ready. And this is what I am telling you now. You must always be ready. You don't know when the owner of the house will come back. He might come in the afternoon, or at mid- night, or in the early morning, or when the sun rises. If you are always ready, he will not find you sleeping, even if he comes back earlier than expected."

KEY THOUGHT

Jesus' preferred title for himself is the "Son of Man." Taken from both Ezekiel and Daniel, Jesus plays on the human emphasis (Ezekiel) and messianic emphasis (Daniel) of this title to link his two "comings" together. His first coming, the incarnation, involved his earthly ministry as a human being who was God living among us. The second coming will be when he comes in his glory with the angels of heaven. The real issue is not if or when he will return; the issue is whether or not his followers will be ready for his return. Will we be doing his work in the world? Will we be found faithful at his return? Will we be longing and expecting his return? When Jesus left earth, he gave his followers a mission: they were to be his representatives, his bodily presence, in the world until his return. Let's be vigilantly living out our mission until the day of his return.

TODAY'S PRAYER

O Father, wake us up and stir us to action. I confess that I sometimes get lethargic in my service to the Kingdom. There are times when I get discouraged and don't long for Jesus' return as I should. Encourage, convict, and motivate me through the power of the Holy Spirit. In Jesus' name I pray. Amen.

CONTEXT: MARK 13:28-37

RELATED PASSAGES: MATTHEW 28:18-20; LUKE 18:1-8; 1 THESSALONIANS 5:5-6

Day 278

WATCH FOR HIS RETURN!

MARK 13:37
"I tell you this, and I say it to everyone: 'Be ready!'"

KEY THOUGHT

When Jesus says this, he is in effect saying, "Watch for my return!" Throughout his ministry, he emphasized that he, the Son of Man, would return in glory and with the angels of heaven. His return would usher in God's ultimate victory and bring complete and eternal salvation for his followers. However, we must be watching and prepared for his return. His voice, his words, his earnest pleading reaches out to us through the centuries and beckons us to be waiting and longing for his return.

TODAY'S PRAYER

O Father, thank you for the assurance that your Son will return and usher your children into your presence and eternal glory. Thank you in Jesus' name. Amen.

CONTEXT: MARK 13:28-37

RELATED PASSAGES: MATTHEW 16:27; MATTHEW 25:31; MARK 8:38

Day 279

THE PASSOVER LAMB

MARK 14:1

It was now only two days before the Passover and the Festival of Unleavened Bread. The leading priests and teachers of the law were trying to find a way to arrest Jesus without the people seeing it. Then they could kill him.

KEY THOUGHT

In all four Gospels, the Passover festival plays a huge part. This is partially because Passover was so important to the Jewish people and the Hebrew faith. Jesus came to earth to be the Passover lamb that was slain for the sin of all people. For Mark's Gospel, the images of Isaiah 53 merge with the theme of Passover and Jesus' paying the ransom to set sinners free. Jesus is our Passover lamb, the sacrifice that brings our freedom from sin.

TODAY'S PRAYER

Father, thank you for providing the sacrifice for my sin at such a great cost. Thank you, Lord Jesus, for paying the price for my sin. Amen.

CONTEXT: MARK 14:1-11

RELATED PASSAGES: JOHN 1:29-34; 1 CORINTHIANS 5:7; JOHN 2:13

Day 280

PREMEDITATION

MARK 14:1-2

It was now only two days before the Passover and the Festival of Unleavened Bread. The leading priests and teachers of the law were trying to find a way to arrest Jesus without the people seeing it. Then they could kill him. They said, "But we cannot arrest Jesus during the festival. We don't want the people to be angry and cause a riot."

KEY THOUGHT

Jesus' enemies were determined to kill him. But they knew that he was popular with the people. With Jerusalem flooded with annual visitors for Passover, a time that was very volatile, they worried that to go after Jesus during this time could backfire. Mark wants us to see that their murder of Jesus on the cross was calculated and premeditated. They were not looking for justice or truth; they were out for blood. Little did they know that the blood they shed would be the atoning blood of the new covenant that would bring our salvation. What they meant for the worst kind of harm, God used for unbelievable good—our good!

TODAY'S PRAYER

O Father, I cannot understand how you withheld your power and allowed the schemes of wicked men to murder your Son, especially when those wicked men claimed to honor you. I am sorry that we can be so misguided and wrong. Please forgive us. Please forgive me. I want to believe that I would have followed Jesus and welcomed him, but part of me fears that I might have been as misguided as those who hated him. Purify my heart and give me wisdom to know and follow your truth always. In Jesus' name I pray. Amen.

CONTEXT: MARK 14:1-11

RELATED PASSAGES: MARK 10:2; MARK 3:1-6; MARK 8:31

Day 281

Beauty in the Broken Things

Mark 14:3

Jesus was in Bethany at the house of Simon the leper. While he was eating there, a woman came to him. She had an alabaster jar filled with expensive perfume made of pure nard. She opened the jar and poured the perfume on Jesus' head.

Key Thought

Mark moves us from a scene of some of the worst of human motivations against Jesus (verses 1-2) to this scene, one of the most precious stories of loving extravagance and genuine appreciation for Jesus that we find in the Gospels. This woman's expensive sacrifice prepares both Jesus and us for his sacrifice that lies ahead. What genuine and extravagant demonstration of love have I shared with the Lord?

Today's Prayer

O Father, may my life be a fragrant sacrifice of praise to you. In Jesus' name and for your glory I pray. Amen.

Context: Mark 14:1-11

Related Passages: Romans 12:1-2; Hebrews 13:15-16; Philippians 2:5-11

Day 282

SCOLDED FOR LOVE

MARK 14:4-5

*Some of the followers there saw this. They were upset and complained
to each other. They said, "Why waste that perfume? It was worth a full
year's pay. It could have been sold and the money given to those who are
poor." And they told the woman what a bad thing she had done.*

KEY THOUGHT

Isn't it sadly strange that people often criticize the gifts others make?
I'm not sure if it is jealousy, greed, or pure pettiness that makes us so quick
to criticize other's generosity. However, God loves a cheerful and generous
giver. Part of the reason is that we are most like God when we give generously
and joyously. If only we were as generous with our giving as we are with our
criticism! May the example of this one woman stir our hearts to renounce our
critical spirit and replace it with a spirit of generous love.

TODAY'S PRAYER

*Loving God and Almighty Father in heaven, please use me as a conduit of your
love, mercy, and grace. I want my heart to be generous with others even if those
around me cannot understand that generosity. Thank you for being so generous
with me. May I never hoard your blessings, but always be quick to share them
in ways that bring you joy. In Jesus' name and for your glory I pray. Amen.*

CONTEXT: MARK 14:1-11

RELATED PASSAGES: 1 TIMOTHY 6:17-19; 2 CORINTHIANS 8:1-4;
2 CORINTHIANS 8:9

Day 283

WHY, IF IT IS FOR ME?

MARK 14:6
Jesus said, "Leave her alone. Why are you giving her such trouble? She did a very good thing for me."

KEY THOUGHT
As Jesus did so often in his earthly ministry, he protected a vulnerable person from criticism and attack and also found a way to affirm and bless her. He emphasized the good this woman had done. May we be willing to do the same to others who are generous, kind, and loving to the Lord Jesus! Let's find and affirm those who are generous with God!

TODAY'S PRAYER
Gracious Father, open my eyes and help me see those who are doing good things in the name of Jesus. Use me to affirm their work and bring them a blessing. In Jesus' name I pray. Amen.

CONTEXT: MARK 14:1-11

RELATED PASSAGES: MARK 5:25-34; LUKE 21:1-4; MARK 2:3-5

Day 284

ONLY FOR A LITTLE WHILE!

MARK 14:7-8

"You will always have the poor with you, and you can help them any time you want. But you will not always have me. This woman did the only thing she could do for me. She poured perfume on my body before I die to prepare it for burial."

KEY THOUGHT

So often we have people we love dearly and greatly respect that we never praise, honor, or thank until after they are dead. This story of the woman's expensive gift to Jesus should remind us not to wait till people are dead to give them the thanks they deserve. Let's thank others and honor them in ways that are appropriate for their service.

TODAY'S PRAYER

Father, there are many people in my life who have blessed me. Please forgive me for not being more affirming and appreciative to them. Help me see the opportunities I have to thank and honor people, always to your glory, before their time on earth is ended. In Jesus' name I pray. Amen.

CONTEXT: MARK 14:1-11

RELATED PASSAGES: 1 THESSALONIANS 5:12-13;
2 TIMOTHY 1:15-18; HEBREWS 13:7

Day 285

WHEREVER

MARK 14:9

"The Good News will be told to people all over the world. And I can assure you that everywhere the Good News is told, the story of what this woman did will also be told, and people will remember her."

KEY THOUGHT

Some events are too precious to forget. Jesus wanted the sacrificial love shown by this woman to be wedded to the Good News of his life—the story of his sacrificial love. They fit together. Wouldn't it be great if when we die our lives have been lived in such a way that they would also fit naturally with Jesus' life, the story of God's Good News?

TODAY'S PRAYER

Lord God Almighty, my Abba Father, help me live my life in such a way that it is consistent with and complementary to the Gospel. May my life honor you and your Son Jesus, in whose name I pray. Amen.

CONTEXT: MARK 14:1-11

RELATED PASSAGES: MARK 1:1; MARK 1:14-15; MARK 10:28-31

Day 286

THE WRONG THING AT THE RIGHT TIME

MARK 14:10-11

Then Judas Iscariot, one of the twelve apostles, went to talk to the leading priests about handing Jesus over to them. They were very happy about this, and they promised to pay him. So he waited for the best time to hand Jesus over to them.

KEY THOUGHT

This section of Mark began (in 14:1) with the enemies of Jesus plotting his death. It now ends with one of Jesus' own close followers offering to betray him to death. How sad! Rather than looking closely at Jesus' ministry and hearing what he had to say, his enemies were looking for the right time and place to kill him while Judas was looking for a way to betray Jesus. Jealousy and hate blind us to the truth about other people. That is why Jesus was so critical of the self-righteous religious leaders. Let's remember that hate always blinds us to the truth about others and closes down our hearts about their true identities and value.

TODAY'S PRAYER

O Father, forgive me when I've judged the actions of others negatively because of my ill feelings toward them. Lead me gently to love them more generously and fully. In Jesus' name I pray and ask for your grace. Amen.

CONTEXT: MARK 14:1-11

RELATED PASSAGES: MATTHEW 5:43-48; MARK 13:13; JOHN 15:21

Day 287

Anticipating the Sacrifice

Mark 14:12

It was now the first day of the Festival of Unleavened Bread—the day the lambs were killed for the Passover. Jesus' followers came to him and said, "We will go and prepare everything for you to eat the Passover meal. Where do you want us to have the meal?"

Key Thought

Jesus is our Passover Lamb. Mark wants us to know that Jesus will go to his death in the context of the Jewish Passover and God's great deliverance of his people from Egypt. Jesus brings us deliverance through the events that lie ahead of him. That deliverance, however, will require a sacrifice. Jesus chooses to be that perfect sacrifice for our sins because of his love for us and his willingness to honor his Father's will.

Today's Prayer

Righteous and holy Father, God Almighty, thank you for my deliverance from sin. Thank you for the sacrifice that Jesus made in his body to deliver me from sin and death. And thank you Lord Jesus, in whose name I pray, for the incredible price you paid to cleanse me. Amen.

Context: Mark 14:12-26

Related Passages: Hebrews 9:14; 1 John 2:1-2; Mark 10:42-45

Day 288

JUST AS JESUS SAID

MARK 14:13-16

Jesus sent two of his followers into the city. He said to them, "Go into the city. You will see a man carrying a jar of water. He will come to you. Follow him. He will go into a house. Tell the owner of the house, 'The Teacher asks that you show us the room where he and his followers can eat the Passover meal.' The owner will show you a large room upstairs that is ready for us. Prepare the meal for us there."

So the followers left and went into the city. Everything happened the way Jesus said. So the followers prepared the Passover meal.

KEY THOUGHT

The disciples of Jesus found that "Everything happened the way Jesus said." In large and small things, Jesus knew what lay ahead and chose to face them even though the cost was great. What great comfort! And today, as we look back at the promises of Jesus, this is another reminder that we will find that "Everything happened the way Jesus said."

TODAY'S PRAYER

O Father in heaven, give me the faith to live passionately and confidently, knowing that all of Jesus' promises can be trusted. In the mighty name of the Lord Jesus I pray. Amen.

CONTEXT: MARK 14:12-26

RELATED PASSAGES: JOHN 14:1-4; JOHN 14:12-23; MATTHEW 28:18-20

Day 289

ONE OF YOU!

MARK 14:17-18

In the evening, Jesus went to that house with the twelve apostles. While they were all at the table eating, he said, "Believe me when I say that one of you will hand me over to my enemies—one of you eating with me now."

KEY THOUGHT

Imagine how it hurt the followers of Jesus to hear these words! Imagine how much more it hurt Jesus to have to say this about one of his closest friends and followers. Betrayal by a friend hurts terribly and wounds us grievously. But, when we are heartbroken because of the faithlessness of a friend, a spouse, or another loved one, we can go to the Lord and know that he cares and that he hears us. He's been down this road himself. While I am deeply grieved that Jesus experienced the heartbreak of betrayal, I am comforted in those moments when I have felt betrayed because I know that the Lord knows, cares, and is present with me through my loneliest times.

TODAY'S PRAYER

O Father, be near. O Jesus, please draw me close to you. O Spirit, fill me with your presence. I cannot exist without the constant assurance of your presence in my life. Thank you in Jesus' name. Amen.

CONTEXT: MARK 14:12-26

RELATED PASSAGES: HEBREWS 13:5-6; MATTHEW 10:19-22; ROMANS 8:38-39

Day 290

I'M NOT THE ONE, AM I?

MARK 14:19

The followers were very sad to hear this. Each one said to Jesus, "Surely I am not the one!"

KEY THOUGHT

This is exactly the question we should ask ourselves. "Surely I am not the one!" Pride and a false sense of our own strength in the face of trial and temptation must never be a part of our spiritual character. We will fail and fall. Instead, we need to examine ourselves and put ourselves to the test, but then take those results back to the Lord and pray for his power and grace.

TODAY'S PRAYER

O Father, I know that I cannot be the person I want to be without your help, power, and presence. Fill me and empower me with your Holy Spirit. In Jesus' name I ask for your strength and grace. Amen.

CONTEXT: MARK 14:12-26

RELATED PASSAGES: EPHESIANS 3:14-21; ROMANS 7:21-25; LUKE 22:61

Day 291

ONE OF YOU!

MARK 14:20

*Jesus answered, "It is one of you twelve—the one who is
dipping his bread in the same bowl with me."*

KEY THOUGHT

How sad Jesus' words must have been to the apostles when they first
heard them. How sad these words must have been as they remembered them.
What a powerful reminder to us of our ability to falter and to let our Lord
down. All of us have let the Lord down and betrayed him at some point in our
lives. Thank the Lord Jesus that he paid the price to ransom us back from our
weakness, hypocrisy, betrayal, and failure. Each time we come to the Lord's
Table, let's be reminded of the price of our forgiveness, of our vulnerability to
letting the Lord down, and of the opportunity we have to live passionately for
him. Most of all, let's remember that we can begin again, fresh and forgiven,
when we falter. Let's get back up, ask for the Lord's forgiveness, receive his
cleansing, and faithfully live for his glory.

TODAY'S PRAYER

*LORD of all heaven and earth, my Abba Father, please help me trust in your
forgiveness and the Holy Spirit's power so that I will not be crushed by my failures
and sins. Instead, as you cleanse me, please empower me to live vibrantly and
faithfully for you. This is my heart's desire. In Jesus' name I pray. Amen.*

CONTEXT: MARK 14:12-26

RELATED PASSAGES: 1 JOHN 1:5-2:2; 2 CORINTHIANS 13:5; GALATIANS 6:1

Day 292

THE HUMAN TRAGEDY OF THE DIVINE GRACE

MARK 14:21

*"The Son of Man will suffer what the Scriptures say will happen to him.
But it will be very bad for the one who hands over the Son of Man to
be killed. It would be better for him if he had never been born."*

KEY THOUGHT

While God planned for Jesus' death to be the atoning sacrifice for sin and
while Jesus died willingly for us, this does not mitigate the sin of those who
orchestrated his murder. Both God's plan and the plot of evil men placed
Jesus on the cross. The one who betrayed Jesus will have to face judgment for
what he did.

TODAY'S PRAYER

*Father, may I never, ever outlive my love and loyalty to you
and your Son. In Jesus' name I pray. Amen.*

CONTEXT: MARK 14:12-26

RELATED PASSAGES: JOHN 19:7-11; 2 TIMOTHY 2:11-13; MARK 8:38

Day 293

MY BODY

MARK 14:22

While they were eating, Jesus took some bread and thanked God for it. He broke off some pieces, gave them to his followers and said, "Take and eat this bread. It is my body."

KEY THOUGHT

For Jesus and his early followers, bread was the "staff of life"—the essence of food and nourishment to people in Jesus' culture. Jesus had already taught his closest followers that he was the bread of life (John 6). Now, Jesus was providing these followers with a way to remember him, his life-giving place in their lives, and the sacrifice he was about to make for them. In addition, he was providing his followers with a way of understanding their role in the world: they were to be his bodily presence. When we take of the Lord's Supper on Sunday as the early followers of Jesus did, we do so to remember him and to commit to keep alive his ministry to the world as we pledge to be his Body. We must never take this meal for granted.

TODAY'S PRAYER

O Father, thank you for leaving us a reminder of Jesus' sacrifice, his life-giving grace, and our responsibility to keep his memory and ministry alive as his Body, the church. In Jesus' name I pray. Amen.

CONTEXT: MARK 14:12-26

RELATED PASSAGES: 1 CORINTHIANS 10:16-17;
1 CORINTHIANS 11:23-24; ACTS 20:7

Day 294

THE GIFT OF MY BLOOD

MARK 14:23-24

Then he took a cup of wine, thanked God for it, and gave it to them. They all drank from the cup. Then he said, "This wine is my blood, which will be poured out for many to begin the new agreement from God to his people."

KEY THOUGHT

Jesus' blood, remembered in this last supper with his followers and continually celebrated by his followers today, seals a new agreement, a new covenant, between God and Jesus' followers. This is a covenant of grace and love brought about by the sacrifice of Jesus on the cross. This new covenant is our way of life as Jesus' followers and is a blessing provided to us by the blood of Jesus.

TODAY'S PRAYER

Father in heaven, thank you for the price that was paid to bring me into a new covenant relationship with you. May my life be lived to honor that price and to fulfill my part in that covenant. In Jesus' name I pray. Amen.

CONTEXT: MARK 14:12-26

RELATED PASSAGES: 1 CORINTHIANS 11:25; 2 CORINTHIANS 3:6-11; HEBREWS 8:6-13

Day 295

I Will Drink It New

MARK 14:24-26

Then he said, "This wine is my blood, which will be poured out for many to begin the new agreement from God to his people. I want you to know, I will not drink this wine again until that day when I drink it in God's kingdom and the wine is new."

They all sang a song and then went out to the Mount of Olives.

KEY THOUGHT

Some debate what Jesus means when he says, "I will drink it new in the Kingdom of God." Some believe he is referring to sharing in the Lord's Supper with those who believe in him—in other words, when we share in the Lord's Supper as his church, he joins us in this meal. Others think he is referring to the great reunion meal in heaven. I personally believe that his reference is all encompassing because the Lord's Supper is anticipatory: we remember his death until he comes. He joins us in that meal just as he joined his followers on the road to Emmaus and shared that meal with them (Luke 24). At the same time we celebrate the Lord's Supper in anticipation of the great meal in heaven with all of God's redeemed. What a great reminder! What a great way to anticipate the future! What a great way to pledge ourselves to one another and help one another see that glorious day of victorious celebration with our Lord!

TODAY'S PRAYER

Almighty God and eternal LORD, thank you for the presence of your Son as we share in the Lord's Supper. Thank you even more for the promise that we will share the victorious meal with our Savior when he returns and takes us home to you. In Jesus' name I thank you for all of your blessings. Amen.

CONTEXT: MARK 14:12-26

RELATED PASSAGES: LUKE 24:28-35; REVELATION 19:5-9; 1 CORINTHIANS 11:26

Day 296

ALL OF YOU!

MARK 14:27

*Then Jesus told the followers, "You will all lose your faith. The Scriptures say,
'I will kill the shepherd, and the sheep will run away.'"*

KEY THOUGHT

Jesus knows that he will face the horrors of the cross alone. He has no illusions about what will happen. Scripture has foretold it. His heart knows it. He lies on the verge of experiencing it. Ray Overholt's hymn, "Ten Thousand Angels," powerfully recognizes the truth of Jesus' words:

He could have called ten thousand angels
To destroy the world and set Him free.
He could have called ten thousand angels,
But He died alone, for you and me.

Jesus knows his death is coming. He knows he will be abandoned, betrayed, denied, and ultimately crucified. He goes through it anyway . . . for you and me.

TODAY'S PRAYER

Loving Father and Almighty God, I am humbled and appreciative of the incredible love your Son demonstrated for me. Please accept my life as my thank you for such grace. In deep appreciation for Jesus' sacrifice and in his name, I pray. Amen.

CONTEXT: MARK 14:27-31

RELATED PASSAGES: MARK 14:45-50; ISAIAH 53:1-3; JOHN 16:32

Day 297

I'll Go Ahead of You

MARK 14:28
*"But after I am killed, I will rise from death. Then I will
go to Galilee. I will be there before you come."*

KEY THOUGHT

Facing his own death and the desertion of his friends, Jesus' faith was strong. He trusted that God would raise him from the dead and bring him back to his disciples to finish his work of preparing them for the future. Jesus' faith in the face of death and his victory over death in the resurrection have reassured Christians for centuries that they would again see those that they love in the Lord after death. May God give us such faith.

TODAY'S PRAYER
Eternal Father, please give me such faith! In Jesus' powerful name I pray. Amen.

CONTEXT: MARK 14:27-31

RELATED PASSAGES: PHILIPPIANS 1:19-24; 2 TIMOTHY 4:6-8; 1
THESSALONIANS 4:13-18

NOT ME!

MARK 14:29

Peter said, "All the other followers may lose their faith. But my faith will never be shaken."

KEY THOUGHT

Peter, seemingly always wanting to be more important than Jesus' other followers, overstates his faith. While Peter initially backs up his words by drawing a sword and being ready to defend his Lord when Jesus is arrested, he also runs away with the other followers when Jesus won't fight. In fact, he later denies his Lord three times. Peter is the great reminder that even those of us who possess great faith can run into confusing times when our faith wavers and our resolve melts. Let's heed Jesus' warning to Peter (that follow in the next few verses) and never over-state our loyalty or be overly critical of those whose loyalty seems to waver for a time. Instead, let's commit to be faithful and to reclaim those who falter.

TODAY'S PRAYER

LORD God Almighty, I am not even close to being invincible. My faith is fallible. I don't want to waver or fall. However, dear LORD, I know that without your powerful help, I will. I humbly ask for your strength and pray that I will not disappoint you or fail you. In Jesus' name I pray. Amen.

CONTEXT: MARK 14:27-31

RELATED PASSAGES: GALATIANS 6:1-3; JAMES 5:19-20; JAMES 5:15-19

Day 299

PETER'S REAL TRUTH

MARK 14:30

*Jesus answered, "The truth is, tonight you will say you don't know
me. You will say it three times before the rooster crows twice."*

KEY THOUGHT

"The truth is, tonight you will . . . ." Ouch! "You can't stand the truth!" is
the old movie line delivered by Jack Nicholson. I'm afraid we might not be able
to stand the full truth of our own weakness. Yet because of the forgiveness of
the Lord and power of the Holy Spirit, we can be resilient and useable to the
Master. Three denials do not mean banishment forever from grace. They are
just a sobering reminder of our desperate need for honest humility and the
power of God's Spirit to strengthen us in times of distress.

TODAY'S PRAYER

*O LORD, please give me the strength I need this day to be strong in your service, faithful
in my promises, and tender in my dealings with others. In Jesus' name I pray. Amen.*

CONTEXT: MARK 14:27-31

RELATED PASSAGES: LUKE 22:32; 1 JOHN 1:7-9; PROVERBS 16:18

Day 300

ALL THE OTHERS SAY THE SAME

MARK 14:31

But Peter strongly protested, "I will never say I don't know you! I will even die with you!" And all the other followers said the same thing.

KEY THOUGHT

Peter's bravado and protest was not a solo performance. All the followers of Jesus felt that they would follow him to whatever fate awaited them, even death if necessary. Little did they know that they would all forsake and abandon Jesus before the night was over. How true to life! When we look in Scripture, we find quite a number of people who lost their way and their loyalty to the Lord. How wonderful that the Lord found a way to reclaim so many of them! May he do so with us! May we do so with others!

TODAY'S PRAYER

Lord God, make me an instrument of your reconciliation. Use me to bring back those who have lost their way. In Jesus' name I pray. Amen.

CONTEXT: MARK 14:27-31

RELATED PASSAGES: MATTHEW 18:12-14; JAMES 5:19-20; LUKE 15:1-7

Day 301

DEEP DISTRESS

MARK 14:32-33

*Jesus and his followers went to a place named Gethsemane. He said
to them, "Sit here while I pray." But he told Peter, James, and John to
come with him. He began to be very distressed and troubled . . . .*

KEY THOUGHT

Never underestimate the emotional and spiritual challenges that Jesus
faced as his rejection, desertion, and crucifixion approached. The battle for
our souls takes place at Gethsemane as much as it does at the cross. Here
Jesus will not just battle those who hate him and those who will crucify him;
he also has to battle his own humanity and will. In Gethsemane, the path that
Jesus will follow—the path to the humiliation of the cross—is determined by
the only one who can accept it. Jesus offers himself to the Father, and gives
himself as an offering for our sins, knowing the dire consequences of his
decision.

TODAY'S PRAYER

*O precious and Almighty Father, words cannot express my sadness. I know
that Jesus realized what lay ahead of him and I know that this caused him
great anguish. Thank you for such love. And to you, Lord Jesus, what can I
say but thank you, bless you, and praise you for your obedient and sacrificial
love. To you, dear Father, belongs all glory, honor, and praise. To you, dear
Savior, belongs all respect, reverence, and humble appreciation. Amen.*

CONTEXT: MARK 14:32-42

RELATED PASSAGES: ROMANS 12:1-2; HEBREWS 2:14; ROMANS 8:26-30

Day 302

STAY WITH ME!

MARK 14:34

*. . . and he [Jesus] said to them, "My heart is so heavy with grief,
I feel as if I am dying. Wait here and stay awake."*

KEY THOUGHT

We desperately need the presence of friends who love and support us in
our times of struggle and distress. Jesus needed these closest three followers,
Peter, James, and John, to be there with him and help him bear his burdens.
Often we don't ask for help when we need it, and we often forget to "stand
with" those in need of support. Jesus' honesty in his moment of anguish is
a powerful reminder that we need to both ask for help when we need it and
provide help when others need it.

TODAY'S PRAYER

*O Father, help me "stand with" those around me who are facing hardships.
Use me to help them bear their burdens and to pray with them. In addition,
dear Father, give me the honesty to share my burdens with those who can
"stand with" me in my times of distress. In Jesus' name I pray. Amen.*

CONTEXT: MARK 14:32-42

RELATED PASSAGES: GALATIANS 6:2; JAMES 5:13-16; 1 THESSALONIANS 4:18

Day 303

IF POSSIBLE?

MARK 14:35

*Jesus went on a little farther away from them, fell to the ground, and prayed.
He asked that, if possible, he would not have this time of suffering.*

KEY THOUGHT

Jesus was honest in his prayers to the Father. He demonstrated his need both verbally and physically. Jesus shows us in this story an important dimension of genuine prayer. In these verses he shares his agony with the Father in humility and honesty. In the verses that follow, he offers himself to do whatever the Father wills, not just what is easiest for himself. As we pray, we need to follow our Lord's example of genuine prayer—honesty, humility, and submission. Not only did Jesus teach us to pray in his teaching on earth, he also demonstrated how to pray in his own walk with the Father.

TODAY'S PRAYER

Dear Father, I come before you recognizing your majesty and my need. You are the glorious God of all creation, the Father of all peoples, and the Sovereign LORD of all nations. I come on my knees, dear Father, offering myself to you. Please use me in the ways that bring you glory and ensure that I am drawn ever closer to you in character and compassion. Please heal me of my infirmities—both the physical ones and the spiritual ones. Bring yourself glory through my life. In Jesus' name I pray. Amen.

CONTEXT: MARK 14:32-42

RELATED PASSAGES: HEBREWS 5:7-9; PSALM 10:14-18; 1 KINGS 8:28

Day 304

YOUR WILL, NOT MINE!

MARK 14:36
*He said, "Abba, Father! You can do all things. Don't make me drink
from this cup. But do what you want, not what I want."*

KEY THOUGHT

Jesus recognizes two crucial realities. First, God can do anything he wants
to do; he is God, the Sovereign ruler of all things. Second, his life must be
governed by God's will and not his own. The whole of human salvation
history hinges on Jesus' following through on one heart-felt phrase from his
own lips: "But do what you want, not what I want." In a similar way, our future
is also connected to our own willingness to follow our Savior's example and
saying, "Father, do what you want, not what I want."

TODAY'S PRAYER
*Father in heaven, I praise your Son for submitting to your will for my
eternal good. Like Jesus, dear Father, I want so much to mean the following
words when I pray them, "Do what you want, not what I want." In Jesus'
name I pray for grace and strength to follow his example. Amen.*

CONTEXT: MARK 14:32-42

RELATED PASSAGES: JAMES 4:13-16; ROMANS 8:26-27; ROMANS 12:1-2

Day 305

Couldn't You Watch with Me?

Mark 14:37

Then he went back to his followers and found them sleeping. He said to Peter,
"Simon, why are you sleeping? Could you not stay awake with me for one hour?"

Key Thought

How this must have hurt the Lord. My heart breaks for Jesus as he endures this time in the Garden. He knows he is going to the cross. He knows Judas will betray him. He knows his closest followers will abandon him. He knows that Peter will deny him. He knows the other ten will run away and leave him alone. He knows that he will be ridiculed and mocked. He knows all those things and still doesn't have anyone care for him enough to pray with him an hour. I'm so thankful that the Lord knows what it feels like to be forsaken and let down by those closest to you. Let's pray and work to never let him down like this again.

Today's Prayer

O Father, I am so sorry for my failures to be faithful! Please, dear Lord, make me stronger and more courageous. Don't ever let me outlive my love for you and my willingness to show that love in my life no matter the circumstances. In Jesus' name I ask. Amen.

Context: Mark 14:32-42

Related Passages: Mark 14:43-50; Hebrews 2:14-18; Hebrews 4:14-16

Day 306

KEEP ALERT!

MARK 14:37-38

Then he went back to his followers and found them sleeping. He said to Peter, "Simon, why are you sleeping? Could you could not stay awake with me for one hour? Stay awake and pray for strength against temptation. Your spirit wants to do what is right, but your body is weak."

KEY THOUGHT

We often underestimate our own weakness. We know what we want to do and be, but so often we fall far short of that. Our intentions are good, but our follow-through is flawed. Thank God for his grace! Thank God that we can rely on the Holy Spirit to strengthen us and help us in our times of weakness.

TODAY'S PRAYER

Father, I know that without the help of your Holy Spirit, I will fall far short of what I want to do and who I want to be. Please strengthen me with your might through your Holy Spirit. In Jesus' name I pray. Amen.

CONTEXT: MARK 14:32-42

RELATED PASSAGES: ROMANS 7:18-8:4; ROMANS 8:12-14; EPHESIANS 3:14-16

Day 307

REPEATED PLEADINGS!

MARK 14:39
Again Jesus went away and prayed the same thing.

KEY THOUGHT

We often find ourselves praying the same prayer, just as Jesus repeatedly asks the Father to let the cross be lifted from him. Yet Jesus also prayed for his Father's will to be done and not his own. While Jesus' repeated requests to be spared the cross were not granted, we know that Jesus' prayer was heard and God was glorified in what happened (Heb. 5:7-9). Sometimes, God's answer to our prayer is "No." He may have other and bigger plans for us as we submit to his will. So while we continue to pray and not lose heart, we also ask for God's will to be accomplished and God's glory to be achieved in our lives (Luke 18:1-8). Like Jesus, we are assured that the Father hears our repeated prayers—not just our words, but the unspeakable emotions of our hearts—and his will is done in our lives (Rom. 8:26-29).

TODAY'S PRAYER

Father, please hear the prayer of my heart. I want to ask you to please . . . .
(add your own prayer concern here.) Yet Father, not what I want, but your will
be done and your glory be seen in my life. In Jesus' name I pray. Amen.

CONTEXT: MARK 14:32-42

RELATED PASSAGES: HEBREWS 5:7-9; 2 CORINTHIANS 12:7-10;
ROMANS 8:26-27

Day 308

They Didn't Know What to Say!

MARK 14:40

Then he went back to the followers and again found them sleeping. They could not stay awake. They did not know what they should say to him.

Key Thought

Sometimes we just fail. Maybe it's because we don't understand the gravity of a behavior. Maybe it's because we're just too weary and distraught to do what we need to do. Maybe it's because we're weak or lazy or . . . . The bottom line is that we are flawed people living in a fallen world. Despite our best intentions, our flesh sometimes triumphs over our faith. I can't think of anything that reminds us of our desperate need for Jesus to be our Savior more than Jesus' closest followers' letting him down in his moment of greatest need. Yet he dies for them and then calls them back to his service. What a message of grace triumphing over sin, disappointment, and failure.

Today's Prayer

Lord Jesus, I pray in your name so often to praise, thank, and request things from the Father, that I sometimes forget to thank you for your incomparable love, mercy, and grace to die for me when I have let you down and hurt you with my sin. Thank you! Thank you, dear Father, for such a divine plan to deal with human weakness and sin. All praise be to you, and to your Son, in whose name I praise and thank you. Amen.

Context: Mark 14:32-42

RELATED PASSAGES: ROMANS 5:6-11; COLOSSIANS 1:18-22; EPHESIANS 2:1-10

Day 309

BETRAYED INTO SINNERS' HANDS

MARK 14:41-42

After Jesus prayed a third time, he went back to his followers. He said to them, "Are you still sleeping and resting? That's enough! The time has come for the Son of Man to be handed over to the control of sinful men. Stand up! We must go. Here comes the man who is handing me over to them."

KEY THOUGHT

Jesus returns from praying for the third time and he knows the Father's answer. The challenge and the horror that he faces will not pass from him. The cross and all that goes with it will be his to bear alone. The inability of Jesus' close friends to remain awake in prayer and the approach of another one of the Lord's close followers to betray him to the soldiers make clear that Jesus' time of sacrifice is about to begin.

TODAY'S PRAYER

Precious Father, the Holy One of Israel, I am saddened by the failure of Jesus' three closest followers and the treachery of Judas. Yet, dear Father, I fear that I also sometimes see a bit of myself in them. Thank you for not letting the story end here. Thank you for Jesus' faithfulness through the arrest, trials, mockery, and the cross. Thank you for giving Jesus victory over death and having him bring us triumph over sin through his resurrection. Thank you, Lord Jesus for all that you endured when you had the power to prevent it. Thank you with all my heart as I pray in the name of the risen Savior. Amen.

CONTEXT: MARK 14:32-42

RELATED PASSAGES: LUKE 23:34; MATTHEW 6:9-15; EPHESIANS 4:30-32

Day 310

INCONGRUITY AT ITS WORST

MARK 14:43

While Jesus was still speaking, Judas, one of the twelve apostles, came there. He had a big crowd of people with him, all carrying swords and clubs. They had been sent from the leading priests, the teachers of the law, and the older Jewish leaders.

KEY THOUGHT

Think of the incongruity: Jesus is in his place of prayer and is being betrayed by one of his own to a mob armed with swords and clubs and sent by religious leaders to arrest him. This travesty should not have occurred. Jesus, the only fully righteous one, dies for the unrighteous. Soldiers armed with crude weapons arrest Jesus, the prince of peace. The experts of God's holy Law hate Jesus, the fulfillment of the Law. Jesus, the ultimate servant leader, is despised and feared by the religious leaders of his day. This doesn't make sense. This isn't fair. Yet this is how Jesus changes everything. What a breath of fresh air for us when things are not right, when circumstances don't fit, and when life is unfair! Jesus shows us he can enter the worst of our circumstances and bring redemption, hope, and victory.

TODAY'S PRAYER

Father, thank you! Thank you for Jesus' victory over sin, death, unfairness, and hatred. Thank you for a victory that was won in the middle of a mess worse than any I have known. Thank you for showing that in the middle of humanity's worst failings, Jesus can bring redemption. I praise you in Jesus' mighty name. Amen.

CONTEXT: MARK 14:43-52

RELATED PASSAGES: 1 PETER 3:18; ISAIAH 53:1-6; GALATIANS 4:3-7

Day 311

WITH A KISS?

MARK 14:44-46

Judas planned to do something to show them which one was Jesus. He said, "The one I kiss will be Jesus. Arrest him and guard him while you lead him away." So Judas went over to Jesus and said, "Teacher!" Then he kissed him. The men grabbed Jesus and arrested him.

KEY THOUGHT

How sadly ironic! Judas betrays the one who loves him most with a kiss. For everyone whose heart has been broken by someone he or she loves, this is a great reminder that Jesus knows those deep feelings of betrayal. Here is a Savior in whom we can confide. He knows our dashed hopes and our broken hearts. He promises to strengthen us and be with us in our dark hours of need. Most of all, he promises to dry every single tear from our eyes and welcome us home.

TODAY'S PRAYER

Father in heaven, betrayal by someone we love is such a deep and cutting wound that many of us never recover. Thank you for reminding us—reminding me— that Jesus knows this bitter sorrow firsthand and can help us in our time of need. In Jesus' name, and because of his sacrifice for me, I thank you. Amen.

CONTEXT: MARK 14:43-52

RELATED PASSAGES: HEBREWS 4:14-16; HEBREWS 7:24-25; HEBREWS 2:14-18

Day 312

PULLING THE SWORD

MARK 14:47

*One of the followers standing near Jesus grabbed his sword and pulled it
out. He swung it at the servant of the high priest and cut off his ear.*

KEY THOUGHT

Peter and the apostles had all agreed that they would die with Jesus if
necessary, yet their view of Jesus as Messiah was misguided. Some thought
he would be a military deliverer. So in an attempt to start the battle for
deliverance, one of them draws a sword and begins the fight. Since Jesus
has raised the dead, healed the sick, restored sight to the blind, mended the
limbs of the lame, opened the ears of the deaf, and given perfect skin to the
leprous, surely he will now use his power for his own victory? So in an act of
faith, defiance, and hope, the sword is drawn and the attack is begun. It is
aimed at those behind this whole evil scheme—the high priest and his gang
of Sadducean allies. This momentary courage and passion are admirable,
yet misguided. When Jesus refuses to be their kind of messiah, his followers
desert him. Passion is good, but if it is misguided, it can be devastating. Our
hearts need to be tuned to the Savior or we will miss his direction and find
ourselves embarrassed, confused, and defeated.

TODAY'S PRAYER

*O LORD God, Ruler of Heaven and Earth, teach me to know your ways
and walk in your will. May I live with passion; but may that passion
always be expressed in the direction of your will. May I live with courage;
but may that courage be demonstrated in righteous actions. Search me, O
God, and correct anything wrong in me, I ask in Jesus' name. Amen.*

CONTEXT: MARK 14:43-52

RELATED PASSAGES: ROMANS 10:2-4; PSALM 119:64-68; PSALM 139:22-23

Day 313

AM I SOME CRIMINAL?

MARK 14:48

*Then Jesus said, "Why do you come to get me with
swords and clubs as if I were a criminal?"*

KEY THOUGHT

Jesus' question helps underscore the crucial travesty of the whole Passion (arrest, trials, and crucifixion) story: Jesus didn't deserve what happened to him. He is holy, righteous, compassionate, and loving. Why should he be treated so unfairly? Why would the religious and political leaders treat him so unjustly? So in the middle of the unfairness that we may well face someday, we can remember that the Lord knows our feelings and cares about our struggles. He has been in our position—abandoned by friends, betrayed by those close to him, and treated unjustly and unfairly. Each of us can go to him for his help and know we will be understood and heard because he has been there!

TODAY'S PRAYER

*O Lord God, thank you for knowing and caring about the unfairness
of our world and promising one to day bring true and lasting
justice to this world. In Jesus' name I pray. Amen.*

CONTEXT: MARK 14:43-52

RELATED PASSAGES: ISAIAH 61:11; 2 CORINTHIANS 5:21; PROVERBS 2:6-9

Day 314

WHY NOT IN THE TEMPLE?

MARK 14:49

"Every day I was with you teaching in the Temple area. You did not arrest me there. But all these things have happened to show the full meaning of what the Scriptures said."

KEY THOUGHT

Just as Jesus used a question in the previous verse to confront his accusers about their injustice, he now confronts their fear and treachery in this verse. They came to arrest him at night in his place of prayer away from the crowds. They feared the people because they believed in him. So rather than conducting their "arrest" of Jesus in the daytime, they slink through the darkened streets to a place where they can arrest him without being seen by the crowds. However, Jesus wants to make clear that their treacherous schemes work only because he allows them to work. Jesus is determined to honor his Father's will and fulfill what the Scriptures had said about him. Jesus will be arrested, brutalized, and murdered by these people. However, their evil deeds happen only because he offers himself for our sins, not because they have power over him.

TODAY'S PRAYER

Father, for your Son's faith, obedience, and sacrifice, I give you thanks. May his example motivate me to be faithful no matter what circumstances I find myself facing. In Jesus' name, and to live for his glory, I pray. Amen.

CONTEXT: MARK 14:43-52

RELATED PASSAGES: LUKE 22:1-6; MARK 11:18, 32; MARK 10:32

Day 315

LEFT ALONE TO FACE THE FURY

MARK 14:50
Then all of Jesus' followers left him and ran away.

KEY THOUGHT

For me, this is one of the most heart-wrenching verses in the entire Bible. Jesus is completely abandoned by those whom he had loved, trained, warned, and prepared. The Son of God, with no friend nearby, will now face the pent-up fury of those who have hated him. He will bear unspeakable brutality and have no one to stand with him in his time of agony. He will die alone. Because he has faced abandonment, we can rest assured that he knows how we feel when we are abandoned, betrayed, and abused. Jesus died alone so we would know that we would never be abandoned (Rom. 8:32-39). He promised to be with us every step of the way, yet he had to face the mob alone!

TODAY'S PRAYER

Father, in those times when I feel most alone and abandoned, please help me remember Jesus and realize that he not only knows those feelings of abandonment, but he also has promised never to abandon me. Thank you for this assurance based on such a costly sacrifice. In Jesus' name I thank you. Amen.

CONTEXT: MARK 14:43-52

RELATED PASSAGES: ROMANS 8:32-39; PSALM 23:4; MATTHEW 28:20B

Day 316

ESCAPED WITHOUT A CLOAK

MARK 14:51-52

One of those following Jesus was a young man wearing only a linen cloth. When the people tried to grab him, he left the cloth in their hands and ran away naked.

KEY THOUGHT

If Mark 14:50 is one of the most heart-wrenching passages of the Bible, these verses are two of the most intriguing. Because this verse does not occur in any of the other Gospels, some have suggested that the young man may have been John Mark, who wrote this gospel—that this is his signature placed in the Gospel to insure its authenticity. If this is so, it is yet another reminder that even those who secretly tried to follow Jesus during his Passion were run off by the violent mob. This left Jesus completely alone when surrounded by a crowd crying for his death. No matter who this young man may have been, he is a reminder of a host of the Lord's followers about whom we know little or nothing.

TODAY'S PRAYER

Father, I thank you for those who followed Jesus who I will never know till heaven. I know you used many more people to support his ministry and carry on his mission than we know about in the New Testament. Help me to be willing to serve him whether I am known or not known as one of his loyal followers by future generations. In Jesus' name I pray. Amen.

CONTEXT: MARK 14:43-52

RELATED PASSAGES: 2 CORINTHIANS 6:3-10; REVELATION 2:10; HEBREWS 11:33-38

Day 317

WATCHING BY THE FIRE FROM FAR AWAY

MARK 14:53-54

Those who arrested Jesus led him to the house of the high priest. All the leading priests, the older Jewish leaders, and the teachers of the law were gathered there. Peter followed Jesus but stayed back at a distance. He followed him to the yard of the high priest's house. He went into the yard and sat there with the guards, warming himself by their fire.

KEY THOUGHT

Jesus was brought before the leaders of the Jewish people, but Peter stood at a cowardly distance sneaking around trying to watch the proceedings. While Jesus faced the cold ridicule of those in power, Peter warmed himself at a fire in the company of those put in charge of Jesus' torture. This seems despicable from the safety of our distance of two thousand years, but if we are honest, haven't we done something similar? When Jesus, his cause, and his people are maligned, haven't some of us have pulled back and tried to be unnoticeable? When a brother or sister in Christ is criticized for his or her faith, haven't many of us hidden in the shadows, disguising our loyalty and connection? If we are honest with ourselves, haven't we warmed ourselves at the wrong fire?

TODAY'S PRAYER

Father, give me wisdom to know how to stand up for your truth, your Son, and your will without totally alienating me from unbelievers. Also, dear Father, help me not to back down from my faith because I am afraid or abandon your children when they are under attack. I want to be wise and courageous in my loyalty to your Son and his people. In Jesus' name I pray. Amen.

CONTEXT: MARK 14:53-65

RELATED PASSAGES: MARK 8:34-37; ROMANS 1:16-17; 2 TIMOTHY 1:12

Day 318

LIARS FOR RENT

MARK 14:55-56

The leading priests and the whole high council tried to find something that Jesus had done wrong so they could kill him. But the council could find no proof that would allow them to kill Jesus. Many people came and told lies against Jesus, but they all said different things. None of them agreed.

KEY THOUGHT

Jesus' opponents were trying to find a liar or two that they could "rent" for the duration of Jesus' trial. Their behavior reminds us once again of two terrible realities. First, religious people can do the most despicable things when they are more concerned with self-preservation than with the truth of God. Second, Jesus is about to undergo a gruesome, horribly unfair ordeal. The first should always make us pause and ask for God's guidance and intervention. We should never let our understanding of truth interfere with his will and his people. The second should drive us to our knees in humility, knowing all that the Lord Jesus unfairly endured because of his love for us.

TODAY'S PRAYER

O Almighty God, you are the one who directs the paths of history and brings kingdoms to nothing when they interfere with your work in the world. Please help me and those with whom I fellowship not to interfere with your will. Please never let me be guilty of trying to preserve my religious understanding at the expense of your Kingdom, your people, and your will. In Jesus' name I ask this. Amen.

CONTEXT: MARK 14:53-65

RELATED PASSAGES: PSALM 2:1-12; JOHN 11:45-50; JOHN 8:24

Day 319

CLOSE, BUT . . . .

MARK 14:57-59

*Then some others stood up and told more lies against Jesus. They said,
"We heard this man say, 'I will destroy this Temple built by human
hands. And three days later, I will build another Temple not made by
human hands.'" But also what these people said did not agree.*

KEY THOUGHT

Yes, Jesus did say something about destroying the Temple and building
it again in three days. Yes, it was confusing to those who heard it, even his
closest followers. But Jesus never intended to say such a thing about the
literal Temple in Jerusalem. He was talking about his own body, which would
be nailed to a cross until he was dead, and then be placed in a tomb. God,
however, would raise Jesus from the dead after three days. The point is that
Jesus' enemies couldn't make the charges stick without lying. He is innocent
and yet they are determined to put him to death. Nothing is quite as brutal or
corrupt as religion that loses its way.

TODAY'S PRAYER

*Guide me, dear Father, into the way that I should go and keep me from
the blindness of my own selfishness. In Jesus' name I pray. Amen.*

CONTEXT: MARK 14:53-65

RELATED PASSAGES: PROVERBS 14:12; JOHN 2:13-22; MATTHEW 27:40

Day 320

No Reply

MARK 14:60-61

Then the high priest stood up before everyone and said to Jesus, "These people said things against you. Do you have something to say about their charges? Are they telling the truth?" But Jesus said nothing to answer him.

The high priest asked Jesus another question: "Are you the Christ, the Son of the blessed God?"

KEY THOUGHT

In fulfillment of Isaiah 53, Jesus does not open his mouth. If the totality of his ministry wasn't enough to silence his critics, then a verbal defense wouldn't help now. Jesus has the power to stop these events, but his silence is just one more way he shows he is obeying the will of God no matter the cost to himself. A priestly system that had grown corrupt and sold out to the Roman political machine could not and would not judge him fairly. Their only desire was to stay in power. Jesus will not dignify them with a self-defense. He needs no defense to prove his innocence and he has already chosen to suffer the humiliation of what he will face to honor God and to save us. His answer will be sacrificial obedience!

TODAY'S PRAYER

Father, please help me use opportunities to influence others in a redemptive way, not a selfish one. I am humbled at Jesus' restraint, sacrifice, and obedience. May I have such wisdom and restraint when it is your will and may I be boldly passionate when that response is needed. I want to honor you in all things. In Jesus' name I pray. Amen.

CONTEXT: MARK 14:53-65

RELATED PASSAGES: ISAIAH 53:7-12; ACTS 8:30-35; 1 PETER 2:21-25

Day 321

You'll See Me and Then Know!

Mark 14:61-62

But Jesus said nothing to answer him.

The high priest asked Jesus another question: "Are you the Christ, the Son of the blessed God?"

Jesus answered, "Yes, I am the Son of God. And in the future you will see the Son of Man sitting at the right side of God All-Powerful. And you will see the Son of Man coming on the clouds of heaven."

Key Thought

Jesus only response—and it is not a defense but a warning to those who think him an enemy—is that he is the Messiah and that they will see him when returns in power. Those who were so sure Jesus was evil, those who were so absorbed in getting him out of the way, those who were so sure it was better that he die, and those who were so sure that Jesus was just a man, will all see him again. This time, however, it will be when he comes in glory. For those of us who long for his return, this will be a day of glorious victory. For those who oppose him, this will be a day of unrivaled sorrow. So let's do all we can so that all people know that Jesus is the Son of God.

Today's Prayer

O Father, may Jesus come soon. Until the day he returns, please use me to serve others and bring them to belief in him. In Jesus' name I pray. Amen.

Context: Mark 14:53-65

Related Passages: 2 Timothy 4:6-8;
1 Thessalonians 5:2-11; Revelation 1:7-8

Day 322

THEY ALL CONDEMNED HIM

MARK 14:63-64

When the high priest heard this, he tore his clothes in anger. He said, "We don't need any more witnesses! You all heard these insults to God. What do you think?"

Everyone agreed that Jesus was guilty and must be killed.

KEY THOUGHT

Jesus comes to us and demands a decision. He offers us his body of work, his life here on earth, as the testimony we can either accept or reject. There is no middle ground: Jesus is either our promised Messiah and Lord, or he is a mad man and lunatic. There is no room for partial acceptance. He is one or the other. What have we decided about Jesus? He doesn't want anyone to stay on the fence of indecision or in the throes of lukewarm discipleship. To refuse to follow with our whole heart is to reject him as our Lord. So the question comes to each of us, "What do you think?"

TODAY'S PRAYER

O Father, I choose Jesus. However, you know that I am sometimes weak and falter. Please forgive me. I never want to be indecisive about my love and loyalty to your Son. Help me live decisively for him. In Jesus' name I ask for this help. Amen.

CONTEXT: MARK 14:53-65

RELATED PASSAGES: 1 JOHN 5:1-5, 13; REVELATION 3:15-22; LUKE 9:26

Day 323

THE JEERS OF THE CRUEL CONDEMNERS

MARK 14:65

*Some of the people there spit at him. They covered his eyes and
hit him with their fists. They said, "Be a prophet and tell us who
hit you!" Then the guards led Jesus away and beat him.*

KEY THOUGHT

I never cease to be amazed at the thoughtless cruelty that human beings
can inflict on one another. No wonder that we needed a perfect Savior, one
who would bear our insults, our violence, our injustice, and our humiliation,
yet still love us. Thank God Jesus came, endured our inhumanity, bore our
sins, and bought our pardon!

TODAY'S PRAYER

*O loving Father, my stomach turns at the inhumanity and senseless violence that
permeates our world. Forgive our propensity for returning violence for violence and our
willingness to inflict violence. Redeem our time and our world through the powerful
reminder of your Son, who bore our sins and carried our sorrows while under the most
inhuman and violent abuse. I thank you for your Son, in whose name I pray. Amen.*

CONTEXT: MARK 14:53-65

RELATED PASSAGES: ISAIAH 53:5; ROMANS 5:6-8; 2 CORINTHIANS 5:21

Day 324

YOU WERE ONE OF THEM!

MARK 14:66-67

While Peter was still in the yard, a servant girl of the high priest came there. She saw him warming himself by the fire. She looked closely at him and said, "You were with Jesus, that man from Nazareth."

KEY THOUGHT

Peter needs to warm his soul, but the fire can warm only his body. The chill that Peter faces is the kind of chill that descends upon those who are profoundly disappointed, confused, and disillusioned with their faith. He could not stay awake in the garden while Jesus prayed. Even though he drew a sword and tried to start a fight with the enemy, when Jesus told him to put the sword away, he didn't know what else to do. When the Lord was arrested by an angry mob led by Judas, one of Peter's friends, Peter's heart was broken and conflicted. So now, as he warms himself in the night chill, he is about to face a deeper chill of his own—the chill of failure, brokenness, and defeat. When we find ourselves battling the same things, remember that Peter's story doesn't end with his weakness, abandonment, and denials. His story ends only after God mightily uses him. Peter is the great reminder that God can use us after our failures if we will only return and let him do so.

TODAY'S PRAYER

Father, please forgive me and heal me. I need your grace, dear Father, but most of all I need you. In Jesus' name I ask for this grace, forgiveness, and healing. Amen.

CONTEXT: MARK 14:66-72

RELATED PASSAGES: LUKE 24:32-34; 2 TIMOTHY 1:15-18; HEBREWS 10:32-34

Day 325

No Way!

MARK 14:68

But Peter said this was not true. "That makes no sense," he said.
"I don't know what you are talking about!" Then he left and
went to the entrance of the yard, and a rooster crowed.

KEY THOUGHT

Peter denies the Lord the first time, just as Jesus had warned him that he would. On cue, the rooster crows as if God is trying to stir Peter's soul to some newfound fortitude or to warn him of his impending failure that has already begun to unfold. As the verses that follow show, Peter does not awaken from his spiritual slumber. He continues down the path of denial and abandonment that was begun in the Garden of Gethsemane. How many times have we been caught in the downward spiral of some spiritual weakness and not heeded the Lord's warning and not found his way of escape?

TODAY'S PRAYER

O God, forgive me for not heeding your warnings, for not asking for your Spirit's power, and for not taking your way of escape. Strengthen me by your Spirit, I pray, and open my eyes to see your way through my times of temptation and sin. In Jesus' name I pray. Amen.

CONTEXT: MARK 14:66-72

RELATED PASSAGES: 1 CORINTHIANS 10:12-13;
EPHESIANS 3:14-16; 1 PETER 5:8-9

Day 326

ONE OF THEM?

MARK 14:69-70

When the servant girl saw him there, she began saying again to the people
standing around, "This man is one of them." Again Peter said it was not true.

A short time later, the people standing there said, "We know
you are one of them, because you are from Galilee."

KEY THOUGHT

Galileans were not very well liked by many in Jerusalem. They had a
different accent. Galilee was even known as Galilee of the Gentiles by the Jews.
Jesus was known as "The Galilean." Peter was branded guilty by association
with "The Galilean." Rather than defending the Lord or accepting this "guilt
by association," Peter continues to deny his association him. We sometimes
talk badly about Peter because of his failure. The real question to face is this:
How many times have I denied or betrayed my Lord for far less than Peter did?
Despite Peter's failures, Jesus reclaimed Peter and used him mightily. Let's use
this example of the Lord's grace, not to justify our failure, but to stiffen our
wills so we won't fail and have the courage to return to him when we do fail.

TODAY'S PRAYER

Father, your grace is incredible. I am encouraged that even after his failure,
you reclaimed Peter and used him in mighty ways. Dear God, I don't
want to fail like this. Help me to never do so. Also, dear Father, use me
to help reclaim those who have failed and don't think they can find their
way back to you. In Jesus' name I humbly ask for this grace. Amen.

CONTEXT: MARK 14:66-72

RELATED PASSAGES: MARK 8:38; GALATIANS 6:1; JOHN 13:31-38

Day 327

AN OATH OF BETRAYAL

MARK 14:70-72

Again Peter said it was not true.

A short time later, the people standing there said, "We know you are one of them, because you are from Galilee."

Then Peter began to curse. He said, "I swear to God, I don't know this man you are talking about!"

As soon as Peter said this, the rooster crowed the second time. Then he remembered what Jesus had told him: "Before the rooster crows twice, you will say three times that you don't know me." Then Peter began to cry.

KEY THOUGHT

Peter swore that he didn't know Jesus. Then he heard the rooster crow and he realized the bitter truth. Not once. Not twice. But three times he had denied his Lord. The third time he even cursed and used an oath! How could he have done it? Only minutes earlier he had been willing to draw a sword and take on the armed soldiers that had come to arrest Jesus. Where had his courage, conviction, and commitment gone? None of us is strong enough to guarantee we won't abandon our Lord for a time. However, the test we face involves two parts. The first is resisting the pressure to sin. If we yield to that temptation and sin, the second part is to have the courage to recognize it as sin, be convicted to the core of our hearts, and to change behavior and renew our allegiance to the Lord.

TODAY'S PRAYER

O Father, I want to demonstrate my allegiance to you, your Son, and your Kingdom no matter what my outward circumstances. But, dear Father, if I fail and sin, please help me to have the courage to recognize it, to be convicted of it, and to be spiritually committed to come back and show that it was an exception to a life wholly devoted to you. In Jesus' name I pray. Amen.

CONTEXT: MARK 14:66-72

RELATED PASSAGES: LUKE 22:31-32; JOHN 21:15-19; MARK 14:38

Day 328

ARE YOU THE KING?

MARK 15:1-2

Very early in the morning, the leading priests, the older Jewish leaders, the teachers of the law, and the whole high council decided what to do with Jesus. They tied him, led him away, and handed him over to Governor Pilate.

Pilate asked Jesus, "Are you the king of the Jews?"

Jesus answered, "Yes, that is right."

KEY THOUGHT

Jesus faced a sham trial and a travesty of justice. The Lord was condemned to die by the Jewish high council and the High Priest along with his priestly conspirators. Pilate had to approve of the execution because the Jews could not carry out that sentence without Roman approval. About the only truth that comes out of this trial is Jesus' acceptance of Pilate's title for him—King of the Jews. Jesus is the king appointed by God. The Lord will not deny his identity even to save his life. He will be recognized at God's time and in God's way, but on this day he will be mocked, beaten, and killed as the rejected King of the Jews.

TODAY'S PRAYER

Father in heaven, according to your promise and your plan, Jesus is King. I gladly accept him and praise him as my King. He reigns on David's throne forever and ever. While I hate that the price of his kingship was so high, I am thrilled that he is the King of glory, and that he will reign forever and ever. Amen.

CONTEXT: MARK 15:1-15

RELATED PASSAGES: PSALM 24:7-10; LUKE 19:35-38; REVELATION 19:6

Day 329

NOT A WORD

MARK 15:3-5

The leading priests accused Jesus of many things. So Pilate asked Jesus another question. He said, "You can see that these people are accusing you of many things. Why don't you answer?"

But Jesus still did not answer, and this really surprised Pilate.

KEY THOUGHT

Once again, as Old Testament Scripture had promised, Jesus does not try to defend himself. He is silent. Pilate is surprised at such silence. Why would Jesus not defend himself? The answer is clear: because the real issue at stake was not Jesus' innocence, but our guilt. He goes to face his crucifixion as the sinless one falsely convicted and sentenced to death for the sins of each of us.

TODAY'S PRAYER

Dear Father, I am ashamed that our sins were responsible for your Son's death. I am horrified that he was treated so barbarically. I am angered that justice was so perverted. I am enraged that political preservation was more important to those in charge than the life of your Son. However, dear Father, I am eternally grateful that your Son loved us enough to endure the cross. And, Lord Jesus, not only do I pray this in your name, but I thank you with all my heart for what you did for me. Amen.

CONTEXT: MARK 15:1-15

RELATED PASSAGES: 2 CORINTHIANS 5:19-21; ISAIAH 53:7-11; JOHN 3:16-17

Day 330

Release!

Mark 15:6-8

Every year at the Passover time the governor would free one prisoner—whichever one the people wanted. There was a man in prison at that time named Barabbas. He and the rebels with him had been put in prison for committing murder during a riot.

The people came to Pilate and asked him to free a prisoner as he always did.

Key Thought

Jesus' ministry was all about release—release from the power of death, release from the power of disease, release from the power of the devil, release from everything that holds us back from being what God wants us to be. We shouldn't find it surprising that Jesus' approaching death sentence coincides with a time when the release of a prisoner is front and center on people's minds. The cross is about release—our release from sin and death at the cost of Jesus' freedom, Jesus' comfort, and Jesus' life.

Today's Prayer

Dear Father, I thank you for my freedom from the power of sin and death. I know it was purchased at a high price, the sacrifice of your Son for my sins. I know that in many ways, I am like Barabbas—deserving punishment but granted freedom because of your Son. Thank you. In Jesus' name I humbly thank you. Amen.

Context: Mark 15:1-15

Related Passages: Luke 4:16-21; Hebrews 2:14-15; Romans 7:24-25

Day 331

PILATE KNOWS THE TRUTH

MARK 15:9-10

Pilate asked them, "Do you want me to free the king of the Jews?" Pilate knew that the leading priests had handed Jesus over to him because they were jealous of him.

KEY THOUGHT

People often make their decisions to honor Jesus based upon the opinion of the crowd around them. Pilate, though armed with Rome's military might, is a puppet in the hands of Jesus' enemies because he is willing to let the crowd decide what he will do with Jesus. What about us? Will we be swayed by the crowd or stand firmly for what we believe about Jesus?

TODAY'S PRAYER

O Father, please give me the courage to be loyal to Jesus no matter which way the crowd goes. In Jesus' name I ask for this courage. Amen.

CONTEXT: MARK 15:1-15

RELATED PASSAGES: MARK 8:38; 1 CORINTHIANS 15:31-34; REVELATION 2:10

Day 332

PRIESTS OF POLITICS

MARK 15:11

But the leading priests persuaded the people to ask Pilate to free Barabbas, not Jesus.

KEY THOUGHT

Pilate knew that the leading priests had handed Jesus over because of envy (Luke 15:10). Now they are orchestrating the events behind the scenes and stirring up the mob for Pilate to release Barabbas. Let's watch their behavior throughout this story and realize how easily we might slip from an honest search for truth into a mad frenzy to defend what we do and believe. Let's pursue Jesus and his truth so we can be set free from our petty desires to protect ourselves and what we have grown accustomed to doing and believing in our religious worlds.

TODAY'S PRAYER

O Father, I want to seek you, your truth, and your Kingdom above all other things, including my own comfort with things I have experienced and known. Lead me to know and to live your truth whatever the cost. In Jesus' name I ask for this grace and strength. Amen.

CONTEXT: MARK 15:1-15

RELATED PASSAGES: MATTHEW 23:29-36; MATTHEW 5:21-26; JAMES 1:26-27

Day 333

CRUCIFY HIM!

MARK 15:12-13

Pilate asked the people again, "So what should I do with this man you call the king of the Jews?"

The people shouted, "Kill him on a cross!"

KEY THOUGHT

The sickening answer to Pilate's question reverberates through time: "Kill him on a cross!" How horrible! Yet as much as evil people are responsible for Jesus' death, this is also God's plan. We should feel the emotional and spiritual agony for our Savior as people he had created now call for his death. When we feel rejected, we have to know that we can talk to Jesus and know that he hears us and cares about us. He has been here . . . all alone . . . abandoned, betrayed, and denied by his closest friends . . . hated by the religious leaders . . . rejected by the people he came to save.

TODAY'S PRAYER

O Father, I sometimes feel isolated and alone, rejected and betrayed by those I trusted. However, dear God, knowing that your Son faced this and now is at your right hand to plead my case to you, I know that I am not alone and that I am never rejected at your throne of mercy and grace. In Jesus' name I thank you. Amen.

CONTEXT: MARK 15:1-15

RELATED PASSAGES: HEBREWS 2:14-16; 1 JOHN 2:1-2; HEBREWS 7:24-25

Day 334

WHY?

MARK 15:14
Pilate asked, "Why? What wrong has he done?"
But the people shouted louder and louder, "Kill him on a cross!"

KEY THOUGHT

Why was Jesus crucified? He was innocent. He had done no crime. He had not committed a single sin. Mark wants us to know that the crowd had lost its collective mind and was thirsty for blood—Jesus' blood. Jesus will not die because he has done wrong. He will be crucified because those who hated him had steered the crowd in a horribly wrong direction and because this was God's eternal plan for our salvation. Jesus is the righteous victim of a crowd out of control and the jealousy and hatred of religious leaders. Jesus is also our righteous Redeemer, who sacrificially gives himself for our sins.

TODAY'S PRAYER

Holy and righteous Father, I hate it when I realize that I have lost my sense of perspective because I have found myself absorbed by the will of the crowd. Please give me the wisdom and the courage to stand against the crowd when the crowd is wrong, even if I have to do it alone. In Jesus' name I pray. Amen.

CONTEXT: MARK 15:1-15

RELATED PASSAGES: 1 PETER 3:18; 2 CORINTHIANS 5:21; ACTS 2:36-40

Day 335

ANXIOUS TO PLEASE THE CROWD

MARK 15:15

Pilate wanted to please the people, so he set Barabbas free for them. And he told the soldiers to beat Jesus with whips. Then he handed him over to the soldiers to be killed on a cross.

KEY THOUGHT

Pilate knew that Jesus was innocent, yet gave in to the wishes of the mob: he first had Jesus beaten with whips and then turned Jesus over to be crucified. Why did he do it? Pilate had to keep Rome happy by maintaining order. This meant appeasing the crowd. Even though he has already pronounced Jesus "not guilty" of any crime, the crowd influences Pilate's choice and his word was law. Jesus, however, knew that Pilate had no power to act, rule, or enforce his verdict apart from God's granting him that power. Pilate unknowingly acted in concert with the crowd's will, Rome's desire, and God's plan for our salvation. Jesus was allowed to be crucified—both by Pilate, to appease the crowd that is being manipulated by its religious leaders, and also by God, who is using this horrifying event to save the world. If God can bring such a great redemption out of such an injustice, imagine what he can do with our suffering for his sake when we are seeking to do his will!

TODAY'S PRAYER

O God, you are the Almighty, the one in control even when I cannot see your control. I believe that you will redeem every injustice brought upon your people at your chosen time. Give me the faith and strength to endure hard times and the courage to live my life in the hope of your deliverance. In Jesus' name I pray. Amen.

CONTEXT: MARK 15:1-15

RELATED PASSAGES: JOHN 19:1-16; ACTS 2:22-23; GALATIANS 1:10

Day 336

THE HUMILIATION BEGINS IN EARNEST

MARK 15:16-19

Pilate's soldiers took Jesus into the governor's palace (called the Praetorium). They called all the other soldiers together. They put a purple robe on Jesus, made a crown from thorny branches, and put it on his head. Then they began shouting, "Welcome, king of the Jews!" They kept on beating his head with a stick and spitting on him. Then they bowed down on their knees and pretended to honor him as a king.

KEY THOUGHT

The purpose of crucifixion wasn't just to kill a criminal. It was also to serve as a deterrent to crime by utterly humiliating the person who was being crucified. So once Pilate signals that Jesus will be crucified, the humiliation begins in earnest. Not only will Jesus be killed on a cross, but he will also be humiliated every step of the way. He had warned his closest followers that this would happen. He knows what is coming. He faces it because it is God's will and the basis of our salvation. How can we not be willing to face embarrassment, ridicule, and even persecution for him?

TODAY'S PRAYER

O Father, help me to never be ashamed of Jesus. After what he endured for me, I want to faithfully stand by him and to courageously stand up for him. Fill me with the Holy Spirit and with genuine courage to honor you and your Son, no matter the cost. In Jesus' name I ask this. Amen.

CONTEXT: MARK 15:16-32

RELATED PASSAGES: HEBREWS 13:12-13; MARK 8:34-37; MARK 10:32-34

Day 337

LED AWAY

MARK 15:20

After they finished making fun of him, they took off the purple robe and put his own clothes on him again. Then they led him out of the palace to be killed on a cross.

KEY THOUGHT

"After they finished making fun of Jesus . . . ." What a sad and sobering commentary! Jesus is not a person in the minds of the soldiers, but a toy for these sadistic persecutors to use to amuse themselves. Mockery, derision, and brutality were their purposes in Jesus' crucifixion journey. They did their job well and were now ready to get him to the destination of their savagery. We must never doubt Jesus' love for us. He didn't die a quick and quiet death for us. He was repeatedly abused, insulted, ridiculed, mocked, and belittled. Not only was he doing this to be our Savior, but also to be our example. He practices what he has taught: turn the other cheek, love your enemies, and pray for those who persecute you. Now he asks us to be willing to follow in his steps.

TODAY'S PRAYER

Dear Heavenly Father, please use me to be a redemptive influence wherever I find myself. Even if I find myself in hostile and unfair circumstances, please help me live up to the example of your Son. In Jesus' name I ask for this strength and grace. Amen.

CONTEXT: MARK 15:16-32

RELATED PASSAGES: MATTHEW 5:38-48; 1 PETER 2:19-24; LUKE 23:34

Day 338

CARRYING THE CROSS!

MARK 15:21

There was a man from Cyrene named Simon walking into the city from the fields. He was the father of Alexander and Rufus. The soldiers forced him to carry Jesus' cross.

KEY THOUGHT

Jesus told his followers, including those of us who follow him today, that they should pick up our crosses and follow him. While Simon was forced to physically to carry Jesus' cross to Golgotha, he also apparently picked up the cross spiritually because his sons, Alexander and Rufus, are known in the Christian community Mark is addressing. Paul also seems to know one of the sons, Rufus, and Paul describes him as one "whom the Lord picked out to be his very own" (Rom. 16:13 NLT). This is a great reminder that if we want to share our faith with our children, "carrying the cross" is the powerful example that helps them follow in our footsteps as we follow in Jesus' steps!

TODAY'S PRAYER

O Father God, please help me live as a powerful example before my family. May they clearly see that I don't just "talk the talk," but that I also "walk the walk." Give me courage as I genuinely commit to carry the cross each day. In Jesus' name I pray. Amen.

CONTEXT: MARK 15:16-32

RELATED PASSAGES: LUKE 9:21-23; DEUTERONOMY 6:1-9; ROMANS 16:13

Day 339

OUR PLACE OF HOPE

MARK 15:22-24

They led Jesus to the place called Golgotha. (Golgotha means "The Place of the Skull.") There they gave him some wine mixed with myrrh, but he refused to drink it. The soldiers nailed Jesus to a cross. Then they divided his clothes among themselves, throwing dice to see who would get what.

KEY THOUGHT

The cross was a Roman tool of torture, shame, and humiliation. The cross that awaited Jesus was on Skull Hill. Not only did the hill look somewhat like a skull, but it was also a place of death, mockery, and pain. In this instance, however, it was also a place of redemption, forgiveness, and hope. What begins here in horror and inhumanity ends in victory and grace for us all.

TODAY'S PRAYER

Holy and loving God, I am humbled and touched by the cross of Christ. Dear Father, help me to remember the grace, power, and victory that are mine because of that cross. In Jesus' name I thank you and praise you. Amen.

CONTEXT: MARK 15:16-32

RELATED PASSAGES: MARK 10:32-34; JOHN 12:27-32; COLOSSIANS 1:18-23

Day 340

THE GAMBLE

MARK 15:24

The soldiers nailed Jesus to a cross. Then they divided his clothes
among themselves, throwing dice to see who would get what.

KEY THOUGHT

Just as the soldiers at the foot of this cross gambled for Jesus' clothes, people still gamble on the cross of Christ today. Anytime people refuse to recognize who was crucified on that cross, they gamble their eternal future, assuming that Jesus was just another piece of human trash to crucify. The stakes of this gamble are incredibly high. Either Jesus offers eternal life with God or he is a delusional, self-appointed messiah. Skull Hill leaves no other places for us to place a wager. God promises life for those who believe in what Jesus did at this cross and commit their lives to him. For those who do not believe, there is only a risky gamble that this Jesus was just another man. We know from Mark 15:39 that at least one soldier acknowledged Jesus as God's Son. What have you decided about the identity of this man, Jesus, on this cross?

TODAY'S PRAYER

Father in heaven, I believe that Jesus died on the cross to save me from my sins. I believe you raised Jesus from the dead. I have been baptized to share in his death and I have been raised to walk in a new life trusting in your saving power. I believe that Jesus' death and resurrection broke the power that Satan and his demons had over me through death. Please help me keep dead the old life I have left. Empower me by your Spirit so that I can be a living witness to the power of your Son's love and your grace. In Jesus' name I pray. Amen.

CONTEXT: MARK 15:16-32

RELATED PASSAGES: 1 CORINTHIANS 1:18-25; COLOSSIANS 2:11-15; GALATIANS 6:14

Day 341

RECOGNIZED AS KING

MARK 15:25-26

It was nine o'clock in the morning when they nailed Jesus to the cross. There was a sign with the charge against him written on it. It said, "The King of the Jews."

KEY THOUGHT

Jesus was recognized as King at his birth by angels, shepherds, and stargazers. Only God truly recognized Jesus as King during the crucifixion. Jesus the Messiah, the King of the Jews was nailed to the cross, with a sign mocking him and stating the charge against him nailed in place as well. While God had shown glimpses of his plan through the words of the prophets, a crucified Messiah was inconceivable to Jesus' contemporaries. So while the sign attached to the cross above Jesus' head is true, only God knows it at the moment of his Son's death. To everyone but the Father, everything seems lost in the mockery of this sign, of this crowd, and of this cross. But God is faithful and Jesus is King, and as awful as these moments on the cross are for Jesus, they become the ultimate proof of his worthiness as Messiah and King. Long may this King reign in our hearts!

TODAY'S PRAYER

O Father, only you would devise such a plan to redeem us. Only you would have your Son revealed as King from the place equated with humiliation, suffering, and death. I confess, dear God, that the message of the cross captures my heart and helps me know your love more fully. I praise you for such love and for such a sacrificial King. In the mighty name of Jesus I praise you. Amen.

CONTEXT: MARK 15:16-32

RELATED PASSAGES: MATTHEW 2:1-2; ACTS 2:32-36; MARK 15:32

Day 342

Among the Criminals

Mark 15:27-28

They also nailed two criminals to crosses beside Jesus—
one on the right and the other on the left.

Key Thought

Jesus came to earth and lived as one of us. He made his home among real people; he wasn't tucked away in some neat and tidy place protected from the agony, sin, and filth of our world. So it is not surprising that when he was killed on the cross, he was placed between two criminals. Jesus demonstrated God's love in a place where any of us, no matter how great or how small, no matter how spiritual or how vile, could find him.

Today's Prayer

Dear God, I am truly saddened that Jesus had to die like a criminal, among criminals, in the most horrible of conditions. At the same time, dear Father, I am truly thankful that your love is shown so clearly and offered in a place so dreadful that none of us could ever legitimately think we could not find it. In Jesus' name I praise and thank you for your grace. Amen.

Context: Mark 15:16-32

Related Passages: Philippians 2:5-11; John 1:10-18; Colossians 1:13

Day 343

SAVE YOURSELF!

MARK 15:29-30

People walked by and said bad things to Jesus. They shook their heads and said, "You said you could destroy the Temple and build it again in three days. So save yourself! Come down from that cross!"

KEY THOUGHT

If you listen carefully, behind the voice of the people shouting abuse at Jesus you can hear the voice of Satan mocking God's Son. Notice how similar these words are to the words of Satan when he tempted Jesus at the beginning of his ministry: "Then the Devil took him to Jerusalem, to the highest point of the Temple, and said, 'If you are the Son of God, jump off! For the Scriptures say, He orders his angels to protect you'" (Matt. 4:5-6). Jesus had refused to use his power and identity as a means for self-protection when Satan tempted earlier. From the beginning of his ministry all the way to the cross, Jesus used his power and his identity as the Son of God to help and bless others. He didn't come to prove his identity, but to give himself as a ransom. His life was lived in the shadow of the cross and he allowed nothing to stop him from his mission. He had the power to preserve himself, but he loved you and me too much to come down from that cross until his work was finished and his life was given for us!

TODAY'S PRAYER

Praise to you, O God, Lord of heaven and earth. Praise to you, King Jesus, for your gracious and sacrificial love. Without your grace, your sacrifice, and your presence, I would be hopelessly lost! In the name of Jesus and through the intercession of the Spirit, I pray. Amen.

CONTEXT: MARK 15:16-32

RELATED PASSAGES: MARK 10:45; ISAIAH 53:3-5; ACTS 2:36-40

Day 344

HE CAN'T SAVE HIMSELF!

MARK 15:31

The leading priests and the teachers of the law were also there. They made fun of Jesus the same as the other people did. They said to each other, "He saved others, but he can't save himself!"

KEY THOUGHT

Wrong! Jesus didn't save himself so he could save others . . . save you . . . save me. Thankfully the religious folks were wrong about Jesus' power to save. Thank God that Jesus loved us enough to bear their ridicule, face their scorn, absorb their hate, suffer their torture, and endure their humiliation. And he did it for you and me!

TODAY'S PRAYER

O Father, my words are inadequate to express my heartfelt gratitude and eternal thanks for your incomparable love. Thank you, dear Father. Thank you, dear Savior; I owe everything to you, and in your name I offer my thanks and praise. Amen.

CONTEXT: MARK 15:16-32

RELATED PASSAGES: JOHN 11:17-18; JOHN 19:6-11; REVELATION 1:7

Day 345

Ridiculed by Everyone!

Mark 15:32

"If he is really the Christ, the king of Israel, he should come down from the cross now. When we see this, then we will believe in him." The criminals on the crosses beside Jesus also said bad things to him.

Key Thought

Jesus is ridiculed by everyone present during his Passion: the crowds cried "Crucify him!" before Pilate, the soldiers beat and mocked him, people who passed by hurled their insults at him, the religious leaders mocked him, and even the criminals who were dying beside him threw in their own ridicule. Jesus faced the cruelty and the humiliation of the cross, alone. His own closest followers had betrayed, denied, and abandoned him. He did it so you and I can have the confidence that he will never abandon us—even if everyone we hold dear abandons us and those who hate us hurl insults at us. Jesus demonstrated that he would pay any price to love us. What a friend! What a King! What a Savior!

Today's Prayer

Father, thank you for the assurance that I will never be alone, abandoned, or forgotten. No matter what others may do to me, I believe that you are never going to forsake me or leave me. Thank you! In Jesus' name I pray. Amen.

Context: Mark 15:16-32

Related Passages: Hebrews 13:5-6; Romans 8:31-39; Psalm 23:4

Day 346

WHY HAVE YOU FORSAKEN ME?

MARK 15:33-34

At noon the whole country became dark. This darkness continued until three o'clock. At three o'clock Jesus cried out loudly, "Eloi, Eloi, lama sabachthani." This means "My God, my God, why have you left me alone?"

KEY THOUGHT

This is the hour of darkness. While the time may be noon, all light was snuffed out as Jesus faced ridicule , shame, brutality, and humiliation alone. He felt absolutely abandoned. But read Psalm 22, the Psalm Jesus partially quoted on the cross and that describes many of the events on the cross. Notice how it speaks of feeling absolutely abandoned and completely being surrounded by enemies. Then read how it finishes: "Those who are not yet born will be told about him. Each generation will tell their children about the good things the Lord has done" (Ps. 22:30-31). In the middle of humanity's worst moment, Jesus looks beyond the horror with the eyes of faith. He will be faithful even though he feels alone. He will trust that the God he honors with his death will also be the Father who will bring him victory.

TODAY'S PRAYER

O Almighty God, my Abba Father, please give me the kind of faith that Jesus had. I want to be able to obey and bring you glory even when I feel abandoned and forsaken. Give me that kind of courage. Empower me with that kind of trust, I pray in Jesus' name. Amen.

CONTEXT: MARK 15:33-41

RELATED PASSAGES: PSALM 22:12-31; HEBREWS 12:2; HEBREWS 4:14-16

Day 347

WILL ELIJAH COME?

MARK 15:35-36

Some of the people standing there heard this. They said, "Listen! He is calling Elijah."

One man there ran and got a sponge. He filled the sponge with sour wine and tied it to a stick. Then he used the stick to give the sponge to Jesus to get a drink from it. The man said, "We should wait now and see if Elijah will come to take him down from the cross."

KEY THOUGHT

From the vantage points of Jesus the Messiah and of the Gospel of Mark, Elijah had already come. John the Baptizer was the Elijah who was to precede the Messiah. Those in power had John murdered; now they were doing the same with Jesus. Those who are at the cross to mock the Lord Jesus misunderstand what he said. They simply turn Jesus' words into another way to mock, belittle, and humiliate him. Little do these mockers know that what Jesus endures on the cross ends up defeating Satan and bringing life to those who call upon him as Lord. Elijah didn't come and take Jesus down from the cross, rather God allowed his Son to die on the cross.

TODAY'S PRAYER

O Father, I am saddened that it took the humiliation of the cross to break through to our hardened hearts. Yet, dear Father, thank you for paying that price. I pray that the story of Jesus will reach hearts that no other story can. Please help me never to be ashamed of the message of that cross. In Jesus' name I pray. Amen.

CONTEXT: MARK 15:33-41

RELATED PASSAGES: COLOSSIANS 2:11-15; HEBREWS 2:14-15; GALATIANS 6:14

Day 348

IT'S FINISHED!

MARK 15:37
Then Jesus cried out loudly and died.

KEY THOUGHT

Jesus finished his work as our ransom from sin and death. Please ponder the incredible words of Mark 15:37. God in human flesh died. He died because he allowed his life to be taken. He died as one of us. He died in pain, humiliation, rejection, and ridicule. He died alone so we won't ever have to doubt his love for us or his presence with us. He died because he loves us and wants to free us from our sin by his blood. He completed the work that God has given him to do for us.

TODAY'S PRAYER

Almighty God, I cannot begin to imagine how Jesus' death impacted your heart and the hosts of heaven. Reading this story breaks my heart knowing that our utter sinfulness placed Jesus on the cross. Thank you for my redemption. Thank you for paying such a horrible price to win that redemption. Hallelujah and thank you in Jesus' name! Amen.

CONTEXT: MARK 15:33-41

RELATED PASSAGES: TITUS 2:14; MARK 10:32-34, 45; ROMANS 6:1-8

Day 349

HOLY OF HOLIES

MARK 15:37-38
Then Jesus cried out loudly and died.

*When Jesus died, the curtain in the Temple was torn into two pieces.
The tear started at the top and tore all the way to the bottom.*

KEY THOUGHT

This event and its symbolism are powerful. The curtain in today's
Scripture was the one between the Holy Place and the Most Holy Place in the
Jewish Temple. For the Jews, the Mercy Seat of God was in the Most Holy
Place and only the High Priest could go before it on behalf of the people. The
tearing of the curtain from top to bottom symbolized that the cross of Christ
opens up the way for us to go straight to the Mercy Seat of God—the place
of ultimate forgiveness in the very presence of God. Jesus is the sacrifice that
completely cleanses us and makes us right with God. Barriers no longer stand
between us and God's grace. Jesus opened up the way for us to the very heart
of God. As horrible as the humiliation of the cross was for Jesus, it was all the
more glorious for us because it ushered in a new way to God for us.

TODAY'S PRAYER
*Loving and sacrificial God, thank you for this gift too wonderful for
words to describe and for paying the price that was too costly for us to
pay. In Jesus' name I offer you my prayer and my life. Amen.*

CONTEXT: MARK 15:33-41

RELATED PASSAGES: HEBREWS 10:1-4, 11-12, 19-22; HEBREWS 8:6-13;
2 CORINTHIANS 5:21

Day 350

SON OF GOD!

MARK 15:39

The army officer who was standing there in front of the cross saw what happened when Jesus died. The officer said, "This man really was the Son of God!"

KEY THOUGHT

While crucifixion was designed to humiliate and torture people, God used this cross to exert power that defies explanation. Something in the message of Jesus' going to this cross reaches out and grabs the hearts of those seeking God. They see the Almighty God's love powerfully demonstrated in the world they know as unfair, brutal, and humiliating. God placed his message of love where all people could see it and be touched by it. One strong evidence of this power is an officer in the Roman army—someone acquainted with the brutal death of crucifixion. This officer saw God's presence in this moment. His confession should be our confession anytime we read the story of Jesus' crucifixion: "This man really was the Son of God!"

TODAY'S PRAYER

Yes, dear Father, I believe that this Jesus who hung on the cross for my sin is your Son! In his name, and to your glory, I offer my thanks and praise to you. Amen.

CONTEXT: MARK 15:33-41

RELATED PASSAGES: JOHN 12:23-33; JOHN 20:30-31; 1 JOHN 5:13

Day 351

THE FAITHFUL WOMEN

MARK 15:40-41

Some women were standing away from the cross, watching. Among these women were Mary Magdalene, Salome, and Mary the mother of James and Joses. (James was her youngest son.) These were the women who had followed Jesus in Galilee and cared for him. Many other women who had come with Jesus to Jerusalem were also there.

KEY THOUGHT

The people of God have been blessed and often sustained by the courageous faithfulness of godly women. While the men who were closest to Jesus betrayed, denied, and abandoned him, the women were different. They followed him as he passed through the streets going to Golgotha, were present at the cross, met him at the empty tomb, and were present in the upper room at Pentecost. Let's never underestimate or devalue the importance of godly women. Jesus never did! Let's also commit to their example of faithfulness, never abandoning our Lord no matter what is happening around us.

TODAY'S PRAYER

O Father, thank you for the godly women in my life who shaped my faith, taught me your truth, served those in my family, and were examples of courage and faith to me. Use me to encourage women of faith and to affirm their importance to your Kingdom. In Jesus' name I pray. Amen.

CONTEXT: MARK 15:33-41

RELATED PASSAGES: MARK 14:43-50; MARK 16:1-7; ACTS 1:9-14

Day 352

DAY OF PREPARATION

MARK 15:42

This day was called Preparation day. (That means the day
before the Sabbath day.) It was becoming dark.

KEY THOUGHT

We have lost almost all sense of a day of preparation for a holy day with God. Yet in the middle of the mayhem and horror of the crucifixion, the Jews in Jesus' day took notice and sought to honor their Sabbath with God. Two judgments are rendered by this one short verse. First, ritual observance of days does not make us holy, because it is so easy to observe the ritual and forget the righteous call of God.Second, in our day, we have lost the sense of holy because we have allowed all days to become the same—busy days to get done what we want to do and then squeeze our "God-time" in where it fits. How sad on both accounts!

TODAY'S PRAYER

O Father, please give me a proper sense of what is holy. I do not want to
be a legalistic ritual keeper; yet at the same time, I do not want to drain
all life of its meaning by secularizing all time. Teach me to know your
will, your time, and your holy ways. In Jesus' name I pray. Amen.

CONTEXT: MARK 15:42-47

RELATED PASSAGES: EPHESIANS 5:15-17; ECCLESIASTES 3:1-14; PSALM 39:4-6

Day 353

GATHERING HIS COURAGE

MARK 15:42-43

This day was called Preparation day. (That means the day before the Sabbath day.) It was becoming dark. A man named Joseph from Arimathea was brave enough to go to Pilate and ask for Jesus' body. Joseph was an important member of the high council. He was one of the people who wanted God's kingdom to come.

KEY THOUGHT

If we love Jesus and remember his suffering and humiliation on the cross, we too can gather our courage and stand up for him—even when there is much to lose and there appears to be nothing to gain. Joseph's show of loyalty and courage is moving. It is the one ray of hope in the dismal scene of the cross. Joseph reminds us that there is always something to be gained in loyalty and faithfulness to the Lord even in the worst of times. God can do great things in our faithfulness in the smallest of tasks and the most dangerous displays of loving faithfulness to the Savior.

TODAY'S PRAYER

O God Almighty, stir my courage and empower me to stand for Jesus even when things do not look promising and many enemies surround me. In Jesus' name I pray. Amen.

CONTEXT: MARK 15:42-47

RELATED PASSAGES: HEBREWS 13:1-3; MARK 8:38; REVELATION 2:10

Day 354

DEAD!

MARK 15:44-45

Pilate was surprised to hear that Jesus was already dead. So he called for the army officer in charge and asked him if Jesus was already dead. When Pilate heard it from the officer, he told Joseph he could have the body.

KEY THOUGHT

We can gather several bits of valuable information from this verse. (1) Jesus died more quickly than most facing crucifixion: the brutal treatment with his beating and scourging, something most who were crucified did not endure, took a heavy physical toll on Jesus' body. (2) Jesus was clearly and legally confirmed dead by those experienced in the work of torture and death. (3) Joseph could not remain a "closet follower of Jesus" and pick up Jesus' body; he had to request it from the one who gave permission for Jesus to be crucified, Pilate himself. These three facts help us know with certainty (1) that Jesus endured a horribly punishing death, (2) that there was no doubt that he died, and (3) that Jesus' death summoned up something deep within people that moved them to honor him. While the first three facts are historically important, these last three are spiritually important to us and move us to honor him with our lives today.

TODAY'S PRAYER

Father, thank you for the death that Jesus faced willingly so that we can be reconciled to you. Please help me let it be a continual reminder that I need to live my life as a daily praise to you. In Jesus' name I pray. Amen.

CONTEXT: MARK 15:42-47

RELATED PASSAGES: MARK 10:32-34, 45; JOHN 12:20-33; JOHN 19:38-42

Day 355

FINAL GOODBYE?

MARK 15:46

Joseph bought some linen cloth. He took the body from the cross, wrapped it in the linen, and put the body in a tomb that was dug in a wall of rock. Then he closed the tomb by rolling a large stone to cover the entrance.

KEY THOUGHT

I can only imagine what this experience must have meant to Joseph. Was it filled with regret for not having been more open about his allegiance to Jesus? Was it filled with deep sorrow for what he felt was lost? Was it filled with anger at seeing the body of Jesus abused, torn, and punctured? Was it a sense of finality that all had been lost and all hopes dashed with Jesus' death? As he placed Jesus in this fresh grave, did he hear a brief echo of a promised resurrection that stirred his hopes? We look at the crucifixion on this side of Jesus' triumphant resurrection. Even when we celebrate the Lord's Supper and remember the death of Jesus, we do so on Sunday, the day of his victory. It is only when one we love comes to the end of this life that we can begin to understand the weight of Joseph's pain and grief. But even then we can be thankful that Joseph's painful task was done in preparation for the glorious Sunday when Jesus rose from the dead and changed everything.

TODAY'S PRAYER

Hallelujah, God Almighty! You have taken death and defeated it through the work of your Son and my Savior Jesus. Thank you. I praise you in the name of my risen Lord, Jesus Christ. Amen.

CONTEXT: MARK 15:42-47

RELATED PASSAGES: JOHN 11:17-26; MARK 16:1-7; 1 CORINTHIANS 15:50-58

Day 356

WHERE HIS BODY WAS PLACED

MARK 15:47

Mary Magdalene and Mary the mother of Joses saw the place where Jesus was put.

KEY THOUGHT

Jesus' death was confirmed by those in authority. Jesus' burial was done by friends: Joseph of Arimathea and Nicodemus (John 19:39) took him down from the cross, wrapped his body, and buried him. Jesus tomb was secured by soldiers (Matt. 27:62-66). The women who had faithfully accompanied Jesus through his whole ordeal now saw his lifeless body placed in that tomb. His followers felt that all hope was gone. The full reality of Jesus' death had settled into the hearts of his followers. There are no doubts about any of the harsh realities of his life's end. They are left in fear in an upper room empty of any real hope. They knew Jesus was dead!

TODAY'S PRAYER

O Father, the witness of these women helps make Jesus' death and burial emotionally and factually real to me. I can only imagine their heartbreak and their deep sense of loss. However, dear Lord, this heartbreak also makes their testimony to Jesus' resurrection even more powerful. Thank you for their faithful witness in anguish that empowers their witness to his resurrection. In Jesus' name I pray. Amen.

CONTEXT: MARK 15:42-47

RELATED PASSAGES: JOHN 19:38-42; LUKE 23:55-56; MARK 16:1-7

Day 357

SETTLING IN ON DEATH'S NECESSITIES

MARK 16:1

The next day after the Sabbath day,

*Mary Magdalene, Salome, and Mary the mother of James bought
some sweet-smelling spices to put on Jesus' body.*

KEY THOUGHT

Death brings with it harsh realities. The physical absence of the person who died and the decay of the physical body are two of the harshest. The women are doing what was expected and what was necessary when a loved one in Jesus' day died. They show their honor and respect by preparing his dead body properly. When people we love die, there are necessities that have to be handled. As difficult as these are, they help reinforce that this person is gone from us. The toughest reality about grief is that the only way past it is to go through it. Though not ready to give up Jesus to death, these women do what is necessary—both for the dead body and for their aching spirits—by taking care of the body properly.

TODAY'S PRAYER

*O Father, to lose a loved one is so terribly difficult. Please give your blessings
and sustaining grace through this time. Help us to take comfort and find hope
that victory and reunion await those who belong to Christ. Give us strength and
courage to hold on to the hope that is ours because your Son came to earth as one
of us, died as one of us, and was raised as the first of us to permanently defeat
death. For this victory, I thank you. In Jesus' mighty name I pray. Amen.*

CONTEXT: MARK 16:1-8

RELATED PASSAGES: COLOSSIANS 1:11-14; 1 CORINTHIANS 15:20;
1 THESSALONIANS 4:14

Day 358

GLOOM OR ANTICIPATION?

MARK 16:2

Very early on that day, the first day of the week, the women were going to the tomb. It was very early after sunrise.

KEY THOUGHT

This verse is filled with anticipation for those of us who live on this side of Jesus' resurrection. However, try to imagine what it was like for those women who had supported Jesus with their funds, had honored him with their discipleship, and were broken-hearted because of his death! In the slowly gathering light of the early morning, their walk to the tomb would have been a walk of agony and deep grief. Despite the danger of being identified with Jesus, despite the heaviness of their hearts, and despite the early hour of their walk, these women still came to honor Christ. What excuse do you and I have for not coming to honor him? Let's approach our times together with believers with anticipation, not gloom. "The Lord's Day" is not only the day these women met the resurrected Jesus; it is also our day of assembling to remember Jesus and his life, death, burial, and resurrection. Let's approach this day with anticipation and joy in our hearts!

TODAY'S PRAYER

Father, make my heart glad to be with your people and meet the resurrected Jesus when we assemble in his name. In Jesus' name I pray. Amen.

CONTEXT: MARK 16:1-8

RELATED PASSAGES: MATTHEW 18:20; REVELATION 1:9-10; HEBREWS 10:19-25

Day 359

WHO WILL ROLL AWAY THE STONE?

MARK 16:3

*The women said to each other, "There is a large stone covering the
entrance of the tomb. Who will move the stone for us?"*

KEY THOUGHT

"Who will move the stone for us?" This was the question of the women
who had followed Jesus. Who will balance the checkbook, service the car,
mow the lawn, take care of the house, do the laundry, prepare the meals, and
on and on we could go about the practical questions that lie behind the death
of a loved one. In the face of death, we often find ourselves with bewildering
and overwhelming questions. These are practical questions. These are hard
questions. These are confusing questions. Jesus' death was no different. Life
goes on for those left behind in grief. More than just offering quiet and nice
platitudes, let's get to work helping "roll away the stone" for each person who
needs help. Let's do practical and helpful things that need doing while they are
overwhelmed with grief.

TODAY'S PRAYER

*Dear God, grief comes back and hits us surprisingly hard. Please be with us and
help us make it through our times of grief. We need you to roll away the stone
that blocks our hearts from life and hope during our times of grief. Give us the
courage to continue. Please provide us with the support of Christian family to
help us do the things that most need doing. And, dear Father, please use me to
help those in grief in very practical ways. In Jesus' name I pray. Amen.*

CONTEXT: MARK 16:1-8

RELATED PASSAGES: LUKE 7:11-15; 1 THESSALONIANS 4:13-18;
1 CORINTHIANS 15:57-58

Day 360

ROLLED AWAY!

MARK 16:3-4

The women said to each other, "There is a large stone covering the entrance of the tomb. Who will move the stone for us?"

Then the women looked and saw that the stone was moved. The stone was very large, but it was moved away from the entrance.

KEY THOUGHT

The question about moving the stone is such a practical one for the women as they approach the tomb. The grave of Jesus has been sealed with a heavy stone. They couldn't manage it—they needed help to move the stone away. Little did they know that God had already taken care of this problem in a far bigger way than they could ever imagine. God raised his Son from death and gives life to us through Jesus. He has rolled away the stone that held us captive to death and brought us hope for all of our tomorrows because of Jesus' resurrection from the dead!

TODAY'S PRAYER

Gracious Father, thank you for rolling the stone of death away and for promising us eternal life. What a great gift! In Jesus' name I pray. Amen.

CONTEXT: MARK 16:1-8

RELATED PASSAGES: HEBREWS 2:14-18; 1 CORINTHIANS 15:54-55; ROMANS 8:11

Day 361

STARTLED BY AN ANGEL

MARK 16:5-6

The women walked into the tomb and saw a young man there wearing a white robe. He was sitting on the right side of the tomb. The women were afraid.

But the man said, "Don't be afraid. You are looking for Jesus from Nazareth, the one who was killed on a cross. He has risen from death! He is not here. Look, here is the place they put him when he was dead."

KEY THOUGHT

These women were more than "touched by an angel"; they were also startled by an angel (Matt. 28:5). They knew where Jesus had been buried. They were wondering about why the stone was rolled away from the tomb. No matter what they could have imagined would happen at the tomb, they had no expectation that an angel would greet them and tell them that Jesus was alive. What an overwhelming and "gloriously frightening" experience! One day angels will startle us as they return with the Lord to take us home to his glory. Let's live each day in expectation of that day and look forward to being "startled by an angel."

TODAY'S PRAYER

O Father, I look forward to the day your Son returns in glory with the holy angels. Help me live with joy, anticipation, and wonder as I await that day. Use my life to help prepare others for your Son's return and to be a blessing to them until that day dawns. In Jesus' name I pray. Amen.

CONTEXT: MARK 16:1-8

RELATED PASSAGES: MARK 8:34-38; MATTHEW 16:27; MATTHEW 25:31-32

Day 362

HE ISN'T HERE!

MARK 16:6

*But the man said, "Don't be afraid. You are looking for Jesus from
Nazareth, the one who was killed on a cross. He has risen from death! He
is not here. Look, here is the place they put him when he was dead."*

KEY THOUGHT

"He has risen from death! He is not here." What incredibly powerful words
and what an even more gloriously important truth! As we reach the end of the
Gospel of Mark, we know at least three important things about Jesus. First,
he is the Nazarene—the one who was from Nazareth and who did the work of
God. Second, he was crucified—he died to ransom us from sin. Third, he has
been raised from the dead—he conquered death and brought life to us. He is
not in the grave. He lives. He is Lord. Praise God, the power of death has been
broken!

TODAY'S PRAYER

*Praise to you, O Father, for Jesus' glorious triumph over sin and death.
Thank you for what his resurrection means. Thank you that because my life
is joined to Jesus in this life, I can be sure that it will be joined with him in
resurrection. Thank you that the tomb is empty and your Son, my Savior,
lives. In Jesus' name and to Jesus' glory I offer this prayer. Amen.*

CONTEXT: MARK 16:1-8

RELATED PASSAGES: 1 PETER 1:3-9; 1 CORINTHIANS 15:20; COLOSSIANS 1:18

Day 363

You Will See Him in the Place of Ministry

MARK 16:7

"Now go and tell his followers. And be sure to tell Peter. Tell them, 'Jesus is going into Galilee and will be there before you come. You will see him there, as he told you before.'"

KEY THOUGHT

Jesus was about ministry. The bulk of that ministry in Mark's gospel occurs in Galilee: it is Jesus' place of ministry. Now that he is raised from the dead, the angels direct his followers to meet him in Galilee, the place of ministry. He wanted his disciples to carry on his ministry and to know that as they ministered in his name he would be with them. They would see him personally raised from the dead after his resurrection, but they would also "see" him after his ascension by ministering to others. Jesus continues to meet his followers, yes even you and me, in our Galilee, the place of ministry.

TODAY'S PRAYER

Gracious, holy, and merciful God, please use me as an instrument of your peace, grace, and reconciliation. May I be a "vessel of honor"—a tool you can use for your purposes in ministry to others. I know, dear Father, that your Son will be present as I minister. Please make his presence real to me and to those I serve in Jesus' name, through whom I now pray. Amen.

CONTEXT: MARK 16:1-8

RELATED PASSAGES: 2 TIMOTHY 2:21; 2 TIMOTHY 3:14-17; MATTHEW 25:31-40

Day 364

BEWILDERED AND FRIGHTENED!

MARK 16:8

The women were very afraid and confused. They left the tomb and ran away.
They did not tell about what happened, because they were afraid.

KEY THOUGHT

Mark wanted us to know two crucial things about Jesus. First, Jesus was mighty and powerful, something even the demons recognized and feared. Second, despite all of his power, he submitted himself to the will of God and went to the cross to ransom us from sin and death. Mark knows Jesus was raised from the dead, but he uses the women and their being "very afraid and confused" to remind us of the resurrection—not because they doubted, but because they believed. Jesus changed everything in their understanding of the Messiah (Mark 1:1). His dying didn't fit and they couldn't understand how it could have happened. All their hopes had been dashed. On this morning, however, they found out he was raised from the dead and they were told this good news by an angel at Jesus' empty tomb. How could they not be "very afraid and confused"? Since Jesus had risen from death, what would happen next? If they followed Jesus, what would the resurrected Jesus do through them? And if Jesus could use them, what will he do through us? So let's join these faithful women at the empty tomb, "very afraid and confused," but full of expectation at the thought of what lies ahead for us!

TODAY'S PRAYER

O God, release the resurrection power of Jesus in our day and in my life. Empower me to live for you and impact my world in a similar way to how these first followers of your Son impacted their world. In Jesus' name and for his glory I pray. Amen.

CONTEXT: MARK 16:1-8

RELATED PASSAGES: ACTS 4:8-20; ACTS 17:6; JOHN 14:12

Day 365

GO INTO ALL THE WORLD

MARK 16:9-20

Jesus rose from death early on the first day of the week. He appeared first to Mary Magdalene. One time in the past Jesus had forced seven demons out of Mary. After Mary saw Jesus, she went and told his followers. They were very sad and were crying. But Mary told them that Jesus was alive. She said that she had seen Jesus, but they did not believe her.

Later, Jesus appeared to two followers while they were walking in the country. But Jesus did not look the same as before he was killed. These followers went back to the other followers and told them what happened. Again, the followers did not believe them. Later, Jesus appeared to the eleven followers while they were eating. He criticized them because they had so little faith. They were stubborn and refused to believe the people who said Jesus had risen from death.

He said to them, "Go everywhere in the world. Tell the Good News to everyone. Whoever believes and is baptized will be saved. But those who do not believe will be judged guilty. And the people who believe will be able to do these things as proof: They will use my name to force demons out of people. They will speak in languages they never learned. If they pick up snakes or drink any poison, they will not be hurt. They will lay their hands on sick people, and they will get well." After the Lord Jesus said these things to his followers, he was carried up into heaven. There, Jesus sat at the right side of God. The followers went everywhere in the world telling people the Good News, and the Lord helped them. By giving them power to do miracles the Lord proved that their message was true.

KEY THOUGHT

What an incredibly wonderful message. Jesus begins as a nobody in a little-regarded place working with insignificant people and changes the world. As powerful a story as this is, we must remember that the story and the power have not ended. Jesus is still looking for people to join him in his work of transforming the world by God's grace.

TODAY'S PRAYER

Dear Father, thank you for the ways you have touched my heart and used my life through the Gospel of Mark. I fervently pray that you will use me in ways I cannot imagine. I want to be part of your work of changing the world. Please wholly use my life until you call me home. In Jesus' name I pray. Amen.

ALSO AVAILABLE

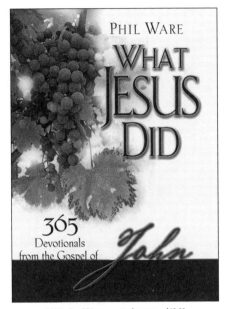

5.125 x 7   374 pages   trade paper $12.99
ISBN 978-0-9767790-5-6   Devotional

What Jesus Did is a one-year devotional guide to the Gospel of John, using one short passage each day and following the Gospel from beginning to end. A wonderful guide for beginning or ending your hectic day in the presence of God.